MW00989833

silence

silence

A Social History of One of the Least Understood Elements of Our Lives

JANE BROX

Houghton Mifflin Harcourt
Boston New York 2019

hmhco.com

Library of Congress Cataloging-in-Publication Data
Names: Brox, Jane, 1956- author.
Title: Silence : a social history of one of the least understood elements of our lives / Jane Brox.
Description: Boston : Houghton Mifflin Harcourt, 2019. |
Includes bibliographical references and index.
Identifiers: LCCN 2018017520 (print) | LCCN 2018029261 (ebook) |
ISBN 9780544702516 (ebook) | ISBN 9780544702486 (hardcover)
Subjects: LCSH: Silence—History. | Silence—Social aspects.
Classification: LCC BJ1499.S5 (ebook) | LCC BJ1499.S5 B76 2018 (print) |
DDC 302/.1—dc23
LC record available at https://lccn.loc.gov/2018017520

Book design by Greta D. Sibley

Printed in the United States of America
DOC 10 9 8 7 6 5 4 3 2 1

Funded in part by a grant from the Maine Arts Commission, an independent state agency supported by the National Endowment for the Arts.

Credits appear on page 300.

for

Cynthia Cannell

and for

Elizabeth Brown

contents

PART V

The Ends of Silence

Coda

PART I

Philadelphia's Eastern State Penitentiary, 1829: Experiment in Silence

Silence is as much a part of history as noise;
the invisible as much a part of history as the visible.

—Max Picard, *The World of Silence*

1

man of sorrows

I FIRST SAW the granite façade of Eastern State Penitentiary on a cold November weekday. I could feel the chill off the rivers. Fairmount Avenue was quiet under a gray sky. The nineteenth-century row houses and the narrow, numbered streets intersecting the avenue were quiet, too, in the afterlife—after the factories, foundries, lumberyards, coal yards, lime kilns, and breweries; after the waves of Irish, German, Polish, and Ukrainian immigrants.

Although today there are white tablecloths and fresh flowers in the restaurants of the Fairmount neighborhood and one of the breweries has become an upscale condominium, the Mid-Atlantic light falls differently on the old working-class streets than it does on the soft red brick of colonial Philadelphia a few miles away. The older part of the city, with its greenery, manila-trimmed windows, and cobblestones, feels swept clean and inhabited by the effort at preservation. Fairmount suggests that the past is still mutable, perhaps because the penitentiary, rather than being preserved, has been stabilized in its slide toward ruin.

Some walls and ceilings have been shored up for safety, and a few early cells have been reconstructed, but mostly its successive histories have collapsed together to create a somber half deterioration. Visitors walk through a world of sunken roofs, rubble, peeling paint, weeds, and weed trees—the detritus of what had once been a dream of order.

The penitentiary isn't as old as it feels. Construction began in 1822, with the intent of providing for the separate and silent incarceration of housebreakers, forgers, highway robbers, horse thieves, and murderers from the eastern counties of Pennsylvania. Not only were the prisoners to remain in their individual cells for the duration of their sentences, but once they passed through the portal their isolation was to be nearly complete. The board of inspectors for Philadelphia's prisons at the time called for "such an entire seclusion of convicts from society and from one another, as that during the period of their confinement, no one shall see or hear, or be seen or heard by any human being, except the jailer, the inspectors, or such other persons, as for highly urgent reasons may be permitted to enter the walls of the prison."

The concept of such extreme silence and solitude—first articulated more than thirty-five years before the cornerstone for the penitentiary was laid—was the vision of Founding Father Benjamin Rush, a well-known public figure in post-Revolutionary Philadelphia. Rush was the city's most prominent physician, an ardent abolitionist, a proponent of hospital reform, and a supporter of the earliest efforts to create a comprehensive public school system. During the last decades of the eighteenth century, he took a particular interest in criminal justice at a time when legislators in the new Republic were seeking to develop a penal code distinct from old-world punishments. His idea for a penitentiary—ambitious, entirely new for its time—would require persistence to see it to fruition, and Rush would need to garner the support of friends and prison advocates who could help him lay decades of groundwork.

The Fairmount neighborhood was still open country when the construction of Eastern State began. Its advocates wanted a rural site to abet the circulation of fresh air and the removal of sewage, and for the sheer space that solitude and silence for hundreds required. It would also stand in contrast to the old jails that often stood in the hearts of towns, where the division between the incarcerated and the free was permeable. There jail windows opened onto the streets, and the jailed could call out to passersby or beg for a little money. Friends of the imprisoned might bring them news and food and drink.

The building commission that oversaw the project had chosen to erect the penitentiary on the site of a modest farm that spanned a small hillside on the outskirts of Philadelphia. Workers tore down or hauled away all its holdings: the cherry orchard (the penitentiary would come to be known as Cherry Hill), the stables and house, the stone troughs, the copper boiler in the milk room. The ten cleared acres then became the site of one of the largest construction projects to be undertaken in early-nineteenth-century America, with a massive wall enclosing most of what was needed to maintain the daily life of hundreds: seven ranges of cells, workshops, storerooms, gardens, a kitchen, a bakery, a laundry room, an apothecary's shop, and a hospital ward for the prisoners; quarters for the prison keepers, the warden, and the watchmen.

The rural location also meant that anyone who approached—prisoners or passersby—would gain a long view of the penitentiary's parapets, Norman-style guard towers, and thirty-foot-high wall built of hewn, squared Schuylkill stone, all of which were meant, the building commissioners declared, to "convey to the mind a cheerless blank indicative of the misery that awaits the unhappy being who enters within its walls."

Now that the city has entirely surrounded the penitentiary—the house for the silent proved to be more enduring than the agricultural world it once imposed itself upon—its wall stands at nearly the same height as the surrounding row houses. I didn't notice it until I came upon it. Vines climb it; a lone tree has gotten a purchase on a capstone; the gray stone is stained with black grit and soot. Still, the one entryway stands massive and imposing. "Let its doors be of iron," Benjamin Rush declared, "and let the grating, occasioned by opening and shutting them, be encreased by an echo from a neighboring mountain, that shall extend and continue a sound that shall deeply pierce the soul."

The original entryway stood twenty-seven feet high and fifteen feet wide. Its oaken double doors, studded with iron rivets, weighed several tons, and a wrought-iron portcullis fronted them. When they were replaced by an electrically operated door in 1938, the wooden planks were burned on the prison grounds, the rivets given away as souvenirs. The door may be different now, but it is still the only entry to the penitentiary, and I trod upon the same stones as the seventy-five thousand prisoners who served their time at Eastern State and all the visitors of nearly two centuries. Once through, I wandered among its decaying corridors with a handful of other visitors, most wearing earphones and listening to a tour tape, trying to match what they have heard to the collapses and rubble, to a place no longer prey to the force of ideas or hopes of control.

I remember it started spitting snow as I stepped through into the yard. The snow quickened and eddies swirled—dense, then spare—before returning to the common drift, as unpredictable as the flow of time itself: some moments come right at you, others rise calmly, mysteriously. I could bring that fluid sense of time with me across the threshold. For the prisoners, their sentences took it away. "Suffering is one very long moment," wrote Oscar Wilde from Reading Gaol. "We cannot divide it by seasons. We can only record its moods, and chronicle their return. With us time itself does not progress. It revolves. It seems to circle round one centre of pain. The paralysing immobility of a life every circumstance of which is regulated after an unchangeable pattern, so that we eat and drink and lie down and pray, or kneel at least for prayer, according to the inflexible laws of an iron formula . . . For us there is only one season, the season of sorrow. The very sun and moon seem taken from us."

I remember, too, the claustrophobia I felt when I looked into one of the remaining original cells from the corridor. The barreled ceiling and funneled light from above hark back to the medieval monasteries of the silent orders: spare, undistracting, penitential, at odds with the Gothic exterior in design and scale. The original cells had no entry doors from the corridors. Only small openings consisting of a peephole and a drawer through which to pass meals pierced the walls between the cells and the corridors. Although the guards could see the prisoners through the peephole, the drawer—even when open—was constructed so that the prisoners could not see who delivered their food. The only entrance to and from the cell was through a private walled-in yard where each prisoner took his one hour of daily exercise. The doorway stood no more than five feet high, so almost every prisoner was forced to stoop in order to pass through.

There's no real way now to sense the magnitude of that initial isolation. Several years after the penitentiary opened, the impracticality of architect John Haviland's design led him to insert doorways between the cells and the corridors, which you now see when you look down the ranges. Even so, nothing prepared me for how close the quarters seemed, or how still the penitentiary was, even with others wandering, too. I couldn't fathom the endurance it took to live in such a way—and to do so obediently.

The first prisoner to arrive at Eastern State: Charles Williams, an eighteen-year-old black farmer who could read and who bore a scar on the bridge of his nose and another from a dirk on his thigh. For breaking into a house and stealing a silver watch, a gold seal, and a gold key worth, in total, $25, he was sentenced to two years of solitary and silent confinement. What did he imagine as he was transported through the countryside from the Delaware County Jail on October 25, 1829? The horses' hooves raised the old dust of the season, the wagon wheels creaked, the late birds called as he breathed in the last open life he would know for two years.

After he passed through the penitentiary gate, a ritual to prepare him for his cell began. It was almost as elaborate as that required of a postulant entering a monastery. He took off his street clothes, was given a bath, and had his hair cut short. He was examined by a physician, and his scars were noted. He was issued two handkerchiefs, two pairs of socks, a pair of shoes, trousers, a jacket, and a shirt of a plain weave. His identity as Prisoner No. 1 would be sewn into his clothing and hung above the entrance to his cell. He was not to be called Charles again for the duration of his stay.

He wouldn't be able to receive or write letters. Although he might exchange occasional words with a guard or inspector, and he would receive regular visits from moral and spiritual instructors, no friends or family would be allowed to visit him. He was not to talk unless instructed to. He was not to make any unnecessary noise. He'd be almost totally cut off from modern speech and its ancient history, and would hear no more than small scurryings in the walls or the sighs of his own making.

Although nine other prisoners would be admitted in those first months of the penitentiary—everyday criminals like himself, horse thieves and highway robbers—Charles Williams would not know whether he lived among nine or ninety. While each prisoner was being escorted to his cell, he was hooded both to shield him from seeing others and to disorient him within the penitentiary. Not only would he not know his fellow prisoners, but he was never to know where in the compound his cell was located. Nor would he be allowed to leave it except in sickness or during an emergency.

When Williams's hood was lifted, he stood on a stone floor, a soul wrapped in rough cloth and surrounded by a twelve-by-eight-foot whitewashed cell, containing an iron bed, a straw mattress, a sheet, a blanket, some scrubbing and sweeping brushes, a clothes rail, a washbasin, a mirror, a crude flush toilet, a tin cup, a victuals pan, a stool, and a workbench where he was to spend his time making shoes. There would be coffee or cocoa in the morning; a ration of one pound of bread a day; potatoes and meat at noon; Indian mush in the evening; a half gallon of molasses a month. He could ask for salt. He'd be given vinegar as a favor. Come Christmas, he'd receive a pound of pork, potatoes, and an apple.

Other than during his daily hour of exercise, the sun in all its seasons would be restricted to what glinted through the iron lattice of the door to his exercise yard—when the exterior oak door hadn't been secured—or what shone down from the eight-inch circular window cut into the barreled ceiling. Enough light by which to read the New Testament. It's said the window came to be known as the "Eye of God," though the architect called it a "deadeye," and it could be darkened by covering it with a half cask should a prisoner need to be disciplined.

Darkening a cell meant the prisoner also lost his only means of measuring the days. As long as the sun wasn't taken entirely from him, he could concentrate on what light was granted to him: though he could not orient himself in space, he could orient himself in time. British writer and social theorist Harriet Martineau, who visited Eastern State in the mid-1830s, wrote: "I never met with one who could in the least tell what the form of the central part of the prison was, or which of the radii his cell was placed in, though they make very accurate observations of the times at which the sun shines in."

It was hoped there would be an expansiveness in the silence, and in the sunlight squeezing through the small aperture, casting undistracted shadows on the whitewashed walls. Charles

Williams's sentence was meant to punish him for his crimes and deter others from committing the same, but it was also meant to alter his soul. "I already hear the inhabitants of our villages and townships counting the years that shall complete the reformation of one of their citizens," proclaimed Benjamin Rush. "I behold them running to meet him on the day of his deliverance. His friends and family bathe his cheeks with tears of joy; and the universal shout of the neighborhood is, 'This our brother was lost, and is found—was dead and is alive.'"

I tried to imagine Williams there—lumpen in his official clothing, disoriented, unseen—in the prickling silence he woke to and slept to, sometimes read in. His thoughts roamed in it; the small sounds of his work as a shoemaker accompanied it. The limit of his world—where he ate and slept and dreamed and worked and took the air—was narrower than the recommended space for a cherry tree.

2

benjamin rush's vision

THE SILENCE AND solitude that surrounded Charles Williams as he worked and read and slept within the tight confines of Schuylkill stone was no simple thing. Not only had the idea of the penitentiary been decades in the making, but it had unfolded in the rapidly shifting world of the industrial age and the first years of the American Republic. As much as it was specific to the Quaker roots of Philadelphia and Benjamin Rush, it was also the culmination of decades of Enlightenment debates that spanned Europe and America, and it involved concepts of justice, punishment, and reform that were sometimes complementary, sometimes competing. Beliefs concerning redemption were intertwined with concepts of control and punishment; the practicalities of this world were tied up with faith in the next. And there was a political stake in Williams's sentence as well. In seeking to establish a justice system independent from that of Europe, American legislators were also looking to define and support the ideals of the nation with an orderly and humane means of justice that would replace the hangings, brandings, and whippings of its colonial past.

As Eastern State was imagined, its practices could not have been more distinct from those traditional blood punishments. Under the old system of justice, jails—in both England and the American colonies—rarely served for lengthy incarceration. Detention in them was usually limited to those awaiting trial or sentencing; only debtors were confined for extended periods. In the colonies—a largely rural society in which travel was difficult and slow—justice was administered locally, and even a small village had some means of temporarily confining the accused, perhaps nothing more than quarters set aside in a house where a prisoner could be fettered. At best, there might be a small, dedicated building for such cases. The early-seventeenth-century village of Pemaquid—where New Harbor, Maine, now stands—was perched at the end of a peninsula on the northern border of what was then British territory. Today the stone foundation of its jail lies exposed on a grassy slope just a short distance from the foundations of a handful of village houses, the trading post, tavern, and warehouse. Outlined in granite are two rooms, each so small that an average-size man of that time would not be able to spread his arms without touching the walls on either side.

Confinement in the cities was more substantial, and rarely orderly or quiet. The outer walls of Boston's seventeenth-century jail were three feet thick and built of stone. The cells, partitioned by wooden planks, were secured by oak doors studded with iron spikes. Barred and unglazed windows let in a little sunlight and air, but snow and rain drove right through them. The cold, dank jail, claimed one prisoner, was "the nearest resemblance to a hell upon earth." But its separate cells marked an improvement over London's Newgate Prison, where young, old, women, men, innocent, guilty, thugs, thieves, debtors, and those condemned to death were at best separated loosely into dank, dirty, stinking common rooms, with only a handful of guards to watch over them. Sometimes they weren't even given straw to sleep on. The stench wafted onto the streets, and passersby could hear the prisoners' curses and cries.

For those without resources, incarceration in Newgate was especially trying. Each prisoner, responsible for all of his or her expenses, had to live by his or her wits. The keeper was hardly disinterested. He made his money by charging for the putting on and removal of chains, and by selling food, stout ale, and tobacco to the prisoners. If a prisoner had no money, he might "angle for farthings" through the windows or grilles from passersby on the street. Sometimes prisoners sold their shirts—or stripped an unfortunate newcomer of his clothes—to buy ale.

More than a few died from "jail fever"—a kind of typhus—or other contagious diseases. Judges and physicians, who also succumbed to jail fever, feared the disorder and disease so much that they hesitated to enter Newgate. In the early eighteenth century it was described as "a bottomless pit of violence, a Tower of Babel where all are speakers and no hearers." Its reputation lasted long after its demise. Twentieth-century British writer Aldous Huxley remarked: "Behind the façade of Newgate . . . there existed, not a world of men and women, not even a world of animals, but a chaos, a pandemonium."

When punishment came, in both England and the colonies, it was public, swift, and physically brutal. For lesser crimes, the convicted could be pilloried, whipped, branded, ducked, or set in stocks in the public square. During the colonial period a free black man who'd committed a crime similar to Charles Williams's might have been whipped or sentenced to stand in the pillory, then branded on the right hand for a first offense. Had he stolen on the Sabbath, his brand might have been set on his forehead. His sentence probably would have been carried out in the town square on market day, though he could have been chained to the end of a cart and run through the streets while being lashed. Any cries of pain would likely have been drowned out by the taunts and mocking of the people gathered around him. Then the scarred felon would have been released back among them. Such punishment was meant not only to impose pain and suffering upon the perpetrator, but also to stand as a warning to the community of the cost of violating its laws: both the crime and the criminal were meant to be remembered.

For all crimes, the punishment for repeated offenses was increasingly harsh. If caught stealing a third time, a thief would be sentenced to hang, and hangings were a world unto themselves. They drew jeering crowds who sometimes egged the condemned. William Hogarth's 1747 engraving *The Idle 'Prentice Executed at Tyburn* suggests the aroused swarm of citizens was its own force of nature. The foreground is full of rambunctious children, old people leaning on canes, and purveyors with their apple carts and baskets of ginger cakes for sale. As uncountable humanity flows toward the horizon, the individuals lose their features and become a sea filling the valley and surging into the distance until bounded by the far hills. The cart carrying the condemned man appears to be helplessly tossed upon it, as does the Tyburn gallows.

In England during the eighteenth century, hundreds of crimes were punishable by death. One could be hanged for murder or piracy but also for stealing a handkerchief or blacking one's face to go about the streets at night, though for lesser crimes the judges often set the penalty aside. In the colonies, far fewer crimes were punishable by death, though in seventeenth-century Massachusetts, for instance, they included witchcraft, children cursing or smiting parents, and sons rebelling against parents. In practice, colonial judges also frequently laid aside the death penalty in favor of lesser punishments. Still, hangings were just as public as in England and drew crowds: the community violated, the community warned. And, also as in England, sometimes hanging alone wasn't enough.

For the most heinous crimes, such as piracy, a wife killing a husband, or slaves killing their masters, the offender's corpse might be hung at a crossroads or town square and sheathed in a cage of iron that had been specifically fashioned for the condemned by the local blacksmith: straight rods secured the limbs, which were also ringed with iron; latticework surrounded the ribs; and a length of iron circled the torso from crotch to neck, where it broke to join an iron cage for the head. An iron loop, through which a hook or rope would be slipped, was fastened to its crown. This was called a gibbet iron, and the punishment was known as gibbeting or hanging in chains. The gibbet's embrace was meant to keep the decaying corpse from collapsing, being devoured by birds, or being carried away by the wind. The punished were eventually buried in their chains.

In Massachusetts, in 1755, a slave known only as Mark was gibbeted for poisoning his master with arsenic. His corpse was still hanging on the Charlestown Common three years later. Most likely Mark's remains weren't taken down until shortly before the Revolution, and even afterward lived in memory. Paul Revere, in describing his ride from Boston to Lexington, noted that he had "passed Charlestown Neck, and got nearly opposite where Mark was hung in chains."

The brittle, heavy black iron forged in fire represents everything Charles Williams's punishment at Eastern State was not. Williams—sentenced to be forgotten, hidden behind stone, isolated, stripped of his name—would, at the end of his prescribed sentence, step out of his woven prison garb, which would fall in a soft heap around him. He would dress himself in his old clothes and walk free, it was believed, as a new man.

Although this profound shift from chaotic, filthy jails and blood punishments to silence and solitude evolved over many decades, it had its specific origins in Benjamin Franklin's Philadelphia home. During the winter of 1787 Franklin began to host twice-monthly meetings of the newly formed Society for Promoting Political Inquiries. A dozen or more men—among the most renowned in the commonwealth—gathered in his dining room or library to listen to speakers and discuss ideas meant to foster social and economic improvements in Pennsylvania and the new Republic. Thomas Paine, political activist and author of the pamphlet *Common Sense,* was among the founding members of the group, as was Benjamin Rush, who often dominated the conversation. Rush, it was said, was opinionated, moralistic, and arrogant—once likening himself to the prophet Jeremiah: "a man of *strife* and a man of contention to the whole earth." He loved to argue, perhaps no more emphatically than in the relaxed atmosphere of the evenings at Franklin's house, which followed no regular rules of order. As Rush's biographer David Freeman Hawke notes: "'There was no formality of discussion,' one member later recalled. 'Dr. Rush, who had great powers of conversation, commonly took the lead'; another member, however, held that Rush's 'incessant talking disturbed us very much.'"

At one of the first meetings of the society, in March 1787, Rush was invited to read his pamphlet *An Enquiry into the Effects of Public Punishments upon Criminals, and upon Society.* To the men gathered in the early dark of late winter, he declared: "I cannot help entertaining a hope, that the time is not very distant, when the gallows, the pillory, the stocks, the whipping-post . . . will be connected with the history of the rack and the stake, as marks of the barbarity of the ages and countries, and as melancholy proofs of the feeble operation of reason and religion upon the human mind."

He argued that public punishments only serve to "make bad men worse," and the infamy that ensues "destroys . . . the sense of shame." He believed that, however painful, such punishment was too brief to produce a true change of mind and habit. "A man who has lost his character at a whipping-post, has nothing valuable left to lose in society," he insisted, and further suggested that such measures also adversely affected those who witnessed them by inciting contempt rather than pity: "The men, or perhaps the women whose persons we detest, possess souls and bodies composed of the same materials as those of our friends and relations. They are bone of their bone; and were originally fashioned with the same spirits. What, then, must be the consequence of a familiarity with such objects of horror, upon our attachments and duties to our friends and connections, or to the rest of mankind?"

By that late-eighteenth-century evening, the wharves and warehouses of Philadelphia, dense with shipbuilders and sailmakers, stretched for over a mile along the Delaware River. Along the streets angling away from the river, shopkeepers, saddlemakers, blacksmiths, coppersmiths, brush makers, bookbinders, druggists, and doctors nestled near one another. More than twenty-five thousand residents lived above the shops or along alleyways cutting into back lots that had once been green with gardens. There were pubs on the corners. The watch patrolled amid the smells of night soil and garbage. Franklin himself had worked to see that the streets—full of carriages, pedestrians, and peddlers selling fish and fresh fruit—were paved with cobblestones. The spire of the Episcopal Christ Church, along with those of the Methodist, Baptist, and Roman Catholic churches, rose above the Quaker meetinghouses.

Even so, Rush's ideas were inextricable from the city's Quaker roots. It's doubtful that his concept of the penitentiary could have found widespread support elsewhere in the country. Silence in Philadelphia held a profound and specific meaning that harked back to its first days as a settlement. The early houses of Philadelphia possessed little ornamentation or decoration: whitewash, fresh sand on the floors. No dancing, no gambling, no drinking. Carefully chosen words. Friends gathered for meetings, at first in homes, then in brick or wooden meetinghouses that had no steeples and were domestic in scale. No liturgy, no hierarchy. No sermons or leader. George Fox, the founder of Quakerism in England, had instructed his followers to "stand still in the Light," and so in the spare, simple spaces of the meetinghouses they gathered and waited and listened together for the presence of the divine, for a voice that could only be heard in profound silence.

Although Quakers in England during the seventeenth century were renowned for their active ministry, publicly proclaiming their beliefs and delivering sermons in the streets, the eighteenth century marked a period dominated by the quietism advocated by Spanish priest Miguel de Molinos. In his *Spiritual Guide,* first published in 1675, Molinos notes: "There are three kinds of silence; the first is of words, the second of desires, and the third of thoughts . . . In the first, that is, of words, virtue is acquired. In the second, namely, of desires, quietness is attained. In the third, of thoughts, internal recollection is gained. By not speaking, not desiring, and not thinking, one arrives at the true and perfect mystical silence, wherein God speaks with the soul." This was not an active seeking.

Caroline Stephen, a nineteenth-century Quaker theologian, explained the congregation's abiding respect for the power of silence:

> The one corner-stone of belief upon which the Society of Friends is built is the conviction that God does indeed communicate with each one of the spirits he has made, in a direct and living inbreathing of some measure of the breath of his own life; that he never leaves himself without a witness in the heart as well as in the surroundings of man; and that in order clearly to hear the divine voice thus speaking to us we need to be still; to be alone with him in the secret place of his presence; that all flesh should keep silence before him . . . The silence we value is not the mere outward silence of the lips. It is a deep quietness of heart and mind, a laying aside of all preoccupation with passing things—yes, even with the workings of our own minds; a resolute fixing of the heart upon that which is unchangeable and eternal.

• • •

Not only did silence have a particular meaning in Pennsylvania, justice did as well. Even before its first structures were built, Philadelphia's founder, William Penn, was concerned with fostering a humane and fair means of dealing with transgressions in his new colony. This was belief born of experience. As a convert to Quakerism, he was intimate with both the jails and the courtrooms of London. Since the founding of the religion by George Fox in the 1640s, Quakers had been subject to persecution, but the persecution became especially strong after the mid-1660s. During the twenty-five-year reign of Charles II, the Crown passed various acts in an attempt to weaken dissent and protect the Church of England. During that time—besides being stocked, stoned, and whipped—more than thirteen thousand Quakers were imprisoned in England. Hundreds died while incarcerated.

Fox himself had been imprisoned many times and described being put "amongst the moss-troopers, thieves, and murderers . . . A filthy, nasty place it was, where men and women were put together in a very uncivil manner, and never a house of office to it; and the prisoners were so lousy that one woman was almost eaten to death with lice . . . The jailer was cruel, and the under-jailer very abusive both to me and to Friends that came to see me; for he would beat with a great cudgel Friends who did but come to the window to look in upon me. I could get up to the grate, where sometimes I took in my meat; at which the jailer was often offended. Once he came in a great rage and beat me with his cudgel."

Penn, a close friend of Fox, was also arrested on numerous occasions. Consequently, he endured the dire conditions of Newgate and had firsthand experience with the capricious judicial system in England, in which it wasn't uncommon for judges to reject the verdicts of juries. Penn sought, in his Great Law—a series of statutes by which the Pennsylvania colony was to be governed—to ensure that the procedures for trial and sentencing would be simple, understandable, and equitable. Although the blood punishments didn't disappear, they were fewer and milder than those in England and in other American colonies. The death sentence was abolished for all crimes except premeditated murder, which was in line with the predominant Quaker thinking on capital punishment. Fox argued extensively that the death penalty should only be imposed for murder or treason, and that the opportunity for redemption should not be denied a thief. He maintained that to fail to discern between a murderer and a thief violated God's law. "Who takes away mens lives for such things as goods and Cattel?" wrote Fox. "Is not this crueller then the Law, crueller to the thief, crueller to him that the goods were stollen from? . . . And do you not think you would slay mens thievish natures to let them live and restore four, or five, or seven fold to the owner from whom they stole? or if they had it not, to be sold for their theft? was not this the way to convince them, and to bring them to repentance?"

In Penn's colony every county prison was to be a workhouse, and felons were to be either fined or sentenced to a specific amount of time at hard labor in a "house of Correction." His idea for the workhouse, which was also to house vagrants and "loose and idle persons," likely took its measure from London's workhouses of the time, which had been erected for the relief of the infirm, the sick, and the poor. How soon or effectively a workhouse could realistically be established in colonial Pennsylvania was another matter. In late October of 1682 fewer than two hundred souls arrived to settle the colony on the shores of the Delaware River. During the first winter some of the colonists lived in caves dug into the bluffs along the river. They had to clear woodlands for fields and build shelters. Not only was establishing a workhouse for felons hardly a priority, but long imprisonments weren't practical because they would tie up manpower: the felons would have to be guarded. In addition, the workhouse would have to be maintained and paid for with taxes.

Within a year over five hundred inhabitants were concentrated along the colony's port on the Delaware. It was then that Philadelphia's first jail was built: a seven-by-five-foot cage that was seven feet high. The cage wasn't thought suitable for use, however, so instead a house was rented where prisoners could be confined with fetters and chains. A more substantial jail was constructed sometime between 1686 and 1700.

Questions of justice grew more complex with time. Philadelphia—situated between the Delaware and Schuylkill Rivers, with open routes to the west and fertile farmland surrounding it—became one of the most rapidly growing cities in the colonies. By the early eighteenth century it had begun to draw people of various religious persuasions from all over Europe. Many slaves and indentured servants were counted among its forty-five hundred inhabitants.

As the city grew, a wariness about the leniency of Penn's Great Law set in. The blood punishments had the force of tradition behind them. They had been used in the American colonies since the first settlements, and in England and continental Europe long before that. Penn, having returned to England, saw his influence in the colony wane, and as reality tempered hopes and ideals, the old forms of punishment crept back in. During the early eighteenth century, the criminal code was redrafted several times; in each version some punishments were harsher than first set forth, and included corporal punishments such as branding and whipping. Though more severe than the original code, the Philadelphia laws were still more lenient than those of other colonies or of any place in Europe.

In 1718 Penn's ideals were further compromised when his Great Law was overturned by the Duke of York, and the colony was required to mete out punishments that fell more in line with those elsewhere in the colonies and in England. The more traditional laws would remain in place in Pennsylvania until the American Revolution. Even so, Quaker ideals continued to be influential there, and legislators and civic leaders continued to deliberate about the means and nature of traditional justice, even as new jails were constructed and conditions in them grew dire enough to foster concern among citizens.

During the 1770s Richard Wistar, a glass manufacturer in Philadelphia, began preparing soup in his home to feed prisoners in the city jails, which by then were as dismal and chaotic as most others in the colonies. Prisoners of all ages were housed in filthy common rooms, overseen by corrupt jailers, and left to their own devices to feed and clothe themselves. By the eve of the Revolution, in 1776, Wistar helped organize a group of citizens to promote prison reform—the Philadelphia Society for the Relief of Distressed Prisoners. In addition to advocating for the welfare and fair treatment of those confined in the jails, members of the society went door-to-door soliciting food, which they piled in a canvas-covered wheelbarrow and then distributed to prisoners. They also supplied clothing and wood for prison fireplaces and stoves. The society continued its work until the British entered the city in the autumn of 1777 and took control of the jails.

After the Revolution Benjamin Rush, Benjamin Franklin, and others founded a similar organization, the Philadelphia Society for Alleviating the Miseries of Public Prisons. Additionally, city officials sought ways to relieve the crowded prisons and move away from blood punishments. One effort involved having felons undertake public works projects, such as building, maintaining, and cleaning the streets. It was hoped this would also be economical for the city. The felons were known as "the wheelbarrow men," and there was no mistaking them, since they wore brightly colored or boldly striped uniforms, which were meant both to humiliate them and to help identify them should they escape. The wheelbarrow men attracted crowds who both taunted them and threw coins in support and solidarity. There were escapes and attacks on citizens by escapees. Both their perceived threat to the public and their degradation created unease, for the wheelbarrow men made punishment publicly apparent in an even more emphatic way than had the stocks and whipping posts. Here men were grouped together—their crimes undifferentiated—and sent out to work among the citizens. "They were encumbered with iron collars and chains, to which bomb-shells were attached, to be dragged along while they performed their degrading service, under the eye of keepers armed with swords, blunderbusses, and other weapons of destruction," noted Roberts Vaux, one of the city's most dedicated promulgators of penal reform. "In this very objectionable manner they were brought before the public. The sport of the idle and the vicious, they often became incensed, and naturally took violent revenge upon the aggressors."

The public humiliation of the convicts, who were everywhere present, and the tensions between the convicted and society in general, only strengthened Rush's arguments for a new system of justice. The wheelbarrow men were certainly on his mind on that March evening at Franklin's home when he made his first public arguments for the penitentiary. David Freeman Hawke suggests that these men were his inspiration: "It took an accidental meeting with a group of 'wheelbarrow men' to arouse his interest in penal reform. He came upon them sweeping the street before his house. He offered the men molasses beer, and while chatting as they refreshed themselves he found that he had sympathy, perhaps even respect, for the way they bore their humiliation."

To the men gathered at Franklin's house, Rush asserted: "All *public* punishments tend to make bad men worse, and to increase crimes by their influence upon society." He then directly addressed the situation concerning the wheelbarrow men: "But may not the benefit derived to society, by employing criminals to repair public roads, or to clean streets, overbalance the evils that have been mentioned? I answer, by no means. On the contrary . . . the practice of employing criminals in public labour, will render labour of every kind disreputable." He argued that the spectacle also drew citizens from their businesses and served to trivialize both criminal and onlooker.

Rush not only criticized the accepted methods of punishment. He also articulated specific ideas for the penitentiary, in which silence and solitude would work toward many ends. The secrecy and sense of the extreme fostered by the penitentiary's isolated location, its aura of gloom, and its creaking iron doors would work to magnify the horror in the public mind. For the prisoner, those same qualities would work to make society feel dear once again. "An attachment to kindred and society is one of the strongest feelings of the human heart," insisted Rush. "A separation from them, therefore has ever been considered as one of severest punishments that can be inflicted upon man . . . Personal liberty is so dear to all men, that the loss of it, for an indefinite time, is a punishment so severe that death has often been preferred to it."

Rush was focused on the restoration of the offender's soul, and his idea was as inclusive as it was direct. He considered no one, not even the worst offender, to be lost: "It is the prerogative of God alone, to contemplate the vices of bad men, without withdrawing from them the support of his benevolence. Hence we find, when he appeared in the world in the person of his Son, he did not exclude criminals from the benefits of his goodness. He dismissed a woman caught in the perpetration of a crime, which was capital by the Jewish law, with a friendly admonition; and he opened the gates of paradise to a dying thief."

3

"good by discipline"

BENJAMIN RUSH'S ADVOCACY for the silent and separate incarceration of criminals was not only influenced by his Quaker beliefs and by what he witnessed on the streets and in the jails of Philadelphia. He coalesced his ideas for a new kind of justice through his readings of European Enlightenment thinkers, specifically drawing on Italian philosopher Cesare Beccaria, who was among the first and most influential voices in penal reform. Born in Milan, the son of an Italian aristocrat, Beccaria was educated in the law and wrote on the economic and social issues of his time. But he is most remembered for his essay "On Crimes and Punishments," which was published in Italy in 1764, and soon after was translated into English. Widely available in book catalogs and serialized in some newspapers in the American colonies, his essay would have been well-known in the Philadelphia area. Not only did Rush refer to him, but Thomas Jefferson referenced Beccaria's work in his writings.

In this essay Beccaria maintains that the blood punishments and the vagaries of European legal systems had more to do with power than with justice. He speaks out against torture and in support of the limits of judges, whom, he insists, were not to punish more than the law allowed. He calls for precise sentences and for certainty in punishments rather than severity. "Let the laws be clear and simple," he writes, and "let the entire force of the nation be united in their defence; let them be intended rather to favour every individual, than any particular classes of men; let the laws be feared, and the laws only."

Beccaria also argues for punishments proportionate to the crime, and as to the death penalty he asks: "What *right* . . . have men to cut the throats of their fellow-creatures?" As Rush would later, he claims that public hangings had a detrimental effect on the citizenry; rather than "moderate the ferocity of mankind," they increased it: "What must men think, when they see wise magistrates and grave ministers of justice, with indifference and tranquility, dragging a criminal to death, and whilst a wretch trembles with agony, expecting the fatal stroke." And although he doesn't advocate for the reformation of criminals in his essay, he asserts that "the end of punishment . . . is no other than to prevent the criminal from doing further injury to society, and to prevent others from committing the like offence. Such punishments, therefore, and such a mode of inflicting them, ought to be chosen, as will make strongest and most lasting impressions on the minds of others, with the least torment to the body of the criminal."

Beccaria, steeped in law, laid down philosophical concepts of justice. At the same time, Englishman John Howard, whom Rush also acknowledges in the pamphlet he read at Benjamin Franklin's home, provided concrete evidence of the depravity and injustice of the traditional punishments of the time and, in particular, the deplorable state of England's jails. Howard, a wealthy Londoner, was appointed high sheriff of Bedfordshire in 1773, and among his duties was the supervision of the county jail. It was meant to be a purely political appointment, and Howard, in his late forties by then, had shown little inclination toward involvement in social reforms, but he took the duties of his office seriously and set out to inspect the jails under his jurisdiction. Upon his first examination, he was shocked at the filth and disorder he encountered, and he subsequently began to visit other English jails to assess the situation of incarceration in general. He found the conditions were no better than those of his local jail: prisoners were poorly fed, barely clothed, and crowded into dirty common rooms—men and women together during the daytime; debtors and felons, young and old. In some jails, he notes in his report, "there is no allowance of STRAW for prisoners to sleep on; and if by any means they get a little, it is not changed for months together, so that it is almost worn to dust. Some lie upon rags, others upon the bare floors. When I have complained of this to the keepers, their justification has been, 'The county allows no straw; the prisoners have none but at my cost.'"

Howard's advocacy for prison reform would consume the last seventeen years of his life. Of particular concern to him was the influence that seasoned criminals might have on the young and on misdemeanants. "There the petty offender is committed for instruction to the most profligate," Howard writes. "In some Gaols you see (and who can see it without pain?) boys of twelve or fourteen eagerly listening to the stories told by practiced and experienced criminals, of their adventures, successes, stratagems, and escapes."

Howard found similar conditions when he took his inspections further, throughout Europe and into Russia. The stench of the jails saturated his possessions. "My cloaths were in my first journey so offensive, that in a post-chaise I could not bear the windows drawn up: and was therefore often obliged to travel on horseback," he remarks. "The leaves of my memorandum-book were often so tainted, that I could not use it till after spreading it an hour or two before the fire: and even my antidote, a vial of vinegar, has after using it in a few prisons, become intolerably disagreeable. I did not wonder that in those journies many gaolers made excuses; and did not go with me into the felons wards."

Rush would have been familiar with Howard's work through his publication *The State of the Prisons in England and Wales with Preliminary Observations, and an Account of Some Foreign Prisons.* Howard issued several editions of the book, for he eventually made seven journeys abroad at his own expense—more than fifty thousand miles along the laborious, dangerous roads of the time—to make a record of the prisons of the age. He died during a journey to Russia, in the winter of 1790, having contracted typhus while inspecting a prison in Ukraine, but his writings continued to be influential long after his death.

In addition to exposing dire conditions, his published accounts detailed exemplary institutions, which he advocated as models for prisons in England, and this information was perhaps the most influential for Rush. Howard's examples foreshadowed the order of the penitentiary and the kind of silence that is inextricable from obedience. He was particularly impressed with the workhouse at Ghent, where prisoners regularly washed and shaved and each was identified by a number. All were given specific work hours and were provided with meals and uniforms. "I was present during the whole time the men criminals were at dinner," Howard writes, "and much admired the regularity, decency, and order, with which the whole was conducted. Every thing was done at a word given by a Director; no noise or confusion appeared; and this company of near one hundred and ninety stout criminals was governed with as much apparent ease as the most sober and well-disposed assembly in civil society."

The regular order of the Ghent workhouse also appealed to some of Howard's contemporaries, who joined him in advocating for penal reform. British philanthropist Jonas Hanway published a pamphlet in 1776 detailing nearly every aspect of his vision of prison life down to the type of dinnerware to be used at mealtime. In this pamphlet, he proposes solitary and silent imprisonment for felons: "The idea of being excluded from all human society, to converse with a man's own heart, will operate potently on the minds and manners of the people of every class . . . The terrors of a *temporary solitude* will . . . convince the most abandoned, that we are awakened from the supineness, which gave birth to rapine, and cherishes violence." Hanway suggests that to "keep the greater awe and silence, no coach or wheeled carriage should come within the gates."

Howard does not propose taking silence as far as Hanway does, though he does find value in it. In his concluding recommendations for reform, he suggests that silence and solitude are beneficial to keep the society of thieves from colluding with one another and from recruiting the young, but he also sees hope for reform: "Solitude and silence are favourable to reflection; and may possibly lead them to repentance. Privacy and hours of thoughtfulness are necessary for those who must soon leave the world; and in the Old Newgate there were *fifteen cells* for persons in this situation . . . The like provision for such as return to society, cannot be less needful."

His advocacy for silence and solitude was perhaps most profoundly influenced by a visit to a house of correction for young boys within the Hospice of San Michele along the west bank of the Tiber River in Rome's Trastevere district. Established by Pope Clement XI in 1703, the house of correction detained young offenders in order to keep them from the influence of hardened adult criminals in Rome's prison. It also housed boys too young to be sent to the galleys—a common punishment of the time—as well as disobedient sons of wealthy families, who could choose to send their children to the house of correction for reformation. At the heart of the facility, designed by Roman architect Carlo Fontana, was a large, rectangular common workroom with a vaulted ceiling, which was flanked on its long sides by individual sleeping quarters: three tiers of ten on each side, sixty cells in all, each with a latrine and a window for light and air.

Carved in the stone at the entrance was something Howard would adopt for an epigraph to later editions of his book: "It is of little advantage to restrain the Bad by Punishment unless you render them Good by Discipline." And the discipline at San Michele was specific. Upon entry, the boys gave up their street clothes for coarse linen shirts and trousers, and their heads were shaved. During the day they were chained to two long rows of tables in the common room, where they worked at spinning cotton or knitting stockings and caps. They rarely left their place, and the hours were precisely regulated. They said prayers and ate breakfast before beginning work in the morning. While they spun and knit, they listened to religious instruction, prayers, and blessings. After several hours of work, they turned toward an altar that stood at one of the narrow ends of the room and knelt for Mass. Then they took their midday meal, usually of bread, meat, and dried fruit, during which they listened to a reader. Afterward they set to work again until evening prayers, after which they retired to their individual sleeping quarters, though even there they weren't beyond the watchful eyes of the guards. Large lanterns shone into the cells during the night so the boys could be watched as they slept.

And so each day proceeded, interrupted only when one of the boys was whipped. Opposite the alter, at the other end of the common room, stood a stand for lashing. Sometimes whipping was part of their regular punishment; at other times it was administered for discipline or extra punishment. Those who weren't being punished were required to witness the lashings. The remarkable setup of the workroom—the tables bracketed by the altar at one end and the lashing stand at the other—was, to John Howard, not the most notable aspect of the house of correction, however. Rather, it was the silence. "Here were sixty boys spinning, and in the middle of the room an inscription hung up, SILENTIUM," he notes.

Such silence—woven into the regulation of the day, carved up into precise duties interlaced with prayers and Mass—had kinship with the Church's monastic tradition and the silence that worked toward redemption. But it was a silence with more than one end, for it also aided and abetted surveillance. The guards, it was said, could hear "the softest conversation that the children might generally hold amongst themselves and with others."

• • •

Although Rush, who died in 1813, never lived to see his idea for the penitentiary realized in full, he did witness a limited, and ultimately failed, experiment with silence and solitude. In 1790 the Pennsylvania legislature, looking for ways to alleviate the crowding in other Philadelphia jails, approved funding to remodel the city's Walnut Street Jail. It had been a typical city jail when it was opened in 1773, with the general prison population housed together in large rooms, debtors and felons alike fending for themselves.

In the expanded and renovated Walnut Street Jail, felons were separated from debtors and misdemeanants, men from women. All prisoners were dressed in the same plain clothing. They slept on mattresses, were fed regular meals, and were convened for public worship on Sundays. A physician visited once a week. The keeper received a salary and did not collect fees from the prisoners. There was to be no alcohol on the premises. A separate building with 16 eight-by-six-foot cells was erected on the prison grounds and designated for the solitary confinement of some prisoners, in keeping with Rush's proposal, first expounded upon in Franklin's living room, that cells be "provided for the solitary confinement of such persons as are of a refractory temper." At Walnut Street, these were reserved for serious and often repeat offenders. Those in solitary confinement did not work, while congregate prisoners were tasked with making shoes, beating and scraping flax, polishing marble, beating hemp, and chipping logwood.

The changes at Walnut Street—which has been called "the cradle of the penitentiary"—marked the beginning of the reimagining of incarceration in the new Republic. Although by the late eighteenth century, the country's attitude toward the blood punishments was changing, and many states were shifting from branding and whipping toward extended confinement for convicts, the prisons that existed were often brutish. For instance, at New-Gate, Connecticut's first prison, the incarcerated were housed underground in the tunnels of a played-out copper mine. They were brought to the surface every day to work in shops forging nails or building barrels and casks.

There also remained little consensus, even in Philadelphia, as to what incarceration was for. As Caleb Lownes, the first administrator of the reimagined Walnut Street Jail, noted: "There have been many opinions about the mode of treating the convicts. Some seem to forget that the prisoner is a rational being, *of like feeling and passions* with themselves. Some think he is placed there to be perpetually *tormented and punished.* Some prescribe a *certain time* as necessary to his cure. One will not allow him the *light* of heaven, or the refreshment of the breeze; the comforts of society, or even the voice of his keeper: while another considers a seclusion from his friends and connexions, as a ground for accusation of inhumanity." At Walnut Street, Lownes added, they "adopted a plan, which upon full consideration was deemed best, though not perfect."

Lownes remarked that the prisoners knew that a "second conviction would consign them to the solitary cells, and deprive them of the most distant hopes of pardon. These cells are an object of *real terror* to them all." The solitary cells weren't distinguished only in prisoners' minds, but, as sociologist Orlando Lewis noted, they were also "at the outset branded in the public mind as punishment cells for the protection of society and the infliction of the hardest endurable conditions."

This concept of solitary as a separate and harsher punishment was an idea that was early and often replicated, evident even in a modest jail Thomas Jefferson designed for Cumberland County, Virginia, in 1823. Jefferson's plans provided for one solitary cell to "put ill-behaved prisoners into occasionally as punishment." Looking back on those first efforts, Lewis remarked: "It was probably not much of a step in the course of time from these solitary cells for the worst offenders to the 'dark cell' and the 'dungeon.' At any rate, here was the prototype. In administering these cells as definite places of punishment, the tendency would grow to make them as forbidding and repellent as possible."

Conditions at Walnut Street eventually deteriorated from their orderly imaginings: it became one more overcrowded jail prone to chaos and corruption. But even prior to its decline, support gathered for a dedicated penitentiary, where Rush's idea could be more coherently realized. This was no doubt, at least in part, a result of Rush's persistence, which his biographer David Freeman Hawke likewise observes about his support of independence: "To acquaintances he did appear changeable, fickle, and unstable, but close friends knew he . . . kept faith until the dream became a reality."

Convinced that the silence and solitude he envisioned—and their potential for redemption—were remedies for all manner of criminal behavior, Rush never seemed to waver from the pronouncement he made in Franklin's living room: "I have no more doubt of every crime having its cure in moral and physical influence, than I have of the efficacy of the Peruvian bark in curing the intermittent fever." The comparison to medical treatment wasn't casual. Rush approached penal reform in much the same way he approached the treatment of physical disease, for which he had developed a unifying theory. He believed there was only one type of fever, and posited that the overarching cause of sickness was either excessive or inadequate nervous stimulation, to be treated with depletion therapy—generally bloodletting and purging—to shock the body back to health. He advocated for bloodletting in particular and told his own medical students: "*Venerate the Lancet.* It is the Magna gratia Coeli. The great gift of Heaven."

His allegiance to bloodletting was evident in his response to Philadelphia's yellow fever epidemic of 1793, in which five thousand of its fifty thousand inhabitants died, and many thousands more fled the city in fear. Rush, the most well-known physician in the city at the time, treated his patients—sometimes nearly a hundred a day—with purgation and bloodletting. Neither practice was revolutionary, nor was the tendency toward extreme measures to fight life-threatening disease. As historian Paul E. Kopperman has noted of the time: "To many practitioners, common sense seemed to dictate that violent diseases could best be conquered by violent therapies." What was startling to the medical community in late-eighteenth-century Philadelphia was how far Rush took even heroic measures. He was convinced that he could safely remove most of the blood from his patients, and he applied copious bloodletting even to the weakest of sufferers.

The penitentiary could be said to be his unifying theory of criminal justice. Although the punishment Rush envisioned when he first presented his idea for the penitentiary wasn't fully developed or uniform, eventually his vision was distilled to its essence: the hardened criminal and the first-time offender, the housebreaker and the murderer, would all be subject to the same extreme sentence of silence and solitude, differing only in length.

4

john haviland's star of solitudes

IN 1821, THE same year the Pennsylvania legislature approved funding to build a penitentiary to house prisoners from the eastern counties of Pennsylvania, a young British architect, John Haviland, won the competition for its design. Haviland wasn't the most renowned or experienced architect to bid on the proposal, yet he was taking on what would become not only the largest building project in the country, but one of extraordinary complexity: He had to consider every mundane decision—such as the type of flooring and its construction, and the thickness of the walls—in light of ensuring the silence, isolation, and security of two hundred fifty prisoners. He had to devise ways to deliver food to each individual cell and grant each prisoner a means of secluded exercise. Ventilation, plumbing, and heating, which were often absent in old jails, proved a particular challenge. Centralized systems were still novel, but they were also necessary in the penitentiary, since the use of common latrines and individual coal or wood fires couldn't assure isolation. Eventually the plumbing and heating throughout Eastern

State Penitentiary would be more modern than what could be found in the White House at the time.

In his notes for the project, Haviland dwells on the practical. His record gives no hint that his challenge was to enhance the spiritual lives of the incarcerated through isolation and silence. The circular window in the barrel-vaulted ceiling of each cell might, to others, symbolize the Eye of God and admit a light that could alter souls, but that wasn't his concern: "The windows are inserted in the groined ceiling of sufficient dimensions to light the cell," he writes. The frames "of iron strongly secured in the masonry of the roof . . . [are] best for the admission of light, and desirable on account of . . . being out of reach of the Prisoners climbing up to converse from window to window as is the case when they are situated in the side wall of the cell."

Haviland couldn't look to the American continent for ideas. Walnut Street Jail was hardly a model for his far more ambitious project. Other prisons in the country remained as brutal as Connecticut's New-Gate, if not more so. The first warden of the Maine State Prison at Thomaston believed that prisons should be "dark and comfortless abodes of guilt and wretchedness . . . cut off from all hope of relief." And so Maine's prison was: The cells were four-by-eight-foot holes in the ground, which were nine feet deep. The only opening to each cell was a two-foot-square aperture at the top, by which the prisoner descended to his cell on a ladder that was then drawn up. The aperture, covered by iron bars, was always open even in the worst of storms. The cells, one commentator observed, "were literally *jugs* in which the prisoner could fully and fearfully realize that he was truly jugged . . . When a driving snowstorm came on his side of the prison he had . . . no choice but to let the rain and the snow blow on his head."

There may have been no institutions in the new Republic providing inspiration, but Haviland could look to his home country of England. Born in Somerset in 1792, he studied with the London architect James Elmes before moving to Philadelphia in 1816 to open a school of architectural drawing. Though neither Elmes nor Haviland worked directly on prison design during the apprenticeship, they both likely knew of John Howard's writings on prison reform. They also would have been familiar with some of the new county jails and prisons built during the latter part of the eighteenth century in the wake of Howard's exposure of the grim state of jails in England and abroad. But jails would not have been their only inspiration. During the late eighteenth and early nineteenth centuries, England also embraced lazarettos (for the isolation of patients with infectious diseases), bridewells (for the incarceration of petty offenders), asylums, and infirmaries. Haviland's heating plan for Eastern State, for instance, was based on that of the Derbyshire Infirmary in England, which was built in 1810.

Most of the new English jails were modest rectangular buildings, but several were constructed in an innovative radial design. The Suffolk County Jail in Ipswich, built in 1790, could have particularly influenced Haviland. Its architect, William Blackburn, placed the prison governor's house at the center of the compound. Four short corridors radiated out from this central building to form the shape of a cross. Airing grounds and kitchen gardens surrounded the jail. The governor could monitor the corridors from his residence, though it's unlikely he could have observed all corridors simultaneously. Haviland's original design of seven ranges and a pathway all radiating out from a central building to form an eight-pointed star of solitudes was a more complex expansion of Blackburn's radial design. Haviland also took the idea of centralized surveillance further. At the center of Eastern State was not the warden's house, but an eight-sided rotunda that served as a dedicated observation center, "best calculated for *watching, convenience, economy* and *ventilation.*"

If Ipswich suggested the radial design to Haviland, the emphasis on surveillance likely had another inspiration—English philosopher and social reformer Jeremy Bentham's plans for a circular prison called the panopticon. Although Bentham based his panopticon on an idea for a Russian factory that his brother had designed for Catherine the Great, his vision for its application was sweeping. He saw it as being equally applicable to "any sort of establishment, in which persons of any description are to be kept under inspection; and in particular to penitentiary-houses, prisons, houses of industry, work-houses, poor-houses, lazarettos, manufactories, hospitals, mad-houses, and schools."

As Bentham worked and reworked his design throughout the last decade of the eighteenth century, though, he clearly considered the surveillance of prisoners to be paramount. The panopticon, as he imagined it, consisted of a series of concentric rings. At its center would stand a circular observation booth, known as the lantern. Between the center and the circumference, which was ringed with cells, a vacant area would serve to open up the inspector's view to the cells at the perimeter. Each prisoner, confined in his own cell, would be partitioned from his neighbors by solid walls and divided from the observation booth by an iron grating. A window at the back of each cell, illuminated by a reflector and light at night, would assure that the prisoner, in his place between the bars and the backlight, could always be seen by the inspector at the center, who could even observe half of the panopticon without moving. Bentham wrote of this arrangement: "To the keeper, a *multitude,* though not a *crowd;* to themselves, they are *solitary* and *sequestered* individuals." Such solitude would, Bentham imagined, feel all the more constraining because each prisoner was to be made to feel as if he was under surveillance. "Ideal perfection, if that were the object," Bentham wrote, "would require that each person should actually be in that predicament [of being watched], during every instant of time. This being impossible, the next thing to be wished for is, that, at every instant, seeing reason to believe as much, and not being able to satisfy himself to the contrary, he should *conceive* himself to be so."

Although Bentham would have known of John Howard's speculations on the consequences of conversations among prisoners, he did not imagine silence. He did remark on the particular challenges the human voice presented within a prison, for it proved in its way the hardest thing to confine. "Noise," he wrote, being "the only offence by which a man thus engaged could render himself troublesome (an offence, bye the bye, against which irons themselves afford no security), might, if found otherwise incorrigible, be subdued by *gagging.*"

Human voices presented challenges particular to the panopticon and undercut the effectiveness of surveillance: "To save the troublesome exertion of voice that might otherwise be necessary, and to prevent one prisoner from knowing that the inspector was occupied by another prisoner at a distance, a small *tin tube* might reach from each cell to the inspector's lodge, passing across the area, and so in the side of the correspondent window of the lodge. By means of this implement, the slightest whisper of the one might be heard by the other, especially if he had proper notice to apply his ear to the tube." Voices traveling across the void between the observer and the observed would create a world of whispers, and Bentham's pipes strangely foreshadow how prisoners would quickly find one way, unforeseen by Haviland, of communicating with one another at Eastern State: through the plumbing and the heating vents.

As Aldous Huxley noted, Bentham's panopticon stood at odds with the spirit of all his other endeavors. Although he promoted abolition of the death penalty, freedom of expression, and equal rights for women, for the last twenty-five years of his life he expended much of his time and effort in repeatedly and unsuccessfully trying to convince the British House of Lords to approve construction of a panopticon as a prison. "Only in one field did Bentham ever sow the teeth of dragons," wrote Huxley. "He had the logician's passion for order and consistency; and he wanted to impose his ideas of tidiness not only on thoughts and words, but also on things and institutions . . . In human affairs the extreme of messiness is anarchy, the extreme of tidiness, an army or a penitentiary."

Although Bentham was ultimately unsuccessful in his effort, other structures based on his design have been erected, though they fall short of his rigorous measures, often disastrously, and none more so than Eastern State's counterpart, Western State Penitentiary, in Pittsburgh, the construction of which began in 1818. It took eight years before the first prisoner was admitted, and from the very beginning the penitentiary was plagued by problems. The architect, William Strickland—a rival of Haviland's who lost the bid for Eastern State—drafted some of Bentham's ideas into his design. One critic claimed he appropriated the worst of them. The circular prison consisted of a double row of back-to-back seven-by-nine-foot cells. None of the cells had windows; the only light came from the barred doorways. The inner cells faced a vacant interior, which had no central watch station, so there was no way to effectively supervise the prisoners. The inmates couldn't work or exercise, and problems with ventilation spread illness among them. When, eventually, Haviland was called on to redesign the prison, he had to dismantle much of it and completely rework the plan.

What proved enduring about Bentham's panopticon was his obsessive idea. The word itself now suggests total surveillance of any kind, and designs that have little in common with his original vision are sometimes called panopticons. Even Haviland's Eastern State on occasion has been labeled as one, but the simple need to entomb each prisoner in his own cell meant that any view of the incarcerated was limited, especially during the first years of operation. To actually observe a prisoner in his cell, the guards had to peer through the peephole in the food drawer that pierced the wall between the cell and the wing corridor as they made their rounds or passed the prisoner his coffee and bread in the morning, his meat and potatoes at noon, his Indian mush in the evening.

The Eastern State guards had to depend on their ears more than their eyes. During the first years of operation, the meal cart wheels were covered in leather and the guards wore socks over their shoes so as to muffle their approach as much as possible. In part this was to intensify the silence within, but it also keyed into Bentham's ambitions: hearing no approach, a prisoner would have no way of knowing when his every movement was being tracked or by whom. Charles Williams might not even have known his meal was arriving until he heard the drawer open. The guards might always be right outside listening for tappings on the pipes, for a whisper or a cough, so Williams would have come to believe that he was always being watched. And anything that was not silence might also fire the imagination of the guards, for sound bends and travels in baffling ways, carrying unexpectedly through hollows and stone. The ear is never as certain as the eye.

Although visual surveillance was quite limited at Eastern State, the sheer scale of the prison, the height and solidity of its walls, and its Gothic exterior with its turreted towers meant that, just as Bentham had strived for with the panopticon, the idea of being watched was palpable. When the Marquis de Lafayette, who'd spent years imprisoned in the Bastille, saw the façade of the penitentiary, he remarked: "I have been subjected to all of this; and of all the sufferings of my life, none have exceeded —none have equalled that single oppression of being, for three whole years . . . exposed to the view of two eyes, watching my every motion, taking from my very thoughts every idea of privacy."

How complicated and seemingly jerry-rigged the solitude and silence of Eastern State were. Drafting fear from the Gothic, concerned with security in tandem with the concept of redemption, the penitentiary couldn't help but be at odds with the spiritual. Even so, the eight-sided central rotunda, filled with light from tall windows on all sides, was the shape of a baptismal font, and the prescribed and invariable rituals of Charles Williams's entry into Eastern State—being washed, shorn, and stripped of his former identity—were reminiscent of a postulant's journey. Hooded, blind, he could hear doors open before him and close behind, and with each portal he passed through, his relation to the outside world receded until finally he arrived at his solitary cell with its plain lime-washed walls, its barrel-vaulted ceiling and circular window.

What Williams thought and how he may have changed during his two-year sentence is left to be gleaned from the bare facts of the penitentiary logbooks, the wardens' journals, and a few recorded encounters with visitors, most prominently Gustave de Beaumont and Alexis de Tocqueville, who spoke with Williams in his cell when they toured Eastern State in 1831, near the end of his time there. "This man works with ardor," they remarked. "His mind seems tranquil; his disposition excellent. He considers his being brought to the Penitentiary as a signal benefit of Providence. His thoughts are in general religious. He read to us in the Gospel the parable of the Good Shepherd, the meaning of which touched him deeply." Imagine him there, his voice hoarse from silence, reciting: "I am the good shepherd, and know my *sheep,* and am known of mine . . . And other sheep I have, which are not of this fold: them also I must bring, and they shall hear my voice; and there shall be one fold, *and* one shepherd."

Aldous Huxley observed that "each living solitude is dependent upon other living solitudes and, more completely still, upon the ocean of being from which it lifts its little reef of individuality." Each prisoner, cut off even from the other living solitudes around him, must have been conscious not only of his own forced silence but also that of the others confined along with him. It's not only that they couldn't speak. They couldn't hear one another. All they had to listen to was the heat through the vents, the wind in the chinks, the feed slots opening and promptly closing.

The prisoners never even gathered for Sunday worship at Eastern State. Although Benjamin Rush calls for a common space in his paper read at Franklin's home, and Haviland mentions an idea for a chapel in his notebook, it was never built into the original construction. Instead, long before radio broadcasts and phonographs and telephones separated the ear from the eye, the inmates listened to the clergy through the same small opening that was used to spy into the cells. Louis Dwight, an early visitor to the penitentiary, described this scene:

> But if there is a chaplain, he might stand in a long and lofty avenue, between the solitary cells, and the little feed-hole drawers, as they are called, might be set open, and a veil hung up between them, so that no one prisoner could look across the avenue and see another; and then, if thirty-six prisoners, being the number arranged on either side of one avenue, will put their heads close to the feed-hole drawers, and the chaplain will stand at the end of the avenue, and speak loud enough, and with a slow and distinct articulation, they can hear his voice, but they cannot see his face. This is the preached gospel as they have it in the New Penitentiary in Philadelphia.

Those who first imagined the penitentiary saw the stone cell and prison sentence of silence as penance, a prescribed time to both suffer and be cleansed, much like that endured by the penitents in Dante's Purgatory. In the *Divine Comedy*, the souls in Heaven and Hell aren't subject to time. Paolo and Francesca, the famed couple condemned to one of the first circles of Hell, will be eternally buffeted by the wind, eternally without volition: "Hither, thither, downward, upward it drives them. No hope of less pain, not to say of rest, ever comforts them." But Purgatory is different. To prepare for his ascent up Mount Purgatory, Dante—as with Charles Williams before his blindfolded walk to his cell—undergoes ablutions. Cato, the guardian of Purgatory, instructs Dante's guide, Virgil: "Go, then, and see that you gird him with a smooth rush, and that you bathe his face so that you remove all defilement from it." And the penitential souls Dante encounters in Purgatory are still governed by time. Things will change for them. They are looking upward and forward even as they are goaded: "When lo, the venerable old man, crying, 'What is this, you laggard spirits? What negligence, what stay is this? Haste to the mountain to strip off the slough that lets not God be manifest to you.'" They anticipate their future cleansed of sin as they begin to circle the mount, their own prayers and the prayers of others lifting them higher and spurring them on.

In his earthly vision of purgatory, Benjamin Rush envisioned a silence and solitude that asked much of the prisoner, but also asked something of the citizens of the new Republic. As ethicist Andrew Skotnicki has noted: "The criminal is what the culture wants the criminal to be; if it wants a demon, a demon it will have, and the demon will be properly accused and treated in the fashion meriting a fiend. If it envisions a person who is 'little less than a god,' then, to a commensurate degree it is God who will be tried, sentenced, and punished."

Who, then, did the citizens of the new Republic want Williams to be? To Rush and the promulgators of the penitentiary, he may have been little less than God. To the guards and warden intent on the practical, he may have been simply a man to be watched and constrained while he served his precise sentence. To society, he may have been a curiosity: Eastern State would become a tourist destination drawing countless visitors, famed writers and reporters among them. But unlike those imprisoned in the jails in the center of Philadelphia, or the wheelbarrow men who worked on the city's streets, he might also have become a forgotten soul. The men and women going about their daily errands in the heart of bustling Philadelphia did not have to think of him much out there beyond the outskirts of the city, stripped of his name and hidden behind stone.

PART II

The Monastic World: A History of Silence

Silence is not acoustic. It is a
change of mind, a turning around.

—John Cage

5

in proportion

BENJAMIN RUSH'S IDEA of redemption through imposed silence and solitude, however well-intentioned and rooted in the concept of spiritual silence, inevitably became its own terrain, distinct from both monastic practice and communal, integrated Quaker silence. The advocates of Eastern State don't seem to have anticipated the consequences of meager support for such a sentence, nor to have considered how a single cell—which may appear to be the most uncomplicated form of shelter, with its unadorned stone, spare light, tight quarters, and few furnishings—is no simple thing and, even when chosen, can prove precarious for body, mind, and soul.

Twelfth-century abbot and theologian William of St. Thierry understood the tenuous stability of a solitary life: how one's state of mind, one's heart, one's beliefs, determine whether solitude and silence engender spiritual growth or despair. In his letter to the novices at the monastery of Mont Dieu in France, St. Thierry declares: "You have one cell outwardly, another within you. The outward cell is the house in which your soul dwells together with your body; the inner cell is your conscience." He urges the novices: "Love your inner cell then, love your outward cell too, and give to each of them the care which belongs to it. Let the outward cell shelter you, not hide you away." Ultimately, he warns, "if anyone among you does not possess . . .[piety] in his heart, display it in his life, practice it in his cell, he is to be called not a solitary but a man who is alone, and his cell is not a cell for him but a prison in which he is immured."

Perhaps as Benjamin Rush and his fellow advocates crafted their vision of the penitentiary, they imagined the lives of hermits and anchorites—those religious souls who live an almost entirely cloistered existence. During the Middle Ages some were so secluded they viewed the church altar through a squint and depended upon others to bring meals to their door. But among monastics, they are the exceptions. As Thomas Aquinas maintained: "Solitude, like poverty, is not the essence of perfection, but a means of perfection." Not only is complete seclusion a rarity, but communal support has long been a component of contemplative life, and monks to this day are infrequently given permission by a superior to live apart and alone. The few who undertake such an extreme way of life do so only after rigorous preparation among fellow monastics.

The place of community in monastic life has been emphasized at least as far back as the time of the Desert Fathers. In fourth-century Syria and Egypt, when Christian ascetics left their cities and towns for a more secluded life in the desert, they were undertaking a solitary journey, searching for purity in their practice at a time of growth in the religion. But they soon attracted followers, and their lives of individual contemplation became quilted with a communal ascetic life. Some leaders, in order to effectively govern the communities that grew up around them, set down rules that not only assured an atmosphere conducive to prayer and contemplation, but also emphasized care and concern for one another. "Like doves are those monks of the associations," writes Pachomius in the earliest of these rules, "gentle as a dove, with knowledge and wisdom and love for their neighbor."

In the sixth century, Benedict of Nursia drew on earlier rules to compose his own, which was written as a general guide for the community of monks he established at Monte Cassino. His Rule of Benedict remains the preeminent guide to monastic life even into modern times. Benedict himself spent years in seclusion prior to founding his monastery atop a mountain in the countryside between Naples and Rome, so he knew well the rigors of solitude. In the first chapter of his Rule, he emphasizes the necessity of community by articulating the demands of a secluded life. Hermits "are not neophytes," he insists. "They have spent much time in the monastery testing themselves . . . They have prepared themselves in the fraternal line of battle for the single combat of the hermit."

In the succeeding chapters of his Rule, which are sometimes only a sentence or two, and at most a few paragraphs in length, he promotes both interdependence and respect within the community. The Rule governs the mundane and the sacred, describing the liturgical offices of the day (also known as the Divine Office or the Liturgy of the Hours), the hymns that should be sung, the special qualities of the night, how and when meals might be taken, the arrangements for sleep, how the sick should be treated, how the abbot should be elected. As for silence: though the contemplative orders orient their lives toward silence, it isn't among the four solemn vows of stability, poverty, chastity, and obedience. Benedict addresses silence, but no more emphatically than many other subjects. Perhaps his most specific dictum concerning it comes in his forty-second chapter: "Monks should try to speak as little as possible, but especially at night."

What becomes clear throughout his Rule is that, although profound solitude and silence—essential for creating an atmosphere favorable to waiting, to listening, to prayer—stand at the heart of the contemplative life, community is not merely a practical necessity. It, too, is integral to the spiritual life. In the best circumstances, the community supports each individual soul, anchors its members, and encourages them to be invested in one another's care. It offers the chance for a monk to turn outward, to build a common world, to encounter the human and the divine in others.

Although some contemplative orders are more hermetic than others, all to some degree work together and share meals together. Up until modern times many orders slept collectively in dormitories. And while silence comprises a considerable part of the day, it is woven through with voices in chant and prayer. The communal observance of Mass and the Liturgy of the Hours—Vigils, Lauds, Prime, Terce, Sext, None, Vespers, and Compline—possess their own qualities, distinct from private prayer. Modern theologian and priest Pius Parsch has remarked: "In liturgical prayer . . . it is not primarily *I* who am praying, but the Church . . . The object of her prayer is broader, too: all the needs of God's kingdom here on earth. In liturgical prayer I feel more like a member of a great community, like a little leaf on the great living tree of the Church. I share her life and her problems."

Likewise, communal silence contains a distinct power, as twentieth-century monk Thomas Merton noted upon witnessing one of his first services at the Abbey of Gethsemani in Kentucky, which would become his home: "The silence with people moving in it was ten times more gripping than it had been in my own empty room." It wasn't, for Merton, separate from the ritual, the chant, or the architecture, and he found it overwhelming: "How did I live through that next hour? It is a mystery to me. The silence, the solemnity, the dignity of these Masses and of the church, and the overpowering atmosphere of the prayers so fervent that they were almost tangible choked me with love and reverence that robbed me of the power to breathe. I could only get the air in gasps."

Nothing could be further from the regimen established for Charles Williams and his fellow inmates in the penitentiary. It was community the penitentiary sought to thwart, after all, cognizant of John Howard's observations that fraternizing in the common rooms of jails only contributed to the corruption of the innocent and the further degradation of the guilty. Benedict, in composing his Rule, always had in mind the power of community, even concerning the disciplining of wayward monks. If private, then public, admonishments failed, progressively stricter isolation from fellow monks was required: "This exclusion means that he shall not intone a psalm or antiphon or read a lesson in the oratory, until he makes his amends. His meals will be taken alone, after the others have finished. If the brothers eat at the sixth hour, he will do so at the ninth . . . A brother guilty of a graver fault is to be excluded from the common table and the oratory. No one shall speak or meet with him. He shall work alone, remaining in penance and sorrow. He shall eat alone . . . He is not to be blessed as he passes nor is his food to be blessed."

Such exclusion within the monastery, intended to be neither vindictive nor retributive, was understood as a means of bringing the offender to a realization of his faults. There was no prescribed sentence of certain length; rather, the period of punishment was measured by repentance and forgiveness. Atonement, which at its root means *at onement,* worked toward a reconciliation with the community and with God. Monastic punishments were meant to be temporary, to foster a renewed respect for both the community and oneself, and presented an opportunity for the transgressor to return to the fold. They were not meant to plague the fallen monk afterward.

What eventually transpired at Eastern State hewed more closely to the corruption of Benedict's concepts. During the Middle Ages some monasteries, contrary to the Rule, began to seclude errant monks in cells. The cruel history of those punishments is recorded in Dom Jean Mabillon's "Reflections on the Prisons of the Monastic Orders," published in 1724, some seventeen years after his death. Mabillon, a member of the Order of Saint Benedict, or Benedictines, served as the assistant to the librarian of the Abbey of St-Germain des Prés in Paris, and in that capacity he made extensive visits to the Benedictine libraries and monasteries of Germany and Italy, bringing manuscripts and books back to Paris in order to write a history of the order.

In his "Reflections," he observes that at first punishment cells, which were generally a chamber and a workroom, were "more retreat than a prison since there was a heated room and workshop." But he notes the cruelties of certain monasteries: "The harshness of some priors went to such an excess (it seems difficult to believe it) that they mutilated the limbs and sometimes struck out the eyes of those of their monks who had fallen into considerable errors." And the cells also became crueler, often built partially underground, without windows. They comprised "a frightful kind of prison, where daylight never entered . . . and since it was designed for those who should finish their lives in it, it received the name *Vade in pace.*" Go in peace.

Mabillon, insisting that punishment must be approached with compassion, was much aggrieved by this historical turn of events, and he knew its usual ends: "The measure of unhappiness of these unfortunates was caused to overflow by their being cut off from all human consolations and that was at least as hard for them to bear as their inability to see the light of day . . . That is why one sees so little fruit from the prisons and penances imposed by the superiors on those who fall and why these poor unfortunates so often lose their mind or all sensitiveness; in other words that they either become insane or hardened and desperate."

Mabillon lists suggestions for improving the prisons of the monastic orders that hewed closely to Benedict's Rule. Harshness should be banished, he advises, and justice should take on a paternal tone. He imagines cellular confinement, but of a humane dimension. He suggests that this cell should be similar to that of the seventh-century monk John Climacus, who retired to live in solitude at the base of Mount Sinai for twenty years: a comfortable cell furnished with good books "to entertain them, sustain them, and fortify them." He proposes that the monks should be able to attend Mass and be occupied by some kind of labor; that each have a workshop and garden; and that they join with others for the Divine Office. Their food was to be simple and coarse; they would be comforted by visits from superiors, but there were to be no outsiders, and strict solitude otherwise. More than the physical surroundings, Mabillon emphasizes the recognition that every prisoner was Christ.

If Dom Mabillon had been able to peer into Eastern State, surely he'd have seen that the sentence of prescribed time, which was rarely under two years for a prisoner, and at times twelve or more, would likely break most. "One knows but too well," he writes, "that it is sufficiently hard to pass only a few days in silence and spiritual exercises which are voluntarily done . . . And then one imagines that the poor wretches overwhelmed by shame and sorrow, could pass entire years in a narrow prison without conversation and human consolations?"

John Haviland's stone-and-mortar design for Eastern State emphasized the isolation of each prisoner. In the monastery it is the idea of community that is set in stone, perhaps most evidently in the architecture of the Cistercian Order, which arose during the eleventh and twelfth centuries in France. The Cistercians were established as a reaction to what its founders perceived as increasing slackness in the members of Benedict's order, who had begun to be preoccupied with elaborate Church rituals and, rather than supporting themselves through their labors as Benedict had instructed, had turned to the selling of indulgences, not only for support but also as a means of increasing their wealth. In some Benedictine monasteries, the surroundings grew ornate; the meals, extravagant.

Cistercians sought a return to a less elaborate liturgy, to a life of poverty, and to supporting themselves with their labor. Bernard de Clairvaux, one of the founders of the Cistercian order, called for humility and simplicity in the design of the monasteries, which were to remain close to the earth, with no high bell towers. There should be nothing to suggest riches or human ambition—no gargoyles, statuary, or tracery; just plain grisaille glass in the windows. "There must be no decoration, only proportion," Bernard insisted. And in a letter to William of St. Thierry he asks: "In the cloister, under the eyes of the Brethren who read there, what profit is there in those ridiculous monsters, in the marvellous and deformed comeliness, that comely deformity?"

Centuries later, Thomas Merton, whose Trappist order is also known as the Order of Cistercians of the Strict Observance, remarked: "The Churches of our Fathers expressed their humility and their silence. There was nothing superfluous about either the office of our Fathers or their architecture . . . They did not use up stone and time in an appeal to sentimental taste or in reverence to some false, arbitrary criterion of piety in art." He made his observation after encountering photographs of one of the earliest Cistercian monasteries, the Abbey of Notre Dame de Sénanque, settled on the floor of the Sénacole Valley, outside the village of Gordes in the Vaucluse region of France: "They knew a good building would praise God better than a bad one . . . Their churches were built around the psalms. Their cloisters were like the chant . . . The simplicity of Sénanque . . . could only house a community . . . A monastery of hermits is necessarily so clumsy that it can only be an architectural monster."

It may have been practically true that by the time the Cistercian Order arose in the eleventh and twelfth centuries, the best land in southern France was already claimed by village and farm, and the land available to build on—the order was dependent on gifts of land for their monasteries—was thorny, marshy, and rough. But Bernard de Clairvaux, besides insisting on austerity in the design, directed that monasteries be built at a remove from villages and cities in an attempt to re-create the solitude of the desert, to abet attention to God and prayer, and to foster stability in the community. He also directed that Cistercian fields and granges were to be no more than a day's journey from the monastery, which was a reinforcement of the Rule of Benedict: "The monastery should be planned, if possible, with all the necessities—water, mill, garden, shops—within the walls. Thus the monks will not need to wander about outside, for this is not good for their souls."

The remoteness that assured a monastery's seclusion also meant construction was slow, even by twelfth-century standards. Before the builders set the first course of stones for the oratory at Sénanque, they drained the land by banking the Sénacole River to create a reservoir on low ground, then cleared brush, brambles, and rocks; felled oak trees and sawed the trunks into planks; and lay the lumber out to dry. Planks for doors and benches and tables; other wood to fuel the lime kiln and forge they'd build. They quarried their own limestone blocks from the valley walls, the stone dust swelling their eyes and settling into their lungs. They split stone by drilling holes along the faults, setting oak pegs into the holes, and then flooding the stone with water until the pegs expanded and the stone cracked. Then they dressed the stone and loaded the blocks onto wagons to haul them to the building site.

They gleaned the building techniques from the ruins of Rome that were scattered throughout the region. The monks worked alongside and learned from the masons and cutters—perhaps itinerants from Lombardy—who left their marks, clear to this day, on the stone. Patience and their patient imagination, and faith in the duration of their vision, carried them through: none of those who began the work would live to see it finished. Undertaken by a sequence of monks, masons, and master builders, the first stage of the construction took thirty years. By then only the choir had been completed, but the church could be consecrated. The nave would take nearly another thirty years, and the dormitory, refectory, chapter house, warming room, library, cloister, and accommodations for lay brothers wouldn't be completed for a century.

Although the oratory doors at Sénanque are plain—without statuary or flourishes to catch the eye of strangers, as the entry to a pilgrim church might have—it, like any Cistercian monastery, however remote, was meant to accommodate outsiders. "*All* guests to the monastery should be welcomed as Christ," instructs Benedict in his Rule, "because He will say, 'I was a stranger, and you took me in.'" He also notes: "A wise old monk should guard the gates of the monastery. He shall know how to receive and answer a question, and be old enough so that he will not be able to wander far. His cell should be nearby; thus, all who arrive will find someone to give information."

The monks at Sénanque welcome visitors to this day to tour parts of the twelfth-century abbey that have survived the wars, dissolutions, and corruptions of the ages. The rooms have been emptied of temporal traces: no bedding or scent of straw in the dormitory; no desks, ink, awls, or parchment in the warming room where the scribes once worked. The residue of soot in the fireplace—so large that the monks could burn tree trunks standing upright—seems to be part of the shadows. Even so, the spaces, in their austerity, precision, and proportion, feel as if they lack nothing. "Medieval comfort is the comfort of space," observed historian Siegfried Giedion. "A medieval room seems finished even when it contains no furniture. It is never bare . . . It lives in its proportions, its materials, its form . . . This sense for the dignity of space did not end with the Middle Ages . . . Yet no later age so emphatically renounced bodily comfort. The ascetic ways of monasticism invisibly shaped the period to its own image . . . There should be peace in man's intimate surroundings. And this is what one breathes in medieval chambers, quietude and contemplation."

The architecture was also meant to serve as an allegory. A thirteenth-century anonymous manuscript known as "La Sainte Abbaye" declares: "Confession shall be the chapter house, because it tells the truth. Preaching shall be the refectory because it feeds souls. Prayer shall be the chapel which must be high according to contemplation and beyond all worldly cares. Compassion shall be the infirmary; devotion the store-room; meditation, the grange."

The play of light and shadow is its own language, and the lack of ornamentation and the plain grisaille glass in the monastery windows stabilize both: nothing fanciful to make light waiver or to create intricate shadows or to take the mind wandering. A solidity meant to foster attention to prayer, reading, hymns, and contemplation. Order and proportion meant to reflect the nature of God. Eight hundred years after the founding of the Cistercian Order, Le Corbusier felt a kinship with it. "The whole and its details are one," he said of Cistercian architecture. "None of these things are there to catch the eye."

These unadorned spaces, with their balance and simplicity,

feel as if they've streamed unaffected through centuries of ornamentation and colored leaded glass, past gargoyles and grotesques: solid shafts of sunlight on the bare limestone floors and against spare scrolls on the cloister capitals; light filling entries and recessed window wells; shadows lying deep in the corners of the warming room, settled beneath the arches of the doorways, in the ribs of the vaulted ceilings and the fine chisel marks of the stonemasons. The plain lime-washed walls and the grisaille glass, the solid light and shadow, help to focus attention, but the spare light is also divine. Twentieth-century thinker Marshall McLuhan remarked that "any medieval person would be puzzled at our idea of looking through something. He would assume that reality looked through at us, and that by contemplation we bathed in the divine light, rather than looked at it." And more particularly, as art historian Roger Hinks has suggested, "it is as though we were invited to focus our eyes not only on the physical surface of the object, but on infinity as seen through the lattice . . . ; the object exists—as it were—merely to define and detach a certain portion of infinite space, and make it manageable and apprehensible."

But the austerity of the architecture is not for the eye alone. "Why do you strain to see?" asked Bernard de Clairvaux. "It is necessary to lend the ear. The hearing, moreover, will restore vision to us, if our attention is pious, faithful and vigilant." In the many silences of their day, the monks were listening for the divine. As Paul in his letter to the Romans wrote: "So then faith *cometh* by hearing, and hearing by the word of God."

Silence is also an integral part of all monastic chants and prayers. Voices rise out of silence and descend back into it, and music and silence are interdependent in a house imagined and built for the glory of God. One of the aims of the architecture in a world without mechanical amplification was to create space where the human voice could resonate deeply and harmoniously and the sacred readings could be heard clearly. The voices of any monastic community are inevitably varied in their gifts and their abilities. The halting, the raspy, the frail, the confident, and the powerful sing as one, striving toward praise. In the most perfectly proportioned oratories, the absence of fanciful design, just as it does not distract light, also does not distort the human voice.

When Robert Lawlor, an authority on sacred geometry, visited Le Thoronet, one of Sénanque's sister abbeys in southern France, he remarked:

> The eye does not see what causes the intense change of mind and body. But something compels one to listen, and the ear to resonate . . . I understood why St. Bernard . . . insisted on vaulted chambers built to a relatively small scale. Their size undoubtedly had been determined as the perfect acoustical volume to enhance the human voice . . . The Abbey . . . does not promote a fundamental tone, but instead allows all notes to resound equally . . . Standing next to a certain pillar in the nave, one's hearing seems suddenly turned inside-out; the heartbeat and internal workings of the organs are magnified; even external sounds seem to originate from within.

And, Lawlor observes, there would have been almost nothing to interfere with the purity of the voices: "No outside sound of man or nature could penetrate the thick walls of stone, and here the mind, wrapped in silence, was able to follow the ear to a confrontation with the eternal."

When I imagine the silence Charles Williams endured at Eastern State, I imagine its weight—how it must have been almost entirely unchanging and unforgiving, pressing down so completely that it shattered all the smaller silences of the day. And then I imagine the monastery, where both silence and the breaking of it are considered sacred, and the days are interwoven with silences of varying purposes and duration: the silences of single souls praying in solitude, reading in solitude, working in solitude; the silences of a community harvesting together in the fields or baking in the kitchen; the silences within the rituals of the Liturgy of the Hours and the Mass, which may be as brief as a handful of heartbeats.

While chanting the psalms, one half of the monastic community faces the other half in the oratory. Half sing the first part of the verse of a psalm, and then all is silent for a moment before the other half of the community completes it. Here, in Psalm 34, the asterisks mark the breaks:

> I will always give thanks unto the Lord; * his praise shall
> ever be in my mouth.
> My soul shall make her boast in the Lord; * the humble shall
> hear thereof, and be glad.
> O praise the Lórd with me, * and let us magnify his Name
> together.

And so they proceed: voices, then silence, then completing voices. The brief silence in the middle of the line allows sound to reverberate; allows the community to listen, to anticipate, to wait. It is a pause for the beauty of the music, for the spirit, for the breath, for the mind. Historian Emma Hornby has explained that in the Middle Ages this *media distinctio* "was considered to be a ceremonial pause, enhancing the solemnity of the chanting. It sometimes served as an architectural pause, lasting until the echo of the previous pitch had died away; the length of the pause depended on the acoustics of the building. The pause would also have promoted meditation: psalm verses often have two statements that mirror each other, and pausing in the middle gives time for reflecting . . . An important aspect . . . was the unity it embodied: the unity of the monastery breathing and singing together."

The silence, Hornby observed, also allows the spirit in: "Both the Hebrew and Greek words for 'spirit' also mean 'breath' or 'wind' and, in Christian teaching the Holy Spirit is said to have come to the disciples first as a wind." I have sat as a visitor among a community of faith at Vespers, surrounded by ancient limestone and deepening shadows, and have witnessed that briefest of silences. The peace, the psalms, the sense of the ancient—nothing stunned me as much as encountering the first brief interval of silence between verses. It was more than fifteen years ago now, and to this day I can't say why.

6

speech and silence

AND WHAT OF simple talk within such a prescribed world of voices and silences? It's meant to be rare, and during medieval times was nearly as regulated as it would be at Eastern State Penitentiary. Benedict in his Rule, evoking Psalm 39, insists that monks are not to converse, not with their tongue or eyes or gestures: "Let us do as the prophet says: 'I have said: I will keep my ways so that I will not offend with my tongue. I have guarded my speech. I held my peace and humbled myself and was silent, even from speaking good things.'"

Although the restriction on speech for contemplative monastics during the Middle Ages wasn't absolute, it was formal. Cistercians were limited as to when, where, and about what they spoke, and speaking was to be used with discipline, most often by monks in specialized positions, such as the abbot, the cellarer, the porter, and the master of the novices. They were required, after all, to conduct the business of the abbey, procure supplies, take care of guests, or teach. To this day obedience is a given in the conversations that do take place between a monk and his superior, student and teacher, confessor and priest. "The master should speak and teach," notes Benedict, "the disciple should quietly listen and learn. No matter what must be asked of a superior, it must be done with humility and reverent submission."

Such obedience in conversation can't help but seem strange and constricting now, but there is an implied dignity in it, a devotion to the depth and true import of human speech, for the root meaning of the verb "obey" establishes just how essential silence is to speech. The word is from the Latin *oboedire,* which in turn comes from *audire,* "to hear." To obey is *to be subject to, to serve, to pay attention to, to give ear to, to listen to, to perceive.*

To listen fully requires silence. To engage in meaningful conversation requires silence. "Speech and silence belong together," observed twentieth-century Swiss philosopher Max Picard. "To see speech without silence is like seeing Shakespeare's fools without the solidity of Shakespeare's heroes." Even in everyday conversation, the qualities of their interrelation are as nuanced as the *media distinctio* in the chant. The silence in which a speaker pauses to think, to choose the right word. The silence in which another listens as a sign of respect, that allows time to comprehend the weight and meaning of what is said, that affirms the import of language itself. Also: the silence to which a speaker turns an attentive ear after her last word rises. "Listening requires that I come out of myself, so as to make room for speech," wrote French philosopher Jean-Louis Chrétien. "It is a listening that is freed from everything sticky and clinging in its psychological representations, a listening without glue, a listening that is free and liberating."

In his Rule, Benedict specifically warns against the most breathless kinds of talk: murmuring, gossip, and grumbling, which he groups with stubbornness, disobedience, pride, and joking. It is not only that gossip is almost void of silence even when quietly whispered in another's ear; consider its synonyms: hearsay, chitchat, scuttlebutt. Gossip also suggests a loose or ungoverned tongue. If monks, believing themselves created in the image of the divine, spent their voices on gossip, they'd undercut their efforts to prove worthy of God. More than a dozen centuries after Benedict, Thomas Merton instructed his scholastics: "Silence itself is a human value." He explained further: "Restraint from useless words has a human value."

The rule against unnecessary talk may have also had a practical side for Benedict. Gossip and grumbling may be primarily regarded as an offense against God, but in any isolated community—a monastery as much as an island town or a village—gossip can be destructive, so restrictions on speech may have helped the community cohere. In addition, the reasons monks had for entering the monastery were diverse. Some joined because their place in the family left them little alternative; some because of their belief; others for shelter, security, and food. And in the hierarchical world of the early Christian era and the Middle Ages, monastics from different social classes lived and worked together, which could create conflict. But a closed community also holds challenges in modern times. "With all the mixture of men they have there, they get along better without it," explained one of Merton's mentors regarding casual talk in the monastery. "Lawyers and farmers and soldiers and schoolboys, they all live together, and go everywhere together and do everything together. They stand in choir together and go out to work together and sit together in the same place when they read and study. It's a good thing they don't talk."

Once Merton arrived at the Abbey of Gethsemani, he discovered that within the monastery, the expectations for the community were high. "The imperfections are much smaller and more trivial than the defects and vices of people outside in the world," he wrote, "and yet somehow you tend to notice them more and feel them more, because they get to be so greatly magnified by the responsibilities and ideals of the religious state, through which you cannot help looking at them."

Gossip and grumbling would have been particularly tempting when the community gathered for meals, which may be part of the reason Benedict specifically calls for silence in the rectory. Mealtime is considered sacred, in imitation of the Last Supper, and to serve the community is considered an essential part of monastic life. "The brothers should wait on one another," Benedict instructs. "No one is to be excused from kitchen duty unless he is ill or he is engaged in a task of greater import, for he can thus obtain greater charity and commendation."

Meals themselves were structured to keep the inner constancy of the monk's attention on the divine. In the Middle Ages, even the arrangement of the table was meant to abet silence. Each monk had an assigned place at the table, and monks did not usually face one another at meals. Typically, chairs were placed only on one long side of each rectangular table, and the tables were set in rows, with each monk facing forward—a life side by side, not face-to-face. All ate the same meal, close to peasant fare: milk, vegetables, beans, bread, pottage, fish, and cheese. (Cistercians do not eat meat, nothing with four legs, unless they're sick, and then some of the restrictions on food are lifted.) While they ate off wooden plates and sipped their porridge from rough wooden bowls, the monks listened to a reader, as Bernard instructed, who was carefully chosen from the ranks for the quality of his voice and its strength—there was nothing to amplify his words save the stone—so that it "may uplift the listeners."

Most of us are inclined to think of mealtime as a special province of human companionship, perhaps never more beautifully depicted than in the humble meal shared by five peasants in Vincent van Gogh's *The Potato Eaters.* You can see their long day in their eyes and in their posture, which makes their gathering all the more gratifying. "The colour they're painted now *is something like the colour of a really dusty potato, unpeeled of course,*" wrote Van Gogh to his brother Theo. "While I was doing it I thought again about what has so rightly been said of Millet's peasants—'*His peasants seem to have been painted with the soil they sow.*'"

The small table Van Gogh's five souls gather around may be square, but all else accentuates a circle of intimacy. The light from above circumscribes them in its warmth. Beyond, the cottage lies in shadow, the province of Old Night, immense and inarticulate. But around the lit table they are sharing cups, sharing food. Their gnarled hands are larger than the vessels they grasp. Communication is everywhere within the circle. They are turned to one another, speaking perhaps with voices, but also—and most evidently—with their eyes and gestures, which convey a long familiarity. A child has her back to the viewer, the young face among them unseen. We are privy to the weathered faces of their world, and their long intimacies and knowing conversations.

It may be difficult to conjure the same closeness among those who shared a meal sitting side by side in silence as they ate, looking into the backs of their fellow monks. Surely they knew one another as well as Van Gogh's peasants. They lived within the community and raised crops together, repaired walls, baked bread, and worshipped together. But they weren't to betray that through gestures or words during the meal. If a monk wished for more bread or fish, he'd use a sign language comprised mainly of nouns—water, soup, carrots, potatoes, cabbage, bread. It was a language useful only for brief and specific communication, so the monks wouldn't be tempted by casual talk even with signs.

Some sign lists come down to us from the Middle Ages. At Cluny, a medieval Benedictine monastery, the list of signs for food was remarkably extensive and specific. "For the sign of bread make a circle with the thumb and its two adjacent fingers because bread is customarily round . . . For the sign of bread, which is cooked in water and which is better than that served on most days, after making the general sign for bread, place the palm of one hand over the outside of the other as if oiling or wetting." There was a sign for marked bread and another for flat cakes. Signs for beans, for food cooked with oil, for vinegar and honey, and for all the fishes: cuttlefish, eel, lamprey, sturgeon, pike, trout. "For the sign of cheese bring together both hands diagonally, as if pressing cheese," and "for the sign of apples, by far the worst and most evil sign, enclose the thumb with the other fingers."

During the twentieth century, the signs for scythe, horse, and bookbinder fell away, and new signs—for tractor, bulldozer, boiler room, coffee—gained purchase. As well, the rules regarding sign language became less rigid than in the past. Merton recalled observing the novices who "kidded one another in sign language." In general today, although the communities still eat together in silence, formal sign language has gone the way of quill pens, the muttering flames of the fires, and the knocking of wooden spoons against wooden bowls.

Still, among the chuffing of boilers and furnaces, among key clicks and the whir of electric dough mixers, the value of silence isn't questioned, even if speaking is more common. For what was articulated by the congregation at Cluny in the tenth century still holds for monastics today: "The usefulness of silence is supremely necessary in every religious institute; in fact, unless it is properly observed, we cannot speak of the religious life at all, for there can be none."

But just as speech has its degrees of integrity, so does silence, which can become an unthinking exercise or an excuse for noninvolvement. Silence can lie as well as words, and to listen to one another can at times be far more difficult than listening to the large silence of the world. In the end, there is nothing less narrow than human speech, distinguishing and various. And a silence practiced too simply, too much for its own end, is not silence so much as muteness. Which isn't really a synonym for silence. "The two words exclude one another," wrote Italian philosopher Michele Federico Sciacca in the 1950s. "Silence is a kind of communication. What is mute isolates and cuts off from all communication. Rather than being a lack on the sense level, silence is an intensification on the spiritual level."

The monastery, with its own distinct and elaborate silence, with its particular regulations, possesses no less danger of distorted silence than does secular life. It can become as restrictive as the imposed silence of the penitentiary. Sister Joann Ottenstroer, a Dominican nun writing in the late 1960s, suggested that silent monastic meals might be a lost opportunity for deeper human connection, that speaking at mealtime could offer something essential to the community. "An appreciation and respect for the kind of communication which builds real personal relationship and thus a community of united persons must be developed in order to make silence a purposeful rather than a destructive force," she wrote. "Possibly the effort required to develop good table conversation would require much more self-discipline and unselfishness than keeping silence."

And although the silence is less rigid in a contemporary monastery, it may seem more emphatic, for the monastic traditions rose to prominence in a quieter time than our own. Though men and women could certainly be talkative during the Middle Ages, they likely spoke more slowly, and the silences between words were more pronounced. "Do they not talk and think faster in the depot than they did in the stage-office?" Henry David Thoreau asked nearly two centuries ago. The speed of talk has only increased in the ensuing centuries, and now actual voices jostle with recorded and transmitted voices for attention.

Perhaps because monastic silence exists outside of the usual course of human life and social norms, its powers and presumptions are that much more easily distorted. At Gethsemani, Merton discovered that finding the right silence seemed at times far more difficult than finding the right words. "What a disaster to build the contemplative life on the negation of communication," he wrote. "That is what, in fact, our silence often is—because we are obscuring it without really wanting it (yet needing it nonetheless) and without understanding what it is all about." And then:

> That is why there is so much noise in a Trappist monastery. The infernal clatter and hullabaloo, the contin-

ual roar of machinery, the crash of objects falling from the hands of distraught contemplatives—all this protests that we hate silence with all our power because, with our wrong motives for seeking it, it is ruining our lives. Yet the fact remains that silence is our life—but a *silence which is communication and better communication than words!* If only someone could tell us how to find it.

The worse pity of all is that we think we know.

What we have found is our own noise.

No, that is not true. The Paradox is that in spite of all, we have found God and that is probably the trouble. Such a discovery is altogether too much and we beat a hasty retreat into any kind of protection.

Michael Sweetman, a Jesuit priest addressing his fellow religious in the early 1960s, described the way the strangeness of the silent monastic life—with its absence of the simplest human conversation, whether kind, profound, or trivial—can come back to one later: "Those who have enjoyed the gift of ill-health will remember vividly their return, after a long absence, to their religious house. More than the uncarpeted floors, and perhaps the hard bed, the thing that impresses most as different is the observance of silence. After the first greeting people settle down to passing you on the corridor without the flicker of an eyelid; they look for no sign of recognition and give none. Rather they look through you . . . They will sit mute beside you at meals . . . During the previous weeks it would have been considered ill-mannered to ignore a nurse or doctor or patient . . . They would interpret your behaviour as unfriendly and resent it."

Sweetman had no interest in denigrating silence: "The positive reason for silence is, of course, to give ourselves a chance to find God and live in His presence. The enjoyment of His company should be the greatest compensation for the sacrifices entailed . . . [God] does not usually shout down the other voices that clamor for our attention. We must silence them if we are to hear Him." But he also noted how the great expansiveness that silence offers can easily corrupt into useless silence. For Sweetman, the reverse side of silence, the danger in silence becoming an unthinking habit, flickers near the surface: "A silence which is nothing more than not talking may be admitted, generally, to be harmful." He concluded: "Since, then, we adopt a code of manners or conventions so different from the general run of Christians, we must be at pains to make sure it is a better one."

As Merton noted: "*Babel.* Silence not a virtue, noise not a sin." It's an observation that applies equally to the penitentiary and the monastery—both institutions born of human imagination and subject to human frailties. More specifically he wrote: "But if silence itself becomes the *worship of a concept,* then we become prisoners of what we are seeking to escape. And then we judge like the workers in the vineyard—and make our tyrannical concept the measure of everything that happens under the sun."

7

thomas merton: silence and the world

SILENCE DOESN'T KEEP pace with the world. It has nothing to add to material gain, nor to the clamor of daily life. Cistercian monk and writer Michael Casey has written that Benedict "advises his monks 'to make themselves strangers to the actions of the age.'" As a monk in the modern world, Casey has called this becoming "strangers to the city." The noise of the city, he has suggested—the sounds of the busyness and distractions of the times, the sounds of production and material hopes—runs counter to the silence of the natural world: birds calling from a high branch, ice cracking in the cold, trees stirring in the wind. Or that of old villages, which, to Max Picard, "seem to lie in an opening of silence . . . as if silence were itself looking down on the little town."

Thomas Merton's life mapped the journey of a citizen of the city becoming a stranger to it. His childhood was marked by restlessness and loss: his mother dead from cancer when he was six; years shuttling between his grandparents on Long Island and his painter father in Bermuda and then France; his father suffering a lingering death when Merton was still a teenager. His school years in England in the aftermath of that loss were marked by nights of carousing that didn't abate when he returned to the United States to attend Columbia University as an undergraduate.

During his time at Columbia he typically spent evenings with friends in Manhattan, where they "would crawl around the tiny, noisy, and expensive nightclubs that had flowered on the sites of the old speakeasies in the cellars of those dirty brownstone houses. There we would sit for hours, packed in those dark rooms, shoulder to shoulder with a lot of surly strangers and their girls, while the whole place rocked and surged with storms of jazz." He'd stay so late that he often missed the last train back to Long Island, where he was living with his grandparents. "It was nothing unusual for me to sleep on the floor," he recalled, "or in a chair, or on a couch too narrow and too short for comfort—that was the way we lived."

But while he was a student in New York, and during the years immediately following, he also read intensely and broadly—philosophy, spiritual writings, novels, poetry—as he attempted to establish himself as a writer and searched for purpose in his life, for a way not to be superfluous to the times. It was through his reading of Saint Augustine, Thomas à Kempis, John of the Cross, and Jacques Maritain in particular, and in his conversations with friends and teachers—specifically Dan Walsh, who taught a course on Thomas Aquinas at Columbia—that he found himself drawn increasingly to Catholicism. He was eventually baptized into the faith.

Although he looked to his conversion to orient himself in the world, he remained unsettled as to what shape his life within the religion would take. His first efforts aimed toward good works. He taught literacy in Harlem, night school at Columbia, and composition at St. Bonaventure, a Franciscan college in upstate New York. While at St. Bonaventure, he considered joining the Franciscans, a mendicant order, which would likely mean a life of teaching for him. Eventually Merton both retreated from the idea of joining the Franciscans and was discouraged from pursuing it. Years later, when he looked back at this time of casting about for his right place, he wrote: "What I needed was the solitude to expand in breadth and depth and to be simplified out under the gaze of God more or less the way a plant spreads out its leaves in the sun. This meant that I needed a Rule that was almost entirely aimed at detaching me from the world and uniting me with God, not a Rule made to fit me to fight for God in the world. But I did not find out all that in one day."

Monasticism didn't possess an immediate appeal for him. Up until the year before he settled in the Knobs of Kentucky at Gethsemani, he understood little of the actual life of a cloistered contemplative, and the idea of its silence seemed utterly foreign to him. He was, after all, an unfailingly social soul in his way, loving discussion and engagement in the world of ideas, and he imagined monasticism as an absolute: daily life devoid of speech, devoid of community bonds. He thought it cold and cruel, inhuman, an "excessive rejection of the rights of nature." Dan Walsh disabused him of his notions by explaining to him that although the monks didn't casually converse, they did speak at times, and they recited prayers and chanted psalms together. Upon hearing this, Merton recalled, "I was relieved to think that the monks got to choir and exercised their vocal cords. I was afraid that so much silence would wither them up altogether."

During the spring of 1941, while he was at St. Bonaventure, Walsh encouraged him to make a retreat at Gethsemani. Merton was twenty-six years old, exhausted not only by his uncertainty concerning the course of his life, but also by the dark note that had descended upon the world. He himself had described that darkness several years before: "The atmosphere of the city suddenly became terribly tense with some news that came out of the radios. Before I knew what the news was, I began to feel the tension. For I was suddenly aware that the quiet, disparate murmurs of different radios in different houses had imperceptibly merged into one big, ominous unified voice, that moved at you from different directions and followed you down the street . . . I heard 'Germany—Hitler.'"

Gethsemani. "That was where I needed to go," Merton wrote, regarding Walsh's suggestion. "Something had opened out, inside me, in the last months, something that required, demanded at least a week in that silence, in that austerity, praying together with the monks in their cold choir." His Easter retreat proved to be even more profound than he could have imagined. While beyond the monastery gates the world descended ever more deeply into war, he was entranced by the solemnity, the psalms, the ritual, the sense of the eternal he found there. Cistercian traditions and ceremonies had been carried forward nearly unchanged since the Middle Ages. The monastery itself, built of local brick and Indiana limestone in the mid-nineteenth century, had housed a community of monks for nearly a hundred years.

He particularly noticed the anonymity monastic life offered. During the first days of his retreat, Merton saw a postulant, a young man in the choir who stood out with his "dark secular clothes." Later he recalled: "Then suddenly we saw him no more. He was in white. They had given him an oblate's habit, and you could not pick him out from the rest." Above all, however, it was the silence and solitude that drew Merton in: "I had entered into a solitude that was an impregnable fortress. And the silence that enfolded me, spoke to me, and spoke louder and more eloquently than any voice."

After a week he returned to St. Bonaventure, but before the year was out, he was making preparations to join the Trappists. He had received a medical deferment from the local draft board, though he had been prepared to sign up as a conscientious non-combatant "and serve in the medical corps, or as a stretcher bearer, or hospital orderly . . . so long as I did not have to drop bombs on open cities, or shoot at other men."

During his last days at St. Bonaventure, his commitment to entering the monastery deepened as he felt himself letting go of the life he knew. As he walked around the college grounds and the nearby countryside, he remarked with joy and wonder that "for the first time in my life I realized I no longer cared whether I preserved my place in all this or lost it . . . I was in the hands of One Who loved me far better than I could ever love myself: and my heart was filled with peace . . . It was a peace that did not depend on houses, or jobs, or places . . . It was a peace that time and . . . the world could not give."

Then he dismantled his life as he knew it. He sent his clothes to Harlem, where he'd once worked, and left most of the books on the shelf in his room at St. Bonaventure. He ripped up his novels—three finished, one half-finished—and threw them in an incinerator. He was kinder to his poems, which he sent to one of his teachers at Columbia, Mark Van Doren. He wrote a few notes to friends, then boarded a train to Kentucky. On the eve of America's involvement in World War II, he traveled through the bare winter landscape of the Advent season to his new life at Gethsemani.

"And it was appropriate that the beginning of freedom should be as it was," he wrote. "For I entered a garden that was dead and stripped and bare . . . The sun was hidden behind low clouds and an icy wind was blowing . . . In a sense my freedom had already begun, for I minded none of these things." After being shown to his room, he promptly went to the church to attend his first service. "If I expected any grand welcome from Christ and His angels, I did not get it—not in the sensible order. The huge nave was like a tomb and the building was cold as ice. However I did not mind." Given a small measure of time to be unanchored, he moved through his first day, feeling his way, unsure of what would happen next, reading and wondering and attending services. The following morning the novice master knocked on his door, greeted him, and asked simply: "Does the silence scare you?"

Trappists are to possess almost nothing of their own, and the material goods of the monastery are common goods. In his Rule, Benedict declares that "the abbot is to furnish all necessities: cowl, tunic, shoes, stockings, belt, knife, pen, needle, towel and writing tablet. With these, any excuse for need will be vanquished." This concept of communal possessions had a deeply spiritual origin and was considered good for both the individual soul and for the strength of the community. Historian Scott Bruce has noted that the monks of Cluny "could only use the possessive adjective 'my' to refer to their parents or their sins."

When he recalled his first days at the monastery, Merton described a box "that was to represent all the privacy I had left: one small box, in which I would keep a couple of notebooks full of poems and reflections and a volume of St. John of the Cross . . . and the letters I would receive." His letting go of the world would be every bit as extreme as his letting go of the personal. There would be no newspapers, no radio. The world was to disappear from him just as much as he was to disappear from the world. He would give up his name and be known in the community as Frater Louis.

But he was never destined to be an obscure monk. Although he assumed that he'd leave his writing life behind once he entered the order, at the urging of his abbot he wrote the story of his young life, his conversion to Catholicism, and his entry into the monastery. *The Seven Storey Mountain* became one of the best-selling books in the United States when it was published in 1948. The unforeseen, extraordinary success of his autobiography meant that his solitude became, in its way, very public. In addition to his obligations to the community, Merton would always be involved in extensive correspondence with readers. Throughout his life at Gethsemani he received international visitors seeking his opinions and advice, and he fielded frequent requests for books and articles from New York editors and publishers. He befriended writers, scholars, and prominent religious figures from around the world with whom he would correspond, and some of them would come to Gethsemani. The Trappists, too, looked to him to write religious histories and commentary.

The pressures and demands of the writing life were enough to send him dreaming of a hermitage. In his difficult moments he felt that his writing obligations, which were inevitably an obligation to his community and the larger world, were just another thing that intruded on his life of prayer and solitude. And they attached him to his previous life. He called his writerly self "my double, my shadow, my enemy, Thomas Merton, the old man of the sea."

Merton's monastic life may have seemed far from the world of silence he dreamed of, and it often was. It also seemed so to some outsiders. Robert Giroux, his editor, recalled: "One sign of [*The Seven Storey Mountain*'s] impact was the resentment it inspired in certain quarters—not only with hostile reviewers, but with fellow religious, who thought it inappropriate for any monk to write. I remember receiving hate mail saying, 'Tell this talking Trappist who took a vow of silence to shut up!'"

But Merton's desire for solitude almost always went beyond the things writing put in his way. He would also struggle with his duties to the community. During one of his stays in the infirmary, he conflated his obligations to writing and those to the monastic community. His sickroom was his own quiet place, and he was alone in it. "I am a different person!" he declared. "Plenty of time. Plenty of time. No manuscripts, no typewriter. No rushing back and forth to church, no Scriptorium, no breaking your neck to get things done before the next thing happens . . . I moved the table to the window and ate looking out of the window the way the Carthusians do. The clouds flew by, and the huts of the ducks were empty and the frogs sang in the beautiful green pond . . . How close God is in this room! The presence of people around me is always something that divides my attention between the world and God: well, not always, either."

• • •

Monastic life is a radical reorientation that questions the priorities valued by the world beyond its walls, but the world also challenges the monastery and is inextricable from it in many ways. The world has plundered monasteries, monasteries have grown corrupt from within, and their history at times has been steeped in violence. Bernard de Clairvaux, one of the founders of the Cistercian Order, preached the Second Crusade and proved so persuasive that he convinced untold numbers to join the ranks for the war. But the silence at the heart of monastic life continues to attract at least some followers, and often more when the world feels particularly corrupt. It has been said that *The Seven Storey Mountain* drew unforeseen numbers of men to the monastery in the wake of its publication in 1948. The America that emerged from the war was distinctly different from the one Merton left behind to live at Gethsemani. The country was enjoying a massive economic expansion, but not every returning soldier was going to college or settling down to start a family in the suburbs.

The sounds of modern war were exponentially louder than the conflicts of the Middle Ages: the twentieth-century battlefields mired in mud and smoke, the human carnage, the aerial bombings, the open cities on all sides left in ruins. Cathedrals in ruins. Monasteries and remote villages in ruins, too. Hiroshima and Nagasaki. After having endured such a war, young men were willing to sleep on straw, to give up their possessions, to turn their back on the world that had required them to fight.

Father Matthew Torpey, a Cistercian monk at Gethsemani's sister abbey in Conyers, Georgia, remembered that time. "It wasn't by reason of Merton," he said of these men. ". . . The war brought them in." There were so many seeking to enter Gethsemani that the monastery hardly knew what to do with them. "Let us suppose that within four or five years, several hundred men decide that they want lives of silence, prayer, labor, penance, and constant union with God in solitude," Merton wrote. "And suppose they all decide to enter the same monastery . . . and the monastery of seventy grows . . . to two hundred and seventy."

The Trappists built new monasteries to accommodate the startling increase in postulants, but still Gethsemani was overflowing. "The problem of where all these people are going to sleep is becoming acute," wrote Merton in one of his journals. "And now it is really cold, for the first time this winter. The other night the holy water was frozen in the fonts of our dormitory cells when we went up to go to bed. But by the time we got up at two o'clock it had started to melt, because of the presence of so many monks in one room, with all the windows closed."

Perhaps such a life could distance these men from what they had endured, or help them to understand it, or bring them to believe in human goodness again. As Merton himself knew, in spite of all his struggles with community, "the only justification for a life of deliberate solitude is the conviction that it will help you to love not only God but also other men."

8

measures of time

IS IT ANY accident that as time has become more regulated, silence has become scarcer? Of all the mechanical sounds of the modern world, the ticking of the clock is one of the quietest, and the one to which we hold a most specific allegiance. The alarm clock by the bed. The time card and the punch clock. Daybooks. Deadlines. Frederick Taylor's precise tasking, which led to the assembly line. As I go about town on my errands, I stuff my pockets with paper receipts collected at the supermarket, the bank, the hardware store. Each one is stamped with the year, the day, the hour, the minute, and occasionally the second of my forgettable tasks, which have been recorded and perhaps stored along with the days and hours and minutes of the tasks of countless others rushing toward the same ends.

To imagine the far quieter medieval world in which the Cistercian monasteries arose, you need to imagine time absent our stamped slips and stopwatches, absent the equal measure of hours, minutes, and seconds. Prior to the invention of the mechanical clock in the thirteenth century, time was marked by shadow and light, or by falling water, falling sand. Time was attuned to sunrise and sunset; to sowing, harvesting, lambing. In the monasteries, the round loaves and slippered loaves, the marked breads and flat cakes, were baked in ovens whose temperature was noted by the feel of the heat coming from the fire. As for timing, the old recipes say: *Do not burn them.* Or: *When they are done take them from the oven.*

In that world, almost every intentional sound was steeped in meaning, none more so than the ringing of bells. It's likely only the clamor of war was louder than the ringing, so it isn't any wonder that the sound of bells was believed to be powerful enough to repel evil forces. They were struck to ward off lightning during storms; to warn of fire or invasions; to announce Easter, Advent, births, deaths. But they also had a daily significance. They rang for the Angelus—the prayer at dawn, midday, and dusk, the times of which changed as the days lengthened and then shortened with the seasons. The bell ringer measured his pulls on the rope not by counting but by intoning one of the psalms. The absence of ringing also held great meaning. Sound, changing sound, and silence can all tell a story. During the last days of Lent, the altar bells were silenced on Holy Thursday and replaced by the muted sound of a wooden clapper. Quiet upon quiet accompanied fasting in anticipation of Easter Sunday. And then the ringing.

In medieval villages and towns, the pealing of the bell was a cherished sound, and bells were given names: Little John, Hosanna, Marie, Emmanuel. They defined less exacting community borders than a stone boundary or a line drawn on a map. Carrying farther than a town crier's voice, their ringing spread out from the center, growing fainter as the connection to the village grew fainter, as its ring moved across the croplands, then the grazing lands, and into the woods. Sound carried on thc wind, or was obscured by it. Crisp on a still autumn day. Dispersed in the fog.

In the monastery, too, bells gathered the community for profound events such as the death of a monk, but they also apportioned the day. They were struck to call the monks to meals and signal the end of work. Most significantly, they announced the daily liturgical offices of Vigils, Lauds, Prime, Tierce, Sext, None, Vespers, and Compline. As with the Angelus, the times of the offices changed with the seasons, following the light of day and the dark. For instance, Vespers, the office of lighting of the candles, was celebrated at dusk. By our timekeeping it fell between six and seven in the evening during summer, before four p.m. in winter.

But for monks, the ringing of bells—now as then—is not only a means of gathering the community. Obedience to the bells is obedience to something greater than oneself. "They are to us, first of all, *the voice of God,*" Thomas Merton wrote. "*The bells call us to abandon our own will, hence they deliver us from slavery;* they are the voice of liberty and joy, calling us to the freedom of the sons of God! How sad to remain attached to what we are doing! From the time of the Desert Fathers it has been regarded as a sign of a good monk, that at the first sound of the bell he stops what he is doing, even leaving unfinished a letter he may be tracing or a word he is writing." At the end of one of his recorded lectures, Merton stops in midsentence upon hearing the bells. He then recites a brief closing prayer, dismisses his novices, and rushes off to the oratory.

Such obedience, historian Lewis Mumford has suggested, broke with the ancient rhythms of the agricultural world and anticipated our clock time: "If the mechanical clock did not appear until the cities of the thirteenth century demanded an orderly routine, the habit of order itself and the earnest regulation of time-sequences had become almost second nature in the monastery." According to Mumford, the liturgical hours "helped to give human enterprise the regular and collective beat and rhythm of the machine; for the clock is not merely a means of keeping track of the hours, but of synchronizing the actions of men."

If that sense of synchronization first manifested itself in the monastery, it soon spread to villages and towns, where, as the Middle Ages progressed, bells began to ring not just for births, deaths, festivals, and catastrophes, but also to announce work hours and market hours. Although local time varied from village to village, the more sustained use of bells, and then the arrival of the mechanical clock, straightened time. Even the Angelus bells became evenly apportioned throughout the day: six a.m., noon, six p.m. "What was clearly new," wrote historian Jacques Le Goff in the 1980s, "was that instead of a time linked to *events,* which made itself felt only episodically and sporadically, there arose a regular, normal time." Townspeople could not only hear time, but they could see it, and the mechanical clock evenly divided the day. "Rather than the *uncertain* clerical hours of the church bells, there were the *certain* hours," Le Goff noted. ". . . Time was no longer associated with cataclysms or festivals but rather with daily life, a sort of chronological net in which urban life was caught." With the arrival of time's strict sound in towns and villages, there also arrived an urgency not unlike the monk rushing to his devotions at the sound of the bell, although the urban regimentation was entirely secular. The clock "marks a perfection toward which other machines aspire," Mumford has observed. "The clock . . . is a piece of power-machinery whose 'product' is seconds and minutes."

With the passing of time itself, with the secularization of societies and the increased power of *chronos,* however much the liturgical day may have initiated a strict measure of the hours, time within the monastery proceeded at a far more incremental pace than in the world that surrounded it. In our current day, the observance of the offices seems more closely aligned to ancient times than our own, though monastic life has never been entirely immune from the world or from change within. And as the centuries progressed, increased pressure on time affected even the briefest of silences within the monastic tradition.

During the Middle Ages, the mendicant orders rejected the idea of monastic stability. Their lives of preaching, teaching, and administering to the sick and the poor were necessarily more attuned to the world. They were more conscious of worldly time, and more pressured by it. They continued to observe the Liturgy of the Hours, although the length even of the heart-stopping silent pause at the center of the chants, the *media distinctio,* shortened. It was no longer tied to the breath or dependent on the strength of resonances created by the stone architecture of the oratory or the natural time of sound itself. It was no longer tuned to the ear. Emma Hornby explains: "The Franciscans replaced the long pause in the middle of the verse with a 'pausea conveniens' that was the same length whatever the day. The Dominicans had a short pause on working days and a longer one on Feast days."

Today, the small, cut-up things of time have become inextricably mixed with our idea of participation in society. A full calendar and list of obligations stand as marks of our usefulness, and attunement to time keeps us believing we are part of the world. The old have moved beyond time, to the margins of society, for they have nothing calling them urgently in the day. But they are in a double bind—they are conscious of the hours *and* they are waiting for events. "What's your rush?" the old inevitably ask the young.

Rushing, rushing, not unlike Dante's souls in Purgatory: "'What is this, you laggard spirits? What negligence, what stay is this? Haste to the mountain to strip off the slough that lets not God be manifest in you.'" Ethicist Andrew Skotnicki has suggested that this sense of urgency tied to the mechanical clock—all the hurry and consciousness of time—isn't just the result of the advent of industrialization: "Punctuality is the sense of time that we have internalized that is tied directly to productivity and performance. It has been secularized to meet the demands of the capitalist workplace, but the clock entered Western social history not with the modern business enterprise, but with the notion of Purgatory . . . Productivity in the Christian West is first measured in moral and spiritual terms . . . The ticking of the clock is a reminder of eventual judgment for what one does with one's time. Who of us, regardless of religious persuasion, does not grow anxious with the passing of time?" Skotnicki accentuates the fact that our unease with time isn't natural; it's something that has a history and can be traced to "the apprehension and expectancy of people who came to believe that penitential time abides on both sides of the partition between life and death."

To defeat the clock, even for a short time, is often to feel that you've defeated the anxieties and constrictions of modern society. Time freed from time, time unconscious of the passing of the hours. Marshall McLuhan would say that to the extent you are lost in your task, the less it resembles work, and this escape from a sense of time is often tied to the creative life. Poet Adrienne Rich who, in her early years as a writer lived day in and day out with the pressures of motherhood, understands that a creative life cannot thrive on fragmented attention. "For a poem to coalesce, for a character or an action to take shape, there has to be an imaginative transformation of reality which is in no way passive," she has written. "And a certain freedom of the mind is needed—freedom to press on, to enter the currents of your thought like a glider pilot, knowing that your motion can be sustained, that the buoyancy of your attention will not be suddenly snatched away. Moreover, if the imagination is to transcend and transform experience it has to question, to challenge, to conceive of alternatives, perhaps to the very life you are living at that moment."

Likewise, the release from chronological time is essential for the contemplative life. Michael Casey, writing in the time-stressed twenty-first century, holds that leisure time makes contemplation possible. He is not speaking of leisure as we have come to know it, as downtime or recreation, but as "a time and space of freedom in which the deep self can find fuller expression." Casey has argued that leisure is "above all being attentive to the present moment, open to all its implications, living it to the full. This implies a certain looseness in lifestyle that allows the heart and mind to drift away from time to time . . . It is the opposite of being enslaved by the past or living in some hazy anticipation of a desirable future . . . Leisure is a very serious matter because it is the product of an attentive and listening attitude to life." It is, he asserts, citing German philosopher Josef Pieper, a form of silence.

It's not surprising that Thomas Merton was entirely clear about the richness and necessity of leisure time in all its freedoms and complexities:

> The contemplative life must provide an area, a space of liberty, of silence, in which possibilities are allowed to surface and new choices—beyond routine choice—become manifest. It should create a new experience of time, not as stopgap stillness, but a 'temps vierge'—not a blank to be filled or an untouched space to be conquered and violated, but a space which can enjoy its own potentialities and hopes—and its own presence to itself. One's *own* time. But not dominated by one's own ego and its demands. Hence open to others—*compassionate* time, rooted in the sense of common illusion and in criticism of it.

If the origins of the regimented times for prayer within the monastery contain the seeds of our clock time, the overall silence of the monastic day—then and now—emphasizes freedom from it. Even the necessary labor of supporting the monastery has always been understood to be undertaken in a way that allows for the continuity of contemplation and prayer. "So the monks prayed while they worked and worked while they prayed. Wherever they were, rectory, oratory, workshop, cell, the differences were only accidental," noted Catholic priest and historian Robert Taft. "What they sought ultimately was what modern spiritual writers would call a *state of prayer,* a degree of spiritual perfection . . .

in which one's every breath, one's very existence is a continuous prayer not subject to fragmentation into successive acts, nor to interruption by external activities."

Silence allows for that continuity. In work, for instance, background music or small talk might offer a pleasant distraction from menial tasks, but it also changes the course of thought. It divides the task profoundly from what precedes it and what follows it. It fragments. It diminishes the meaning of the work itself. Merton lectured his novices about the value of silent work as a means of praising God and as a way of being in touch with present reality: "Supposing it's my afternoon to be weeding the strawberries . . . [If you are talking] it's much less tedious . . . You don't notice the back is hurting . . . but you've lost the particular value that comes from weeding strawberries . . . To do it right you have to do it in silence . . . If you're doing it in silence it's a penance . . . a fruitful penance . . . Your mind is empty, and you're ready to read . . . Whereas if you have been talking all afternoon . . . you have to go through a ten-minute period of adaptation before you can settle down [to read]."

One of the aims of the monastic vows of poverty and stability, and of the practice of communal ownership, is to reduce necessity so as to preserve time for prayer, for contemplation, for silence. But maintaining a balanced work life could be difficult even in medieval times, as the monks of Sénanque—like those of so many other Cistercian monasteries of the Middle Ages—proved when they expanded their holdings and consolidated both power and wealth. Sénanque may have taken more than a century to build, but before another century was through, its holdings had spread across Provence and included extensive woodlands, at least six barns, and four water mills. The monks pastured their animals in the hills of the Vaucluse and moved them to winter feeding grounds on the plains stretching toward the Mediterranean. The abbey eventually established granges throughout the territory, supported several hospices, owned houses in some of the surrounding villages, and held properties as far away as Arles, more than forty miles away from the Sénacole Valley. This was too far to travel in one day, a distance Bernard de Clairvaux had advised them to avoid. In its ambitions the monastery had grown away from the center of silence fostered by the Rule of Benedict and the dictates of Bernard. Wealth and prosperity eventually invited strife: the monastery was seized upon by peasants, raided, and damaged, some of its hewn stones carted away.

"Silence . . . stands outside the world of profit and utility," wrote Max Picard. "It cannot be exploited for profit, you cannot get anything out of it." Its relationship to time is far more complex than the simple march of hours allows, and is perhaps, in the end, best likened to fruitfulness. "It is not so much the equal measure of the hours, which is the same in every day, which connects one day with another," remarked Picard, "but the equal measure of the silence with which each day is newly born." Silence "does not develop or increase in time, but time increases in silence. It is as though time had been sown into silence, as though silence had absorbed it; as though silence were the soil in which time grows to fullness."

9

the voices of the pages

A FEW THINGS have grown quieter over time. Even on the subway, amid jostles, screeches, conversations, and stares, an aura of silence seems to surround the readers in the car. It may be defensive, but it's silence all the same, and not so unlike the habitual silences of readers in a library or in a chair at home, their absorption distancing voices, engines, and birds alike—the same sounds that can feel amplified and distinct before sleep or just after waking.

To learn to read, after all, is a descent into silence. I can still conjure the room where I first learned to mouth the words on a page: the map of the world rolled up above the chalkboard, the green canvas shades partially drawn over high windows of watery glass, the alphabet in cursive letters strung around the room. Our future lay in learning the efficacy of joined letters as much as it lay in learning to read beyond our first efforts. All our practice and repetition reading aloud, to one another and to the teacher . . . We repeated, repeated, then whispered the pages to ourselves, then silently mouthed them, until the words sped by faster than we could possibly say them. How long that took I have no idea, but I know the silence was an accomplishment.

It accompanies me still, whether I'm skimming a newspaper, mining a website for information, or absorbed in a novel, and it's how I've always imagined readers: silent within themselves. So it's strange to think that all of it—the variety of things I now peruse, the speed with which I read, the silence—would have been impossible for medieval monks and nuns to imagine. Although silent reading wasn't unheard-of in antiquity or the Middle Ages, people then read "usually, not as today, principally with the eyes, but with the lips, pronouncing what they saw, and with the ears, listening to the words pronounced, hearing what is called 'the voices of the pages.'"

"It is a real acoustical reading; *legere* means at the same time *audire;* one understands only what one hears," monastic scholar and monk Jean Leclercq explained in the 1960s. ". . . [It is] an activity which, like chant and writing, requires the participation of the whole body and the whole mind. Doctors of ancient times used to recommend reading to their patients as a physical exercise on an equal level with walking, running or ball-playing." Of course, the murmuring of innumerable readers could be a distraction in the monastery. In his Rule, Benedict urges, "Should anyone desire to read, he should do so without disturbing his brothers."

Such reading was inextricable from a life of prayer and was to be given full attention. "At fixed hours time should be given to certain definite reading. For haphazard reading, constantly varied and as if lighted upon by chance does not edify but makes the mind unstable; taken into the memory lightly, it goes out from it even more lightly," William of St. Thierry noted. "The Scriptures need to be read and understood in the same spirit in which they were written."

The spirit in which books were written and the spirit in which they were read was also meant to be the spirit in which they were to be patiently copied by medieval monastic scribes. Although the practice was necessary for the economic well-being of the monastery and one more assurance against idleness, copying manuscripts might have, above all, been considered a spiritual labor. The work was arduous. Even before a scribe dipped the reed or quill into ink, the parchment had to be dried and stretched, then scraped clean and smoothed with a pumice stone. Each sheet had to be lined with a ruler and awl; the ink, made from lampblack or tree galls; the quills, cut and slit. And, as Leclercq noted, the copying of manuscripts was an endeavor that also required the entire body. Scribes, often the younger members of the monastery who had sharp eyes and steady hands, likely mouthed the words as they copied them, thus embodying the text, though not all of the scribes understood what they were writing. A skilled scribe might produce two books a year. The Bible could take fifteen months to copy.

At Sénanque the scribes worked in the low-vaulted warming room just off the cloister. As the only heated room in the monastery, it was the one place where the ink wouldn't congeal in winter. Imagine them at their desks in their white robes, light from the cloister slanting in. Since candles were often forbidden in scriptoriums for fear of fire and concern that the fats might stain the manuscripts, it's likely that in the dark days of winter, they had only the burning tree trunks in the fireplace for added light.

In general, Cistercian scribes, in keeping with the spareness of the architecture and the simplicity of their lives, produced unornamented texts—perhaps broken only by a modestly illuminated initial letter—which possess an orderly abstract beauty to us now. Upon the completion of a manuscript, a scribe might record his or her name at the end, though not all scribes signed their work, and it is likely that women were more reluctant to do so than men. They also recorded the hour the work was finished, the day, and the year. Sometimes they added a plea. "The work of writing makes one lose his sight, it hunches his back, it breaks ribs and bothers the stomach, it pains the kidneys and causes aches throughout the body," proclaims one inscription. "Therefore, you the reader, turn the pages carefully and keep your fingers from the letters, because just as hail destroys the fields, the useless reader erases the text and destroys the book."

A wealthy medieval monastery might have had no more than a few hundred books in its library—far fewer than I now have in my home—and most monasteries possessed more modest collections, which might be stored in a cupboard or cabinet. However modest or large the collection, only books considered of value would be copied, and each book was considered precious. Some were even chained to lecterns to prevent them from being stolen.

The value of a book wasn't separate from the value of reading itself, which was central to monastic life. At the beginning of Lent, the abbot would distribute a book to each monk or nun who could read, and that book was to be studied throughout the year. Several hours of each monastic day were given over to *lectio divina*—divine reading—but such reading wasn't confined to the time spent bent to the pages. It was expansive and ongoing, linked to all the other activities of the monastery, to be contemplated while a monk or nun tended bees, hoed the garden, or kneaded bread, and then recalled again and again during the vast silence of the day. Their reading worked its way into their prayers, their thoughts, their recollections. "Some part of your daily reading should also each day be committed to memory," William of St. Thierry instructed the novices at Mont Dieu, "taken as it were into the stomach, to be more carefully digested and brought up again for frequent rumination. He also counseled: "You will never enter into Paul's meaning until by constant application to reading him and by giving yourself to constant meditation you have imbibed his spirit. You will never understand David until by experience you have made the very sentiments of the psalms your own . . . There is the same gulf between attentive study and mere reading as there is between friendship and acquaintance with a passing guest."

It is said that readers in the Middle Ages had capacious memories. No doubt the design of books made it a necessity. Without tables of contents, chapter divisions, and indexes—all of which would consistently arrive only after Gutenberg and the printing press in the 1400s—favored passages weren't easy to retrieve. And surely the slow pace of reading, as well as reading aloud, helped with memory, as did the continual engagement with only a few books. But, most essentially for monastics, as Jean Leclercq explained, "to speak, to think, to remember, are the three necessary phases of the same activity. To express what one is thinking and to repeat it enables one to imprint it on one's mind . . . What results is a muscular memory of the words pronounced and an aural memory of the words heard . . . It is what inscribes, so to speak, the sacred text in the body and in the soul."

Progress with *lectio divina* may not always be steady. Some days one needs to return to the literal, trusting the words on the page, rereading, attending, thinking, ingesting again and again: the labyrinthine progress of engaging with one's reading as an essential part of life. In early Cistercian monasteries, where only the slant of natural light and the flickering of small candles accompanied readers, surely the low light and the surrounding world enclosed in shadow narrowed the focus of readers and was integral to the slow progress of *lectio divina.* Perhaps the practice even grew out of the world of light and shadow the monks inhabited, the quality of their concentration inextricable from the limits of their condition, in the same way that modern Japanese writer Jun'icherō Tanizaki has suggested that the quality we call beauty "must always grow from the realities of life, and our ancestors, forced to live in dark rooms, presently came to discover beauty in shadows, ultimately to guide shadows towards beauty's ends."

The meager light that medieval Cistercians so intently read by would now be considered impossibly inadequate by most of us. The realities of our life involve brilliant light and speed, so often associated with the noise of the modern world. And although light and speed have made possible the silence surrounding the act of reading, they also have created the conditions in which words are often quickly consumed, coming and going as passing guests, more swiftly all the time, as the world dissolves into a future where books are accessed through the ether and the main floors of libraries, with their rows of luminous screens, are akin to the decks of starships.

10

the great silence

WHAT IS TRUE of the flickering lamps of the Cistercian monasteries is also true of medieval dusks: we'd hardly know them. Modern urban nights bear almost no resemblance to the gradual waning of the day during the Middle Ages, when no one—not workers in the field, scribes at their desks, women bent to their handiwork, or travelers along the roads—could ignore the fading light. It was, then, its own time—a border hour. Night's meaning, too, was tied to restriction, since the only available human light was costly and small—the difficult flame of a candle or lamp. Limiting as it may have been, night also released almost everyone from the obligations of the day. As the early Church theologian Cyril of Jerusalem remarked: "A servant would have had no rest from his masters, had not the darkness necessarily brought a respite. And often after wearying ourselves in the day, how are we refreshed in the night."

Within the monastery, the approach of darkness retains its enormity to this day and is prepared for, as it has always been, with two liturgical offices. During the first, Vespers, at the onset of dusk, candles are lit against the growing dark. It is an office of gratitude, thanksgiving for the day just finished and all that was accomplished, and is celebrated with the chanting of the Magnificat: "My soul doth magnify the Lord, / And my spirit hath rejoiced."

The mood of Vespers is decidedly different from that of Compline, which follows soon after. This final office of the day is an austere preparation for the hours of darkness ahead. The church is meagerly lit, and the altar is bare. The silence is intensified by the darkness. The two elemental forces increase each other. When British writer Patrick Leigh Fermor, in the heart of the twentieth century, arrived at the Abbey of St. Wandrille in northern France, he concluded that Compline, of all the liturgical hours, belonged most to the medieval Church: "The faces of the seated monks are hidden in their hoods, their heads are bowed; and they themselves are only just discernible under the accumulation of shadows. The solitary voice reading aloud seems to issue from an inner silence even greater than the silence that surrounds them. The reading comes to an end; the single light is extinguished; and the chanted psalms follow one another in total darkness."

As the monks made their way from the oratory and up the night stairs, it's likely they were chanting "Salve Regina," their solemn hymn to the Virgin, reminding them that they are "the banished children of Eve," confronting the dark, with its mysteries, its fears, its vastness, its human vulnerability. Pius Parsch, in writing about the distinction between these two offices, remarked: "I am tempted to say that Adam could well have prayed . . . Vespers in the Garden of Paradise . . . but only after his fall, in exile on this earth, could he pray . . . Compline."

• • •

Benedict thought the hours after Compline, known as the Great Silence, was the holiest of times, and in his Rule he calls for nothing to interfere with the silence and solitude then: "Monks should try to speak as little as possible, but especially at night." Cyril of Jerusalem also understood that profound darkness is its own exposure, providing a time of privacy and mystery, of receptivity and turning inward: "And when is our mind most attuned to Psalmody and Prayer? Is it not at night? And when have we often called our own sins to remembrance? Is it not at night?"

Cyril of Jerusalem was writing at a time when everywhere on earth there was little to obscure the magnitude of the celestial light above, and its enormity enhanced human beings' sense of solitude and the place of the human soul in the infinite. The Great Silence of the monastic night persists today, but the world around it no longer shares in the profound darkness. Its observance stands isolated amid myriad other kinds of nights shot through with activity, alternate possibilities, ease, and obscurities of their own.

"Only man makes himself illuminations he conceives to be solid and eternal," wrote Thomas Merton from his twentieth-century monastery. By then he'd been at Gethsemani for a dozen years, and quiet, solitary dark held a particular attraction for him, perhaps all the more so because much of the struggle of his young adulthood prior to his calling to monastic life was a struggle with his nocturnal self. The New York City he knew in the late 1930s and early 1940s was a city at ease with the twenty-four-hour day, steeped in the instantaneous light that separates the modern era so completely from the Middle Ages. It was Edison's world, and by dusk during the brief days of winter, most of the Midtown office windows appeared as fully illuminated rectangles, the signature of incandescent light. (A candle, as French philosopher Gaston Bachelard observed, "does not illuminate an empty room; it illuminates a book.") The workers in those rooms were all part of a rational grid, connected to the lit streets and the traffic on the avenues below.

If you were to hang your camera from the top of the Empire State Building during a winter dusk, as photographer Berenice Abbott did in the 1930s, you'd capture those city lights and their seeming infinitude. Countless souls in one glance. The photograph that Abbott produced, *Nightview, New York,* is a small gelatin silver print, little more than thirteen by ten inches in size. You need to stand close to contemplate the office lights, apartment lights, streetlights, and headlights from taxis and other cars. The most consistently dark parts of Manhattan are the building roofs. It's as if there is no light from the heavens, obscured as it is by the illumination emanating from the hive.

Long after the offices emptied—except for workers staying late and cleaning crews—after millions of souls were already sleeping in the high-rises, nightlife stayed close to street level in the nightclubs that Merton and his college friends frequented. As he looked back on those nights from the monastery, he remembered a despondency that wasn't allayed when he awoke, clouded and confused, to see men and women alert to the daytime world. "The thing that depressed me most of all," he wrote, "was the shame and despair that invaded my whole nature when the sun came up, and all the laborers were going to work: men healthy and awake and quiet, with their eyes clear, and some rational purpose before them."

If those New York nights seemed to intensify his sense of feeling lost in the world, and superfluous, once he arrived at the monastery, the dark hours seemed to contain everything he both accepted and struggled toward: his search for God, his prayers, his solitude, his embrace of the community. Far from the fractured nights of his youth, the monastic night promised integrity. "I thought of the darkness as a luxury," he wrote, "simplifying and unifying everything, hiding all the accidents that make one monk different from another monk and submerging all distractions in deep obscurity."

Significantly, the epilogue to his journal of his first years at Gethsemani, *The Sign of Jonas,* records his experience moving through the monastery at night on Fire Watch, when all the souls in the monastery were in his keeping. Everything was dark, save for where he focused his flashlight: light as it had been carried for ages, akin to a lantern—vessel, oil, wick—shining on one thing and then another. What had just been seen fell into darkness; what lay ahead struggled into apprehension. The limited light intensified smells, sounds, memories; the silence and dark seemed to amplify his ability to register the world. His was a search, and a syntax, as he scanned the cellar, the scullery, the little cloister, the furnace room, the choir novitiate.

Merton's vow of stability meant that he'd rarely left the monastery. He could make his way in the dark if he had to, being as familiar with his world as people in the Middle Ages would have been intimate with their landscape, at a time when few would have ventured more than a day's journey from home during their lives. Gethsemani was already more than a century old. Generations of monks had worked in its fields and woods, prayed in solitude, prayed in community, undertaken Fire Watch in the heat of the summer. And in the darkness, Merton was as deeply aware of the past as of the present. He apprehended more than merely the walls and rooms. "You hit strange caverns in the monastery's history," he wrote, "layers set down by the years, geological strata: you feel like an archeologist suddenly unearthing ancient civilizations."

Most essentially, he moved through registers of his own road to belief: "The walls of the building have their own stuffy smell and I am suddenly haunted by my first days in religion, the freezing tough winter when I first received the habit and always had a cold, the smell of frozen straw in the dormitory under the chapel and the deep unexpected ecstasy of Christmas." The night revealed, and the night also interrogated: "I have prayed to You in the daytime with thoughts and reasons, and in the nighttime You have confronted me, scattering thought and reason. I have come to You in the morning with light and with desire, and You have descended upon me, with great gentleness, with most forbearing silence, in this inexplicable night, dispersing light, defeating all desire . . . While I am asking questions which You do not answer, You ask me a question which is so simple that I cannot answer. I do not even understand the question . . . This night, and every night, it is the same question."

Fire Watch consolidated all the meanings of the monastery to him. The long silence of the night was both a reward after the busy day and an intensification of what he had entered the religion for. Most particularly, during Fire Watch he was aware not only of the place but of his responsibilities to it and his obligations to the community: "Between the silence of God and the silence of my own soul, stands the silence of the souls entrusted to me."

However much he often felt overwhelmed by the community, struggled with the demands of it, and periodically expressed a wish to leave it behind to join a more reclusive order, he also understood its essential place in monastic life. "I know what I have discovered: that the kind of work I once feared because I thought it would interfere with 'solitude' is, in fact, the only true path to solitude," he wrote. "One must be in some sense a hermit before the care of souls can lead one further into the desert. But once God has called you to solitude, everything you touch leads you further into solitude. Everything that affects you builds you into a hermit, as long as you do not insist on doing the work yourself and building your own kind of hermitage . . . What is my new desert? The name of it is *compassion.* There is no wilderness so terrible, so beautiful, so arid and so fruitful as the wilderness of compassion."

In describing Fire Watch and his singular responsibility to the community, Merton was also describing the responsibilities of the community to the world beyond. The Great Silence was broken by Vigils, or the Night Office, observed during the small hours. "'Vigilers' or 'watchers' is the common term for angels in Syriac Christianity even today," Robert Taft wrote, "and . . . the monks and nuns who keep vigil at night while the world sleeps do so in imitation of the angels, who need no sleep and never interrupt their unending hymn of praise."

When he first came to Gethsemani, Merton found that the hour or so immediately after Vigils was an inspiring time to write poetry. The arts were in his blood, his father having been an artist. "I had learned from my own father that it was almost blasphemy to regard the function of art as merely to reproduce some kind of a sensible pleasure," he remarked. "I had always understood that art was contemplation, and that it involved the action of the highest faculties of man." And so his first inclination was to use those deeply perceptive hours for his creative life: "After two or three hours of prayer your mind is saturated in peace and the richness of the liturgy. The dawn is breaking outside the cold windows. If it is warm, the birds are already beginning to sing. Whole blocks of imagery seem to crystallize out as it were naturally in the silence and the peace, and the lines almost write themselves." But eventually, in the wavering line between writing and prayer, prayer rose: "Or that was the way it went until Father Master told me I must not write poetry then. The Rule would keep that hour sacred for the study of Scripture and the Psalms. And as time went on, I found that this was even better than writing poems."

Merton would study scripture until Lauds, counterpart to Vigils, a celebration of the day to come—an office, too, that could be celebrated in paradise. And the silences of the night would give way to the silences of the day—all the intricacies of the silence of the monastery. The desire, ultimately, as Merton summarized it, was "to deliver oneself up, to hand oneself over, entrust oneself completely to the silence of a wide landscape of woods and hills, or sea, or desert; to sit still while the sun comes up over that land and fills its silences with light. To pray and work in the morning and to labor and rest in the afternoon, and to sit still again in meditation in the evening when night falls upon that land and when the silence fills itself with darkness and with stars."

PART III

Philadelphia: Darkening the Dark

We cannot help thinking of our theories, our systems, our magnificent and futile mental constructions in whose corners some victim can always be found crouching.

—Marguerite Yourcenar, "The Dark Brain of Piranesi"

11

night in stone

THOMAS MERTON WROTE about his encounters with silence and solitude in books, journals, essays, and extensive correspondence that has been gathered in archives and carefully cataloged. But Charles Williams's plight is its own silence: He never set down his thoughts and feelings during his two years in the penitentiary, or if he did, that record hasn't survived. But the community of solitary prisoners knows no time or borders. Williams's experience would have abundant similarities with all those sentenced to solitude and silence with him and in the centuries to come, in North and South America, Europe, Africa, Asia, Australia, Russia, and the Soviet Union.

The similarities exist even when the reasons for imprisonment are distinct. Eugenia Ginzburg was a faculty member at Kazan State University in Russia and a dedicated Communist Party member before being caught up in Stalin's Great Purge. In February 1937 she was arrested and accused of engaging in and concealing counterrevolutionary activity. When first interrogated, and naïve as to the fate that would befall her, she maintained a belief in the integrity of the Soviet state and was incredulous that innocent people would be charged with staged crimes, though she soon began to comprehend the horrors of her times. After her seven-minute trial on charges of being "an enemy of the people," she was sentenced to ten years in prison. During her imprisonment, her second husband was arrested, and she was wrongly told that he had died. Her eldest son died of starvation during the siege of Leningrad. Her youngest, who was four years old when she was first detained, grew into his teens without her.

Most of Ginzburg's sentence was carried out in forced labor in the Gulag, but prior to her long, slow train ride across Siberia to the prison "archipelago," she spent two years confined in regular Soviet prisons, some of it in solitary. She may have spent her entire sentence in isolation had not the number of victims of the Great Purge far exceeded the capacity of the prisons. Unlike Williams, whose sentence was fixed in place and length, Ginzburg was subject to the illogical whims of the Soviet state. She could be moved without warning and was, though she spent most of her confinement in a prison in Yaroslavl, a city about 160 miles northeast of Moscow at the confluence of the Volga and Kotorosi Rivers.

Williams would have surely found Ginzburg's twentieth-century Soviet cell familiar, with its stone walls, its iron door, its flap window and peephole, its width of three paces and its length of five. "At a pinch, by taking very short steps, I could stretch it to five and a quarter," Ginzburg writes in her memoir, *Journey into the Whirlwind*. Surely his eyes would have searched first for the high window of her cell, which was almost completely screened with wood so that "what remained of the pale-blue Yaroslavl sky looked like a narrow trickle of water." And while the machinery of Soviet detention and its aims of political control may have been distinct from the corrective aims of Eastern State Penitentiary, the silence and solitude at Yaroslavl often worked to the same end. "From the authorities' point of view, the ideal was that each of us should feel as though she were the only inmate of the prison," Ginzburg writes. Her statement recalls the elaborate ritual at Eastern State to hood each prisoner before leading him to his cell, so as to disorient him and isolate him within the compound.

Ginzburg records the daily tribulations of her confinement: the struggles with silence, the filthy conditions, and the cruelties of the guards. But it is nighttime that looms particularly large. Within the prison in the city of Yaroslavl, just as in the penitentiary on the outskirts of Philadelphia, almost always when night descended, there was deathly quiet. She could do nothing but wait for sleep or become anxious about insomnia, while on the other side of her cell wall guards patrolled the corridors, listening for tappings and whispers between prisoners. "The time after supper was the worst," she writes. "The silence thickened, became tangible and stifling. Depression attacked not only the mind but the whole body. Even my hair seemed to bristle with despair. I would have given anything to have heard just one sound."

Unlike Charles Williams, who would have had no prior understanding of the sentence that befell him, Ginzburg had some familiarity with the challenges of extended solitary confinement. It had been used previously in Russia, and she had thoroughly read, and could recollect parts of, the revolutionary political activist Vera Figner's nineteenth-century account of her years in a Russian solitary cell, to which she'd been sentenced for her part in the assassination of Tsar Alexander II. Figner's description of her psychological and physical trials and her methods of endurance would prove to be of help to Ginzburg in her efforts to survive.

Upon her incarceration, Figner was assigned a number—her name had sunk into oblivion, she noted—and she, too, was disoriented within the larger prison. At times her depiction of the toll the silence and solitude took on her suggests the way a cloistered religious might describe the experience. "A new life began," she writes. "A life amidst deathly stillness, that stillness to which you always listen and which you hear; the stillness which little by little overpowers you, envelops you, penetrates into all the pores of your body, into your reason, your very soul." You might think she was on the verge of a holy vision, save for her next remark: "How dreadful it is in its dumbness, how terrible it is in its soundlessness and in its chance interruptions." And strangely, after that observation, she returns to a description that could be mistaken for that of a monastic: "Gradually there steals from it to you the sense that some mystery is close at hand; everything becomes unusual, puzzling, as on a moonlit night, in solitude, in the shadow of a still forest. Every thing is mysterious, incomprehensible. In this stillness the real becomes vague and unreal, and the imaginary seems real."

Even those who choose silence and have utter freedom within it are inevitably cornered by it. Writer Sara Maitland, who deliberately spent months alone on a remote Scottish island, noted that after six weeks she "felt that the silence was stripping me down, desiccating, denuding me. I could hear the silence itself screaming." Maitland, who found much fruitfulness in silence, wrote: "My negative experiences have been little ones, but they have been enough to give me some small understanding of how overwhelming and destructive silence can be, and how closely the terrors seem to follow the same paths and patterns as the joys." Maitland could turn on the radio for distraction. She could sing to herself, go for a walk across the moorlands, or even drive to a nearby village if she desired. How much more unendurable the silence must be for those cut off forcibly from loved ones, from cities, forests, fields, voluntary actions, speech itself.

How much more fragile the mind is in such circumstances. In a solitary cell the smallest thing becomes magnified, and random sounds are their own terror. When a person has no comprehension of their surroundings and is at the complete behest of others, the slightest knock can be construed as menacing, as Vera Figner explains: "Accursed sounds which suddenly and unexpectedly break upon you, frighten you, and vanish. Somewhere begins a loud hissing, as though an enormous snake were creeping from under the floor, to enwrap you in its cold, slippery coils. But it is only water hissing somewhere below . . . You imagine people immured within stony sacks. You hear a very soft, suppressed groan, and it seems as though some one were suffocating beneath a heap of stones . . . If a dish clatters somewhere, or the metal leg of a cot drops on the floor, your imagination pictures men rattling their chains and fetters."

And if sleep should come, certainly the nightmares of an imposed silence are of a singular order. Come night, Figner's anxieties couldn't be allayed and seemed to be magnified in sleep: "And the dreams by night! Those mad dreams! You see flights, pursuits, gendarmes, fusillades, arrests . . . But most often you see torture. They torture with hot steam . . . and there is no escape from it . . . Or they torture you with electricity. You sit on a wooden chair, like those they have at the guardhouse, and you cannot rise; some invisible jailer is sending a current through you." Such dreams are far beyond any control, as are the inner voices of the incarcerated, which rise in the small hours, in the unwilling dark, questioning the ends of all the sinister contraptions and innovations dreamed up by the human mind.

If for Ginzburg, as for Figner, there was torture in dreams, there was no balm in sleeplessness either. The endless, immeasurable dark brought forth the true measure and challenges of Ginzburg's sentence: "The worst thing of all was that . . . I was incapable of deliberately making myself go to sleep. The knowledge that the hours to sleep were running out and could not be made up for by day drove me to desperation. Terrified of wasting precious time, I frantically tried to sleep, and this drove sleep away altogether." Her years of education, her experience as a teacher at Kazan State University, and her love of literature meant that she at least had the memory of literature to help her. In the solitude and silence, she sought what consolation she could in words. As she lay in the dark, she recalled her reading. She recited poems to herself that she'd long ago memorized, and she composed her own.

Charles Williams likely had few of Ginzburg's resources to draw on. The intake log notes that he could read, though he probably had only a rudimentary education, enough to get by in an increasingly literate world—to peruse a newspaper, perhaps, and sign his name and write a note. We can only conjecture whether the nights felt longer to him than they did to Ginzburg, though he surely would have understood something she expressed in one of her poems:

> The night grows wider
> And the dreams more bitter.
> How much silence
> Is there in the world?

12

"i get up and hammer my leather"

IT WAS AGAINST the vastness of their nightmares and inner voices that Eastern State prisoners recorded the movement of the sun against their lime-washed walls. And against such vastness they relied, too, on something denied to Eugenia Ginzburg in her Soviet cell: the regularity of their labors. Charles Williams's work as a shoemaker, with its cutting, scraping, hammering, rubbing —sometimes merciless, sometimes soothing—inhabited the hours, and he could draw his knife across the whetstone to allay the tyranny of time. A certain gratitude for work was depended upon, for as Harriet Martineau observed, work was initially withheld during the first days of confinement so that prisoners could begin to perceive the reality of incarceration. "In the Philadelphia penitentiary, work is forbidden to the criminal for two days subsequent to his entrance: he petitions for it before the two days are out, however doggedly he may have declared that he will never work," she wrote. "Small incidents show what a resource it is. A convict shoemaker mentioned to a visitor a very early hour of the winter day as that at which he began to work. 'But how can you see at that time of a winter's morning? it must be nearly dark.'" To which the prisoner replied: "'I hammer my leather. That requires very little light. I get up and hammer my leather.'"

Other visitors also noted the appreciation inmates felt for their work. After their tour of Eastern State in 1831, Gustave de Beaumont and Alexis de Tocqueville wrote: "As solitude is in no other prison more complete than in Philadelphia, nowhere, also, is the necessity of labor more urgent . . . When we visited this penitentiary, we successively conversed with all its inmates. There was not a single one among them who did not speak of labor with a kind of gratitude, and who did not express the idea that without the relief of constant occupation, life would be insufferable . . . Labor gives to the solitary cell an interest; it fatigues the body and relieves the soul."

Yet, long before the cornerstone had been laid at Eastern State, the idea of work for its inmates had been controversial and by no means a given. Would idleness be more conducive to reform than work? Might work, like vinegar, be a favor bestowed for good behavior? While the idea of a penitentiary was still in its planning phase, some supporters favored imprisonment without labor —and not for just the first few days, but for the duration of confinement. They believed idleness would bring the incarcerated to remorse more quickly. One year without labor, they suggested, would be equivalent to three years with it, because "employment diminishes in a very great degree the tediousness of confinement, and thus mitigates the punishment." So they advocated that labor "be abandoned altogether, except as an indulgence to penitent convicts, and as a relaxation from the *much more painful task of being compelled to be idle.*"

But between the planning of the penitentiary and its occupancy in 1829, a number of sobering experiments involving solitude without work occurred in other prisons. The most notorious transpired at Auburn State Prison in New York—one of the oldest prisons in the country—where prisoners labored in congregate workshops during the day and slept in individual cells at night. On Christmas Day 1821, in an attempt to impose order among restive inmates, eighty of the worst offenders were confined entirely to their individual cells. They had no reading material and no work. They were forbidden to lie down during the day. This confinement was not a temporary measure. It was meant to last for the length of each man's sentence. "Let them walk their gloomy abodes and commune with their corrupt hearts and guilty consciences in silence, and brood over the horrors of their solitude, and the enormity of their crimes," the board of inspectors declared. If there was any hope of redemption, it would only be arrived at in the wake of extreme cruelty. "The demands of nature must indeed be complied with: their bodies must be fed and clothed . . . But they ought to be deprived of every enjoyment arising from social or kindred feelings and affections: of all knowledge of each other, the world, and the connections with it. Force them to reflection and let self-tormenting guilt harrow up the tortures of accusing conscience, keener than scorpion stings; until the intensity of their suffering subdues their stubborn spirits, and humbles them to a realizing sense of the enormity of their crimes and their obligation to reform."

Before long, many of those sentenced went insane. One managed to escape from his cell when the door was opened, and he threw himself from the gallery to the pavement below, suffering serious injury. Another beat his head against the walls of his cell until he was bloodied and so gravely battered that he eventually lost an eye. Eighteen months after the experiment began, the governor of New York, on an official visit, was so horrified by what he saw that he ordered the confinements stopped and pardoned most of the remaining solitary prisoners. Auburn subsequently abandoned its practice of confinement without work and moved to the practice of work in closely guarded silence in communal rooms during the day, and solitude and silence at night, which eventually came to be known as the Auburn system.

In part, the failure of New York's experiment in total silence and solitude prompted the Pennsylvania legislature to order those incarcerated at Eastern State to be given work in their solitary cells, though there were practical considerations that went into the decision as well. It was hoped that being taught a useful skill would provide the inmates with a better chance of finding work upon their release. Legislators also hoped that the goods produced by prisoners would offset the cost to the state of their incarceration. Building the penitentiary had been an expensive proposition as well. Haviland's seven ranges, when finally completed in 1844, had a price tag of over $650,000 (equivalent to about $20 million today). The wall alone cost $200,000.

So, within their eight-by-twelve-foot cells, inmates took up traditional trades. Most made shoes. Some fashioned shuttles and lasts. Others worked as weavers. The utterly unskilled were set to picking oakum. Charles Williams's shoemaking skills perhaps fell somewhere between those of an itinerant cobbler, making or mending boots out of a farmer's own leather, and those of a master cordwainer, crafting custom-made footwear. Although the tools of the trade surrounded him—knives, awls, bristles, tacks, and scrapers; wax and dogfish skin; grease and blacking —the atmosphere could not have been further from a typical shoemaker's shop of the time in, say, Lynn, Massachusetts. Such a shop might have been almost as small as Williams's cell—perhaps ten feet by ten feet and called a "ten-footer" because of it. Four or five men and boys—apprentices, masters, journeymen —could be working at benches within, though they weren't necessarily there every day. Shoemaking was often a part-time job for farmers and fishermen, and the rote and undemanding work meant that a shoemaker's shop was known for its talk.: "Every workshop [was] a school and an incipient debating club," wrote Lynn historian David Johnson. "When the discussion waxed warm, one of the defenders of some cherished doctrine might have been seen enforcing his argument with his hammer poised in an imposing manner, or slowly descending upon the shoe he held on his knee."

Williams, by contrast, worked long, solitary, unbroken hours at his repetitive task. The dissimilarities didn't end there. Williams received no pay for his labor, though neither did he need to worry about paying for shelter or where his next meal might come from. Such security was hardly insignificant at a time when the poorest workers in cities lived crowded together in windowless cellars and were unable to find food regularly. In fact, critics of the penitentiary system feared that if the conditions there were better than anything a prisoner could hope to find on the outside, confinement, even within the strictures of Eastern State, might be attractive to some poor workers.

Inmate labor, in the end, failed to fully offset the expenses to the state, as the early annual reports make clear:

> 1830: . . . When the prison has 300 inmates it will be entirely self supporting, including salaries.
>
> 1831: Our convicts have, with but a few exceptions, maintained themselves . . .
>
> 1832: Profits for the past year have met all expenses save salaries. We hope for revenue from convicts when building is completed.
>
> 1833: Labor is attended with difficulties. Have not met expenses.
>
> 1834: Reformation of the prisoner the all-important thing. Our prison was never expected to be self-supporting . . .
>
> 1835: Deficiency, $4,998. Want of capital a bother.
>
> . . .
>
> 1839: Our institution cannot expect to be lucrative to the state.

"Prisons and the social portrait of those who inhabit them are essentially products of human imagination," wrote Andrew Skotnicki. The majority of Eastern State prisoners were from what would come to be called the dangerous classes—immigrants, the poor and the working poor, vagrants, minorities. While many of the proponents of the penitentiary were, like Benjamin Rush, abolitionists, as historian Adam J. Hirsch found, the penitentiary had much in common with the chattel slavery of the American South: "The penitentiary arose in an age of slavery . . . Both institutions subordinated their subjects to the will of others. Like Southern slaves, prison inmates followed a daily routine specified by their superiors. Both institutions reduced their subjects to dependence on others for the supply of basic human services such as food and shelter. Both isolated their subjects from the general population by confining them to a fixed habitat. And both frequently coerced their subjects to work, often for longer hours and for less compensation than free laborers." During the 1830s about forty percent of Eastern State prisoners were black. "Even as they were outlawing slavery," historian Caleb Smith observed, "the Northern states were inventing new instruments of unfree labor, new sites of confinement, and new patterns of inequality."

As an unfree laborer, Charles Williams was more of a competitor than a brother to the others working in his craft. The shoemakers of Philadelphia complained bitterly about the use of prison labor to make shoes. The merchants, they claimed, "are now getting work manufactured by convicts in the Eastern Penitentiary at less than one-half what our bill of rates call for." The ire of the shoemakers must have been compounded by the anxieties of the industrial age, with its competition, materialism, and consumerism. The singular tappings of a hammer, the passing of a shuttle, and the draw of a saw were sounds of the past. Williams would eventually be released into a city where shoemakers were congregating in large shops that supplied ready-made goods to new markets in the South and West more cheaply than ever before along highways, canals, and rivers. Competition had lowered wages.

Still, his particular trade was slower to become mechanized than some others. Shoes would be made by hand until sometime after mid-century, when a sewing machine to make uppers came into use. Then, with the arrival of the McKay sole-sewing machine in 1862, which was able to produce "in one hour what the journeyman did in eighty . . . even prison labor . . . [was] not cheap enough . . . to compete with the product of green hands and steam power."

The directors at Auburn State Prison, home of the competing experiment in silence, were more tuned in to the times. Auburn, with its congregate system that involved inmates working together in large rooms, anticipated the regulations and rigor of a mechanized factory, with its timetables and workstations. At almost all times of the day, an inmate at Auburn was strapped to a strict order of obedience: "He arose at 5:15 in the summer, or at sunrise in other seasons . . . As soon as his cell was unlocked, he marched out carrying three pieces of equipment: a night tube used for calls of nature, a can for drinking water, and a wooden food container called a 'kid.' Holding this paraphernalia with his left hand, he laid his right one upon the shoulder of the felon who occupied the next cell and marched in lockstep to a washroom where the kids and cans were deposited for cleaning . . . After this he marched to his workshop."

Once the inmate was at work, the restrictions were relentless, since order was a means of maintaining silence and solitude within the crowd. Gershon Powers, an agent and keeper of the prison in the 1820s, noted: "The duty of the convicts in this prison, is to obey orders, and labor diligently in silence . . . They are not to speak to each other, on any pretense, except by special direction of a keeper; may not sing, dance, whistle, run, jump, or do any thing which will have the *least tendency* to disturb or alarm the prison. Their every movement and whole demeanor are to be in strict accordance to the most perfect order."

By the time Austin Reed, a young black convict, arrived at Auburn in the 1840s, the workrooms were in a state of decay.

Often filled with smoke and dust, they were intensely hot in summer and cold in winter. The roofs leaked on the workers. Reed, who'd been born a free man, gives an unstinting and detailed firsthand account of life within Auburn in his memoir, *The Life and Adventures of a Haunted Convict.* No matter the decay and disarray around them, Reed affirms, the strictness concerning prisoner behavior still held. He and his fellow inmates were to remain orderly and silent: "When marching, we must keep close together, with our arms folded and our heads to the right, our heads bowed and our eyes a looking down upon the ground."

Just as at Eastern State, inmates were not permitted to hear news from the outside, not even news of family unless there was an emergency. Although they were not allowed visitors, outsiders could view the prisoners. There was a hidden corridor with peepholes along the perimeter of the workrooms which was used not only by guards for surveillance, but also by the famous, the curious, and family members, who could pay 25 cents to peer at the convicts at labor. At times visitors also walked through the workrooms. Reed notes that inmates "must not look up off of your work and cast an uplifted eye at spectators. (I like that rule. It's a good rule. How does it look for convicts to be staring and gazing at spectators and strangers in the face as they are passing through the shops? It looks to me like shame and misery. They came through to gaze and stare at us, and not we at them.)"

What would a visitor see and hear in the workrooms? Gershon Powers noted: "In all the shops, the convicts are arranged, as far as possible, in such a way as not to face each other, and have their work entirely separate . . . In this way, a shop, and business of an hundred men, are so managed, that hours together will frequently pass without a word being spoken." Powers asserted that the inmates "generally admit, that the desire to converse is so great, and the temptation to it so strong, that the convicts will run the hazard of speaking to each other, whenever they think there is any probable chance of escaping detection; but that such is the vigilance of their keepers, generally, that scarcely any thing can be said, and never so as to carry on a connected discourse or to concert conspiracies or rebellion. It is not an uncommon thing for a convict, when discharged, to state, that he did not know the names of his fellow-convicts, who had for months worked by his side, and who had lodged in adjoining cells."

But Reed's account differs from this. He recalls that notes were passed under worktables and inmates communicated with one another in a makeshift sign language, an observation supported by Harriet Martineau, who wrote of Auburn's night cells: "The convicts converse with nearly as much ease, through the air-pipes or otherwise, at night, as they do by speaking behind their teeth, without moving the lips, while at work in the day." With good reason, perhaps, the guards raised their concerns when they discovered that one of the inmates was a ventriloquist.

The rigor of obedience at Auburn never let up, even—or especially—at mealtime. Like Benedict, who took particular care to restrict talking in the monastery during mealtime, the officers at Auburn knew the dangers of a whisper. Reed describes the tables of the dining hall, set with seven hundred or eight hundred wooden plates for breakfast and lunch, the congregate meals of the day. For breakfast: brown bread, beef, potatoes, and a pint of coffee. For lunch: bread, meat, potatoes, soup, and a cup of cold water. "When sitting at the table," he writes, "we must keep our arms folded, our head bowed, with our eyes directly down on our dishes before us, not allowed to touch a knife or a fork, or to unfold our arms until the bell rings as a signal for us to eat. Must not pass a piece of bread or meat or a potato from one man to another, either behind you or before you, at your right hand or at your left hand . . . for if you do, off comes your shirt, and [in] less than a minute's time you are suffering under the pains of the cats."

"Cats" is short for the cat-o'-nine-tails used to whip the prisoners. They would have been quite familiar to Reed. He was an outspoken man, often angry, and had the scars to prove it. According to one of his prison records, he was "5' plus 5½ inches in height. Mulatto. Breasts covered with scars. Scar from burn on left arm. Scar on left side of back." Reed had been whipped for the first time by a farmer near Rochester, New York, to whom he had been indentured at the age of six.

At the end of the workday, the Auburn inmates returned to their cells, where they ate their supper of mush and molasses, washed down with cold water. "Many was the nights that the prisoners returned to their cells with their backs cut and hacked up with the cats, and cursing and damning their makers and uttering hard and horrible oaths," writes Reed. Their cells contained nothing personal, only a sleeping hammock, a Bible and tract, and the spoon with which they ate their mush. They were forbidden to "swing their hammocks" before eight p.m.

However different from Eastern State the daytime routine at Auburn might have been, the stifling silence of the night would have been familiar to those confined in either institution. "When the day is finished, and the prisoners have retired to their cells, the silence within these vast walls, which contain so many prisoners, is that of death," remarked Gustave de Beaumont and Alexis de Tocqueville after their visit to Auburn. "We have often trod during night those monotonous and dumb galleries, where a lamp is always burning: we felt as if we traversed catacombs; there were a thousand living beings, and yet it was a desert solitude."

13

punishment within punishment

COBBLING SHOES OR picking oakum could only do so much to alleviate the weight of time and silence at Eastern State, which took its toll on many of the incarcerated, even though the plan for extreme isolation broke down from the beginning. The warden and the guards may have understood the concept of redemption through silence and solitude, but they were also concerned with the orderly running of the prison, with its specific and immediate demands. During the first years of operation, their task was made all the more challenging because only three of the seven planned ranges of cells had been completed by the time Charles Williams arrived at the gate on that October day in 1829. As a result, the penitentiary was also a worksite. Masters and journeymen arrived daily to dig foundations and build stone walls and floors, and it wasn't uncommon for the incarcerated to help with the construction, as well as with daily operations within the compound.

There is evidence that this practice began soon after the first prisoners arrived. Even Prisoner No. 1 was let outside his cell to help with the construction and upkeep. One of the overseers at the time attested that Williams "worked about the yard, cleaning up, took care of the horse in the stable, attended the masons awhile about the building as a mortar carrier, and stone carrier." Other prisoners were "frequently employed in cooking, in working, in breaking coal, in making fires, occasionally as waiters, in work connected with the building and construction of cells, out of their cells." Some even worked as blacksmiths, which means they were "constantly while at work associated, each with an individual not a convict, who aids in the work."

Work outside their cells wasn't all that allayed the prescribed strictness of the environment. Over time even the austerity of their confines softened. Some inmates mixed plant dyes from weeds they found growing in the exercise yards and painted the walls of their cells. They hung pictures. They kept small gardens in the yards and tamed wild animals to keep as pets, all of which was permitted by the warden and guards. Charles Dickens noted these human touches when he visited Eastern State during his American tour in 1842. His account of his findings, "Philadelphia, and Its Solitary Prison," was included in *American Notes for General Circulation*, which was published later that same year. He remarked on the sour smell of one cell in which a prisoner was allowed to keep rabbits. Another prisoner, he observed, "wore a paper hat of his own making, and was pleased to have it noticed and commended. He had very ingeniously manufactured a sort of Dutch clock from some disregarded odds and ends; and his vinegar bottle served for the pendulum."

Dickens's account of his visit provides the most renowned description of life at Eastern State during its early decades, and while he does note the colored walls and decorations, he largely writes of the psychological despair he saw so clearly among the incarcerated. He describes one inmate as being possessed of "a strange stare as if he had forgotten something." Another "took one of the visitors aside, to ask, with his trembling hands nervously clutching at his coat to detain him, whether there was no hope of his dismal sentence being commuted." Yet another, eleven years in, stared "at his hands and pick[ed] the flesh upon his fingers, and rais[ed] his eyes for an instant, every now and then, to those bare walls which have seen his head turn grey."

"I am . . . convinced that there is a depth of terrible endurance in it which none but the sufferers themselves can fathom, and which no man has a right to inflict upon his fellow-creatures," Dickens writes concerning the silent and solitary sentences at Eastern State. "I hold this slow and daily tampering with the mysteries of the brain, to be immeasurably worse than any torture of the body: and because its ghastly signs and tokens are not so palpable to the eye and sense of touch as scars upon the flesh; because its wounds are not upon the surface, and it extorts few cries that human ears can hear; therefore the more I denounce it, as a secret punishment which slumbering humanity is not roused up to stay."

Dickens was criticized for his empathic view of the inmates, and penitentiary officials expressed concern that the reputation of Eastern State had been compromised by a man "whose note as a writer of fictions, has secured for his crude performance a diffusive popularity." At the request of the Pennsylvania Prison Society, William Peter, Britain's consul general for Pennsylvania, investigated Dickens's claims. After his inspection Peter noted that Eastern State was "*superior* to any thing of the kind that I am acquainted with, either in the old world or the new." Of Dickens's account generally, Peter remarked: “I do not think that he would be guilty—knowingly guilty—of a falsehood for any consideration. But all things are not given to all men; and the very faculty which has enabled him so to excel in one species of composition, almost incapacitates him for some others.”

Peter then methodically compared his findings with those of Dickens. For instance, in describing Charles Langheimer, who was serving five years for larceny, Dickens writes: “A more dejected, heart-broken, wretched creature, it would be difficult to imagine. I never saw such a picture of forlorn affliction and distress of mind.” But Peter noted that “he was in as excellent health and spirits as a mortal need be,—conversed freely about his situation and expressed confident hopes, that he should, through the kindness and recommendations of the governor and others, be able to get into good employment as a paper-stainer, on the expiration of his term of imprisonment. He is an ingenious and clever fellow, but a great hypocrite, and evidently saw Mr. D’s *weak* side.”

Negley Teeters and John Shearer, in their history of the penitentiary, offer the official record of Langheimer’s sentence, gleaned from the wardens’ journals and the penitentiary logbooks. Langheimer, it is recorded, attempted suicide four days after his arrival at Eastern State. He made a second attempt soon afterward and also refused to work (he was tasked with winding bobbins). Upon release he committed subsequent offenses and was imprisoned multiple times both at Eastern State and in the county prison.

Perhaps there was a little bit of Langheimer in all three of these accounts. Yet, however sentimental Dickens’s chronicle of his visit may be, it doesn’t negate the profundity of the suffering, and three brief angles of vision can't begin to mine the complexities of a human being confronted with extreme silence and solitude. Langheimer's last days illustrate how unforeseen the turns of a heart and mind can be. At the end of his life, it could be said that the penitentiary seemed like home to him. Shortly before he died, he appeared at the door of Eastern State and rang the bell. "The guard responded, and outside found a little old man with silver gray hair, cleanly dressed, begging to be allowed to go inside . . . He said he had come back to die. He was taken inside and placed upon a cot. From that day his vitality ebbed away."

The inmates at Eastern State all dressed in the same uniform, wore the same hood when being transported through the prison, were served the same mush and bread and coffee. All were certainly ill-prepared for confinement in a stone room where it was forbidden even to whisper. But the lives that led them to the stone cells were theirs alone. Their crimes, and the reasons they had for committing them—whether they were repeat offenders or first-timers convicted of larceny, burglary, arson, highway robbery, rape, murder, or manslaughter—were distinct. Some had broken the law out of need for food or shelter. More than a few suffered from mental illness. Others were violent and led unapologetic lives of transgression and confrontation. And not all sank into themselves within the silence and solitude.

From all reports, Charles Williams made no trouble during his two years in solitary. But some inmates destroyed the meager furniture in their cells. Others refused to work or intentionally ruined their work. According to one account, "No. 50, was a notorious robber. He had been several years a man-of-war's man; was upwards of six feet in height, robust and athletic, and of remarkable fierce and stubborn temper. He now became careless of his work, and would spoil it, alleging that inasmuch as he was blind of one eye, the other was getting sore, and he could not see to work, and ought to be put on the sick list."

The refusal to work and the spoiling of work may have been ways for prisoners to protest their confinement and attempt to take control of their fate in whatever small ways they could, even though, as one observer suggested, work "is almost universally liked by the convicts in solitary confinement, so much so, that nothing is more common than their asking and begging for light, when the days begin to be short, and lamps are not yet given to the prisoners, in order to work by candlelight." Such methods of protest would have been familiar to many of the incarcerated, for as historian Jennifer Lawrence Janofsky has observed: "The vast majority of inmates came from the laboring classes. Before arriving at Eastern, prisoners had worked as shoemakers, tailors, chair makers, and carpenters . . . Work slowdowns, 'Blue Mondays,' and sabotaging of tools and machines all characterized the labor movement of the early nineteenth century and, for many, became the tools of resistance at Eastern State."

But the situation at the penitentiary was in no way similar to that of a union workshop. The prisoners couldn't negotiate their grievances. The wardens could simply deny work to an intransigent inmate, and often did. After Prisoner No. 50 began to spoil his work, Mr. Griffith, the principal keeper,

> immediately removed his tools and books, and restricted his visits to those of necessity. Before a week had elapsed

> he gave evidence of great uneasiness, by sighs and groans and the rapidity with which he walked his cell, and humbly begged that he might have his work back again . . .
>
> Before the expiration of three weeks, he exhibited strong symptoms of ennui, misery, and despair . . . and when his cell door was opened, he would exclaim to the keeper, "Give me back my work, or I will go crazy;" or, "For G—'s sake, give me a book or some work, or I shall die."
>
> At the expiration of three weeks, Mr. Griffith, by permission of the Warden, restored his tools and materials; he pursued his work with unusual industry, and never after gave cause of complaint.

While the refusal to work might have been the most costly, disruptive, and confrontational form of protest, breaking the silence was the most common infraction during the early years of Eastern State. Just a few miles away, the loquacious world of Philadelphia thrived, with its lecture halls and living room debates, its pubs and streets and shops. At Eastern State prisoners used their tools to tap on the pipes to try to say the merest thing to their neighbors. They sent notes through the pipes, and they called to one another through them. They rapped on the thick stone. They threw notes over the walls of the exercise yards. They tried anything ingenious, really, to say something to the other prisoners. Imagine the determination and ingenuity required to say just a few words—always at the risk of severe punishment. They had to secure writing implements and paper to write notes. They had to develop coherent tapping codes among themselves.

While no known tapping system survives from the solitaries at Eastern State, the simplicity and complexity of such a system can be gleaned from the legendary tap codes used in Russian and Soviet prisons. The same system lived on through the fall of the empire, the establishment of the Soviet state, and Stalin's purges. In her nineteenth-century memoir Vera Figner describes the prisoners' alphabet. The Cyrillic alphabet was imagined as a grid of five horizontal rows, six letters in each row. Each letter was assigned two sets of taps—the first designating the row, the second designating its place in the row. The first letter was 1,1; the second, 1,2; the third, 1,3; and so on. So common was the system's use in Figner's time that guards were continually working to drown out the tappings. She recalls one instance when a man in a neighboring cell began to send a message, "but hardly had he begun his tapping again when the gendarmes forestalled him by snatching up staves and beating furiously on our doors. A din beyond all imagining arose. One who has not spent many years in the silence of a prison, whose ear has not grown unaccustomed to sounds, cannot imagine the pain experienced by an ear grown tender through the constant stillness."

In the Soviet Union of the 1930s, Eugenia Ginzburg heard her prison neighbor tapping day in and day out, and only slowly came to realize that what she was hearing was a code for the word "greetings," which the neighbor—who was escorted daily to the washroom ahead of her—had been writing out in tooth powder on the sinks. The realization prompted her to remember Vera Figner's account of the tap code, which she could recall perfectly. She now had the entire alphabet at her disposal. Ginzburg, it turned out, knew the prisoner in the adjoining cell, which was not uncommon during the purges. "From then on, though outwardly nothing had altered, our days were full of interest," Ginzburg writes in her memoir. It was through her neighbor that she began to gain a true understanding of the scope of Stalin's brutality. His brief tapped-out messages, she remarks, "opened a new world to me, a world of camps, deportations, prisons, tragic twists of fate—a world in which either the spirit was broken and degraded or true courage was born."

In the solitary cells at Eastern State, with its thieves and forgers arriving one by one from across the eastern half of Pennsylvania, each was a stranger to each. What friendships could be established within the penitentiary were likely limited. Some prisoners, with their tappings and notes, could have been planning disruptions or even escapes. They could have been tapping in the hope of finding boon companions to consort with on the outside once their sentences were completed. Or attempting to orient themselves in their environment. Or trying to find out who else shared their common lot and to gain some support in an insupportable solitude. Or simply whiling away the searingly silent hours, or finding delight in transgression, or trying to remain sane against the onslaught of silence.

"The most important thing of all was not to forget how to talk," Ginzburg writes. Even the merest tap or whisper could offer great comfort and was certainly magnified in its import. Small talk, to people deprived of a voice, is no trivial thing. In truth, in a world where any utterance at all is forbidden, there's really no such thing as small talk. As Harriet Martineau observed of prisoners forced into silence: "They are denied the forgetfulness of themselves and their miseries which they might enjoy in free conversation." Certainly, it helped the isolated to know others shared their lot, and sometimes breaking down the boundaries between prisoners didn't require words at all, only a common endeavor —something beyond being ordered by guards, instructed by visitors intent on teaching them the Bible, or preached to on Sundays. Several inmates at Western State Penitentiary, Eastern State's counterpart in Pittsburgh, shared "pets": they trained a rat or mouse and passed it back and forth between cells through the pipes.

Beyond denying work to those who transgressed within the penitentiary, what further means of punishment did the wardens and guards have? How were they to discipline the most recalcitrant prisoners? For even minor infractions, their food might be reduced to bread and water. Their bedding might be taken away, leaving them with only a blanket to sleep upon. They might be denied their daily hour of exercise.

The loss of that one hour of relative freedom in the enclosed stone exercise yard must have been particularly painful. Such hours "were brief intervals of life," Eugenia Ginzburg recalls of her fifteen minutes in an exercise yard in her Soviet prison. "I waited for them impatiently. I remembered them in the evening. To be deprived of exercise—and this was a fairly frequent punishment—was a horrible misfortune. After all, fifteen paces were more than five. And there was the sky." The squared-off sky above was almost all the nature she could see, and it became imbued with beauty beyond measure: "To my dying day I shall not forget the clear, high-vaulted Yaroslavl sky. No other town has anything to compare with it. And besides, one could sometimes see gulls flying over from the Volga . . . And the ships' sirens! How can words convey what they meant to a prisoner in solitary confinement, especially one who, like me, had lived by the Volga? I heard them as the living voices of friends."

Benedict, in his Rule, calls for an errant monk to be whipped if even excommunication fails to reform him. And if physical punishment fails, "if in pride he defends his misconduct, the abbot must behave like a wise physician . . . If all this is to no avail, the abbot must wield the surgeon's knife. As the Apostle says . . . 'If the faithless one depart, let him depart.' Thus the one sick sheep may not infect the flock." An evicted monk could petition to reenter the monastery three times. After that, he would be banished for life.

But in the penitentiary, transgressors could not be turned out. If the denial of basic necessities didn't subdue an offender, the wardens and guards at Eastern State had few other sanctioned options. They were charged to avoid corporal punishment, but one form of discipline they could use for more serious infractions or repeated offenses was to isolate a prisoner even more completely in a punishment cell, also known as a dark cell or dungeon. Usually the dark cell was an ordinary cell where the oculus, the circular window cut into the barreled ceiling, was covered by a half keg and a piece of cloth so that no natural light at all could enter. And in the dark cell, prisoners also could be denied their rations: "No. 132 was put into a cell, and kept forty-two days—six weeks—upon half a pound of bread a day. His offence was cutting up some upper leather of shoes."

Solitary within solitary. The prisoners who were involuntarily subjected to such darkness already had no sense of place within the prison. When deprived of light, they would lose all consciousness of time, which, as Harriet Martineau observed, had taken on an outsized meaning for them. Why else would they make meticulous observations of the movement of the sun shining into their cells? Eugenia Ginzburg recalls that when she was sentenced to five days in a punishment cell after being falsely accused of writing her name on the washroom wall, any sliver of light—even when a guard entered, for instance—was a deep blessing, and keeping track of time helped her survive: "What I must do was to keep count of the days and nights so that they did not all merge into one. They had just offered me bread: this would be the first day, and so I made a rent in the hem of my shirt. When there were five of them I would be let out." In order to keep a level head, she also used sounds to help her orient herself. After a day or so, she could distinguish between the guards by their distinctive footfalls and had concluded by listening to the clangings in the hall that there were at least five other "black holes" besides the one she occupied. As always, she recited poetry to herself in the dark to keep her spirits up and her mind focused, and she composed her own verses in her head.

The wages of disorientation and isolation are now known to be profound. Stuart Grassian, a psychiatrist who has studied the effects of modern-day solitary confinement on the human mind and body, has reported that by the latter part of the nineteenth century, the United States Supreme Court had come to the conclusion that general solitary confinement—not even as severe as a dark cell—gravely affected a prisoner's mental health, that many "fell, after even a short confinement, into a semi-fatuous condition, from which it was next to impossible to arouse them, and others became violently insane; others, still, committed suicide." Grassian has observed that the effects can vary widely from individual to individual. The stable and the disciplined—those who can find a way to retain a sense of time and remain mentally active, as Ginzburg did—fare better. "However all . . . individuals will still experience a degree of stupor, difficulties with thinking and concentration, obsessional thinking, agitation, irritability, and difficulty tolerating external stimuli," he has written. The absence of stimulation intensifies reactions to stimuli: "Ordinary stimuli become intensely unpleasant and small irritations become maddening. Individuals in such confinement brood upon normally unimportant stimuli and minor irritations become the focus of increasing agitation and paranoia." Prisoners often suffer from perceptual distortions and hallucinations.

Confinement in a dark cell when prisoners were already somewhat fragile from their daily solitude must have intensified all these effects. "The brain," neurologist and writer Oliver Sacks has noted, "needs not only perceptual input but perceptual *change,* and the absence of change may cause not only lapses of arousal and attention but perceptual aberrations as well. Whether darkness and solitude is sought by holy men in caves or forced upon prisoners in lightless dungeons, the deprivation of normal visual input can stimulate the inner eye instead, producing dreams, vivid imaginings, or hallucinations," which in modern times have come to be known as "the prisoner's cinema."

Eyewitness accounts by guards who testified about the conditions of prisoners confined in dark cells at Eastern State affirm all of this: "No. 118 . . . looked like a ghost when he came out, and was never hearty afterwards—I . . . never saw a man who suffered so much. His allowance also was eight ounces of bread for 24 hours. His first name was Samuel. My conscience permits me to say, that he was in this dungeon not less than 20 days. He had been punished frequently before . . . when he went in he was hale and hearty."

The deprivation of work and food, and even the dark cell, had been sanctioned as means of punishment within punishment. But sometimes authorities resorted to unprescribed harsher treatments, which eventually came to light in an 1834 investigation into the management and financial matters of Eastern State. Testimony during the proceedings of the investigation revealed that guards at times doused prisoners with water—a particularly severe punishment in the open exercise yard during the cold months, as was the case for Seneca Plumly, who was "tied up against a wall in the depth of winter, while buckets of extreme cold water were thrown upon him, which partly froze on his head and person, and he was shortly after discharged as incurably insane."

In at least one instance, prison authorities resorted to a metal gag to punish an inmate. Prisoner No. 102, Matthias Maccumsey—a laborer in his early forties who, it was noted, could read and write and who bore scars on his eyebrow and chin—arrived at Eastern State in November of 1831 to serve a twelve-year sentence for murder. In the ensuing months he'd repeatedly tried to speak to other prisoners through the pipes and over the exercise wall. In June of 1833 he was gagged for "having on several occasions got the men next to him talking."

The warden at that time, Samuel Wood, who would eventually be exonerated for any wrongdoing, noted in his daily journal on June 27, 1833: "Last evening I ordered . . . the gag on No. 102—this I saw put on about 8 OCK." The gag has been described as a "rough iron instrument resembling the stiff bit of a blind bridle, having an iron palet in the centre, about an inch square, and chains at each end to pass round the neck and fasten behind. This instrument was placed in the prisoners mouth, the iron palet over his tongue, the bit forced in as far as possible, the chains brought round the jaws to the back of the neck; the end of one chain was passed through the ring in the end of the other chain drawn tight to 'the fourth link,' and fastened with a lock, his hands were forced into leather gloves in which were iron staples and crossed behind his back . . . the straps were drawn tight, the hands forced up toward the head."

The entry in Wood's journal concludes: "About 9 OCK I was informed by Wm Griffiths that they had found him in a lifeless state. I immediately went to him and found him warm—but with no pulse. We tried to bleed him and used ammonia and many other things but life was extinct."

As with Seneca Plumly's dousing with water, the gag harked back to the sanguinary laws of colonial days and, like the use of the pillories and stocks, were by the nineteenth century regarded as cruel and unusual punishments that could not be meted out by the courts of the Republic. But it's as if these old practices, once loosed on the world, could not be entirely discarded. They continued to live within the penitentiaries, their purpose now distorted. There was no longer the assumption—so ingrained in the sanguinary laws—that public shaming could work toward the public good by making the criminal think again before committing another such crime. Instead, at Eastern State, in secrecy and seclusion, the old blood punishments were, as the minority report investigating abuse and corruptions stated, "perpetuated in defiance of the law and Legislative enactments." They were nothing more than the enforcement of power and attempts at control. For Matthias Maccumsey, beyond the violence and cruelty of his punishment, there would have been another, more shameful layer of meaning. Silencing under the sanguinary laws was—not always, but primarily—a woman's punishment and a slave's punishment.

14

so that it "may uplift"

DURING HER FIRST few months in Yaroslavl, Eugenia Ginzburg did not have access to the prison library. She spent her time pacing her cell; combing her memory; recollecting her loved ones, her former life, her reading. "I was able to observe the virtuosity that human memory can develop when it is sharpened by loneliness and complete isolation from outside impressions," she writes in her memoir. "One remembers with amazing accuracy everything one has ever read, even quite long ago, and can repeat whole pages of books one had believed long forgotten."

When she was finally granted borrowing privileges, she anticipated the first offerings that were to arrive from the prison library: "This was the end of our loneliness. Tomorrow at this hour I would have visitors: Tolstoy and Blok, Stendhal and Balzac." She soon discovered that in the depths of cruelty and constrained by force, reading helped her maintain a sense of hope and a connection to humanity: "I have never loved human beings so devotedly as in those months and years when, cast away in the inhuman land and imprisoned behind stone walls, I absorbed every line of print as though it were a message radioed from Earth, my distant mother and homeland, where I had lived with my human brothers and sisters, and where they lived still." Not only did books provide a link to the world beyond her cell, but the rewards of reading deepened during her life of restriction. Although she'd been an inveterate reader prior to her sentence, she notes that it was in her cell, "in my stone sepulcher, that I really explored for the first time the inmost meaning of what I read. Up till then I had skimmed the surface, enlarging my mind in breadth but not in depth." Decades later, her experience in the free world affirmed this: "After I came out of prison I found I could no longer read as I had done in my cell at Yaroslavl, where I rediscovered Dostoevsky, Tyutchev, Pasternak, and many others."

In her words there is no small echo of the intensity of reading experienced by medieval monastics and, more currently, of the kind of concentration and depth Thomas Merton voluntarily sought when he arrived at the gates of the Abbey of Gethsemani. "When a human being is isolated from the 'rat-race' of everyday life, he achieves a kind of spiritual serenity," Ginzburg remembered decades after her time in solitary and her release from the Gulag. "Sitting in a cell, one no longer has any call to pursue the phantom of worldly success, to play the diplomat or the hypocrite, to compromise with one's conscience. One can immerse oneself in the lofty problems of existence, and do so with a mind purified by suffering."

Benjamin Rush had imagined that spiritual reading would accomplish much the same thing at Eastern State. He believed he had good reason to place his faith in books. By the time Charles Williams walked through the penitentiary gate, literacy was on the rise in the United States. In Philadelphia there were more bookshops than in Boston, and several newspapers were published daily. Readers all over the city, from all stations of life, glanced at the pages of the *Philadelphia Inquirer,* skimming short passages concerning crimes, accidents, and social and political events connected largely by proximity on the page and in time. While perusing the October 30, 1829, edition of the *Inquirer,* Philadelphians would have encountered, in the first of six narrow columns, election results, the story of a young man acquitted of murdering his father, another story of a hunting accident, and the news that Sheriff Broomhall, "in obedience to the sentence of the court, conveyed Charles Williams, a colored man (indicted for burglary and found guilty) to the new State Penitentiary, near Philadelphia, on Saturday last." This item was followed by an account of a public dinner and information concerning the completion of a new hotel. The space given to each article, whether Williams's historic incarceration or the public dinner, is nearly equal in its measure, and the two events had little in common other than having been deemed by the publisher of the *Inquirer* to be of interest to readers.

This "all at onceness," as Marshall McLuhan called it—events from different places and times joined together only by their proximity on a newspaper page—could not be further from the monastic practice of *lectio divina,* although the perusing of a newspaper was deemed just as essential to the Republic, in its way, as the slow and repetitive study of texts was to monastic life. Cesare Beccaria had foreseen in the mid-eighteenth century how essential the dissemination of the printed word would become for a democracy: "Without written laws, no society will ever acquire a fixed form of government, in which the power is vested in the whole, and not in any part of society; and in which the laws are not to be altered but by the will of the whole, nor corrupted by the force of private interest. Hence we see the use of printing, which alone makes the public, and not a few individuals, the guardians and defenders of the laws."

Thomas Jefferson built upon Beccaria's ideas as he revised the laws of Virginia in the early days of the Republic. His "Bill for the More General Diffusion of Knowledge" advocated for public funds to be used to educate the citizenry, arguing that the best means of preventing tyranny was to "illuminate, as far as practicable, the minds of the people at large, and more especially to give them knowledge of those facts, which history exhibiteth, that, possessed thereby of the experience of other ages and countries, they may be enabled to know ambition under all its shapes, and prompt to exert their natural powers to defeat its purposes."

Jefferson's bill failed to gain traction, in part because many Americans were wary of government-funded education. In the village world of the colonies, education had been largely local, left to families and churches, and communities were reluctant to cede the power of education to the federal government and to pay for schooling with taxes. But efforts to provide a more general education to the public steadily increased. Jefferson's voice was joined by that of Benjamin Rush, who believed that democracy required new responsibilities of its citizens, which education would abet. He recalled Beccaria's words: "When the clouds of ignorance are dispelled by the radiance of knowledge, power trembles but the authority of laws remains immovable."

Rush's staunch belief in education went beyond establishing an informed citizenry. Part of the appeal of education for him was its perceived capacity to increase conformity—not surprising in a man who looked for one cure for all disease and a uniform means of meting out criminal justice. A century after its founding, descendants of the settlers shared the city with immigrants from all parts of Europe, indentured servants, and freed slaves. The crowds and noisy street life created anxiety in the old Quaker city. Rush saw education as a means to alleviate the anxiety by reducing the differences: "Our schools of learning, by producing one general and uniform system of education, will render the mass of people more homogenous and thereby fit them more easily for uniform and peaceable government." His ideas concerning education as a means of conformity would be reinforced in the nineteenth century when proponents of the common school movement advocated general education in part as a means of equipping the citizenry for life in the industrial age, when workers would be required to adhere to the discipline of the factory, with its regimented tasks and precise hours.

Rush further argued that education would decrease the crime rate: "Of the many criminals that have been executed within these seven years, four out of five of them have been foreigners who have arrived here during the war and since the peace." He also suggested that "fewer pillories and whipping posts and smaller jails, with their usual expenses and taxes, will be necessary when our youth are [more] properly educated than at present." He laid out these ideas in an essay published in 1786, around the same time he was imagining the penitentiary.

Decades later, advocates of the penitentiary, echoing Rush's faith in literacy, hoped that the Bible in particular would not only be read by prisoners but become integral to their moral and spiritual life—meditated upon while they hammered at their work in their world of silence. But this hope had a secular tone. "The first object of the officers of this institution is, to turn the thoughts of the convict inwards upon himself and to teach him how to think; in this solitude is a powerful aid," an early annual report from the penitentiary states. It continues, "The character of the convict is generally social to a fault . . . and, when, deprived of the society of his companions in vicious indulgences and guilt, he reads and listens with eagerness, because he is relieved by the variety from the weariness of his solitude. There he can only read and hear, what is calculated to make him industrious and virtuous." The prison library at Eastern State was stocked with Bibles, testaments, and prayer books, "calculated to imbue [prisoners'] minds with moral and religious ideas." Although visitors could peruse the library, prisoners had to request books on a slate, and the books were then delivered to their cells.

Alexis de Tocqueville and Gustave de Beaumont remarked on how eagerly Charles Williams took to the Bible, and William Peter, while countering Charles Dickens's claims, noted that one inmate "was quite ignorant and uninstructed when he entered, but learned whilst in prison to read, write, and cipher; has now a good place as a servant . . . and behaves remarkably well." This may not have been the norm. Although the intake logs at Eastern State indicate that more than a few of the prisoners could read, what that meant is up for conjecture. Most inmates at Eastern State came from the working classes, and a good number were immigrants, whose first language wasn't English. Even free blacks in Philadelphia, who had better opportunities for education than blacks in the South, might not have had extensive schooling. A share of the prisoners also had cognitive and emotional problems.

Most who could read were likely, at best, grade school adequate. In 1833, when there were over one hundred forty prisoners at Eastern State, the warden asserted that "only four have been well educated, and only about six more . . . could read and write tolerably; and we rarely meet with a prisoner who has had attention paid to moral and religious instruction." The next year he noted that nearly half could only "read or write indifferently, [and] many of these, as well as most of those who could read only, were not able to read a sentence without spelling out many of the words." Visitors to the cells could read to the prisoners and could instruct them in the Bible, but as historian Jodie Schorb has noted: "From the start, Pennsylvania reformers and prison authorities lacked consensus about whether reading—even Bible reading—did any good."

Here is a question to ask the silence: What made time in a cell survivable? For Ginzburg, books were of untold value, and we, who depend so much on reading and writing now, might feel that there could be nothing more consoling than reading in that silence. Given that Eastern State's overseers may have been complacent about fostering literacy, those prisoners who could not read well enough to become engaged with books needed to find the merest thing upon which to train their attention: making clocks with vinegar-bottle pendulums, mixing dyes from weeds and painting the cell walls, cultivating gardens in the exercise yards from whatever seeds blew in. Such absorptions, in their way, were less of a threat to order than reading, for the power of reading can't be narrowly defined, nor can its effects, or how it transforms a mind, be controlled.

Reading gave Austin Reed a sense of power and self-possession. When he arrived at Auburn State Prison in 1840, he was angered to find no library and no reading materials other than a Bible and tract in each cell. (No doubt some of the prisoners at Eastern State would hold the same low estimate of the Bible that Reed did.) He found no slate or pencil. "Those was dark days," he observes in his firsthand account, "when no prisoner was allowed to write a letter to his friends or to make one single mark with a pencil . . . Those was the dark and lonesome days when the convict had no library books to read, nothing but his bible and tract, and if he wanted to kill time during the long summer days, he must take his bible or tract from his shelf and wear away the long and lonesome hours that came a hanging on him like a heavy weight by reading them."

Prior to being sentenced to Auburn, Reed had been incarcerated as a juvenile at the House of Refuge in New York City, which is where he learned to read and write. The classroom work that was offered there was reinforced by a fellow inmate: "Every spare minute that Jack could get, he would run to me with his little pointer in his hand and show me which was A, and which was B, and by the space of nine months I was sitting at the head of the ninth class every night, reading and studying pieces from *The English Reader.*" After a year, Reed writes, "I found myself the master of a pen and the reader of a book, and a conqueror of arithmetic. Them was the days when I would challenge old England or America to throw down any history before me and let me read it through just once, and I was the boy who would stand before any historian that ever stood between England and America and argue with him." He would be repeatedly punished for having more than one book at his desk. "I say that I use to crunch on those old fellows until there wasn't a hair's breath of them left —Robinson Crusoe . . . the life of Capt. John Smith."

Auburn had no orientation toward reformation, and perhaps its overseers understood that reading did not necessarily lead one to become a law-abiding citizen. Reed was no more controllable once he learned to read and write than he had been before. He was incarcerated multiple times from 1840 to 1860, with brief stints of freedom in between, and it was during this time that he wrote his memoir of prison life. Historian Caleb Smith, who edited Reed's manuscript, suggests it was written piecemeal, both while he was in prison and when he was living as a free man.

It's impossible to trace the course of his life after his release in 1863 with any certainty. Smith conjectures that he may, for a time, have worked making artificial legs for disabled Civil War veterans. He may have boarded at a temperance hotel in Rochester, New York, the city where he was born. He may have served more time. He may have changed his name to Robert Reed. As Smith notes: "His book is full of men who travel under pseudonyms and call each other by nicknames." He suggests that Reed may have "drifted westward or north into Canada, or maybe he changed his name yet again."

He was as lost to history as his manuscript was lost to the world until 2009, when an antiquarian bookseller discovered the brown and brittle pages at an estate sale in Rochester. Since its discovery, Reed's script has been pored over and analyzed. His account was first published in the twenty-first century, when the incarcerated in America number more than a million and his words can be called up before a reader's eyes in an instant.

15

time again

TIME AT EASTERN STATE had its markers: the daily hour of exercise, visits from wardens and members of the prison society, services on Sunday. The meal slot in the cell door slid open for breakfast, lunch, and dinner. These events that punctuated the prisoners' waking hours must have seemed to rise suddenly out of unmeasured time, akin to bells in the Middle Ages. And the prisoners' days—lived without the precision of minutes and hours—were one more way they were set apart, for the nineteenth-century world beyond the walls was now ruled by the urgencies of clock time.

That doesn't mean that the sound of bells disappeared. Rather, as clocks gained ascendancy, the tolling of bells took on added layers of meaning. In one sense, by the time Charles Williams arrived at Eastern State, the bell had become a vestigial sound at the fringes of awareness, particular and romanticized, as Henry David Thoreau suggests in *Walden.* When the wind was right, in his cabin at Walden Pond Thoreau could hear the

Sunday-morning bells from the towns of Concord, Lincoln, Acton, and Bedford, Massachusetts. (At ten by fifteen feet, Thoreau's wooden cabin, hand-built in the 1840s, was not much larger than Williams's cell. But it was open, light-washed, and furnished with three chairs: one for solitude, two for friendship, three for society.) Walden was beholden to no one center, and Thoreau registered no sense of obedience to the bells. Although their ringing was a town sound, he felt that it was old enough and far enough away that the peals were married to the sounds of the woods: "faint, sweet, and, as it were, a natural melody." He thought their tether "worth importing to the wilderness . . . a melody which the air had strained, and which had conversed with every leaf and needle of the wood, that portion of the sound which the elements had taken up and modulated and echoed from vale to vale. The echo is, to some extent, an original sound, and therein is the magic and charm of it. It is not merely a repetition of what was worth repeating in the bell, but partly the voice of the wood; the same trivial words and notes sung by a wood-nymph."

Among Thoreau's refutations in his attempt to live deliberately was that of industrial time. His brief description of the bells follows his long—and more renowned—discourse on the train, its plume of steam and its whistle; its mechanical sounds, direct and cutting, moving through the landscape: the sounds of the Republic, of commerce and capitalism and world markets. Bringer of time zones and timetables. His description of the steam engine billows, as unconfined as steam itself, but the sound of the train suggests an unmistakable restriction: "The startings and arrivals of the cars are now the epochs in the village day. They go and come with such regularity and precision, and their whistles can be heard so far, that the farmers set their clocks by them, and thus one well conducted institution regulates a whole country. Have not men improved somewhat in punctuality since the railroad was invented?"

Not far from his cabin, at the confluence of the Concord and Merrimack Rivers, in the mills of Lowell, Massachusetts, northern New England farm girls who'd traveled south for work in the weaving and spinning rooms of the city quickly came to understand how fraught the new sounds of time could be. For them, the factory bells held nothing of Thoreau's romanticism. They were married to clock time and were to be obeyed no less vigorously than Merton's monastic bells: "You may see her leaning from the window to watch the glitter of the sunrise on the water, or looking away at the distant forests and fields, while memory wanders to her beloved country home . . . Soon the breakfast bell rings . . . and she hastens to join the throng which is pouring through the open gate."

During winter the young women were summoned to work and released from work in darkness: "The clang of the early bell awakes her to another day, very nearly the counterpart of the one which preceded it. And so the week rolls on." The first, second, and third work bell. The dinner bell, ringing in at noon and ringing out thirty-five minutes later. The evening bell. "It is their station to work. And they *do* work," wrote Charles Dickens, who visited Lowell not long after he toured Eastern State. "They labour in these mills, upon an average, twelve hours a day, which is unquestionably work, and pretty tight work too."

In their life on the farm, though the work was endless, the young women's tasks were varied and could be done in their own time unless the season demanded otherwise; then all hands worked to get in the hay before the rain. In the factory, silence was lost, space was lost, their own time was lost. They needed to accustom themselves to the crowd. "Chairs, chairs—one, two, three, four, and so on to forty," one young woman wrote. "It is really refreshing sometimes, to go where there is only now and then a chair."

Lowell had sprung up almost overnight along the banks of the Merrimack, and the city in its entirety, then, was oriented toward the work in the mills. Philadelphia, by contrast, had been growing in unexpected ways for over a century. It was among the most diverse cities in the country during the rise of the penitentiary, and its adaptations over the years included time. Old measures of it overlapped with new, and the city was crowded with both bells and clocks. Catholic church bells still rang the Angelus; other steeple bells rang for services; bells also announced the hours, reinforcing clock time. Historian Alexis McCrossen has noted that in 1828, civic leaders believed that "the time of the citizens of Philadelphia was of so much importance to them, that there ought to be some accurate means of marking its passage." Additionally, city officials wished to improve the appearance of their city, "which is so deficient in embellishments, which in other cities are considered indispensable." "The city's Select and Common Councils," McCrossen has written, "appropriated $12,000 (about $300,000 in today's dollars) to install a new clock and bell on the Old State House. They also approved the purchase of two new clocks for the market houses, and funding to pay for the upkeep of all the city's clocks."

It was a city growing more and more aware of the hours and minutes, of precious time bargained over by laborers and imposed by bosses. It was hoped that the turret on the steeple of the Old State House would be high enough so that the bell could be heard throughout the city, and that the new clock dials affixed to the tower could be seen everywhere as well. The gaslight illumination of the dials would make the hours visible after dark. Time, inescapable even at night, was visible "from more than one thousand doors and windows." With the bells ringing on the hour and clock faces that never disappeared in the dusk, it was hoped a common time would be established throughout the city, although both clocks and bells proved difficult to synchronize, so the hours were often marked by a confusion of independent accuracies, assertions not quite in tune with each other.

During its first decades of operation, the penitentiary may have been surrounded by open fields, but it was no farther from the center of Philadelphia than Walden Pond was from the center of Concord. It's not difficult to imagine the inmates could hear the city's hours bells and announcing bells. Any inaccuracies hardly mattered to them, for, as Oscar Wilde famously remarked, "it is always twilight in one's cell." Their sound likely meant only one thing to the prisoners: the world was going on without them. So it must have seemed doubly strange that, in its early days, the octagonal tower above the massive entryway to Eastern State contained, in addition to an alarm bell, a clock, which announced time to the open countryside beyond the penitentiary wall and to the occasional wagons jostling past on the road. Its ticking minutes may have meant something to prison employees, but it held no conceivable meaning for the prisoners, who couldn't see it from their cell windows or doors. Besides, for them Eastern State was a house ruled by only one measure of time: the sentence.

"Forth you are from the steep ways, forth from the narrow. See the sun that shines on your brow, see the tender grass, the flowers, the shrubs, which here the earth of itself alone produces," Virgil announces to Dante at the end of their climb up Mount Purgatory. "Free, upright, and whole is your will, and it would be wrong not to act according to its pleasure; wherefore I crown and miter you over yourself." So was Benjamin Rush's hope for the solitary souls after they passed back through the lone gate of Eastern State to open country at the end of their sentence: honest citizens, ready now to rejoin society.

The records still remain, long after the penitentiary fell into ruin. One discharge book after another meticulously charts the inmates' departure—if not from the penitentiary, then from this life. In the first years, one or two prisoners were let back into the world every few weeks. Rarely would two be released on the same day. Young men whose parents were dead. Men who'd reached their middle years who "were deranged, and continued so till discharge." "Intemperate." "An Old Convict." "Could work at wheelwrighting." "Former slave." Tailors, laborers, blacksmiths. Every once in a while someone was pardoned. Charles Williams's 1831 release entry appears halfway down the second page of the first discharge book:

> July 31. William Reys. No. 26 (w) Aged 33. Waterman. Can Read & write. Parents dead. Time Out.
>
> August 17. Shem Loomis, alias Judson. No. 38. (w) Aged 20. Powder Maker. Can read. Parents living. Time Out.
>
> August 17. Wm. Caldwell, alias, Frederick Amey. No. 39 (w) Aged 21. Farmer, cannot read or write, parents dead. Idiotic. Time Out.
>
> August 20. Amos Davis. No. 43. (c) Aged 36. Laborer, Cannot read or write. Died.

October 18. Jacob King. No 77. (w) Aged 33. Miller. Can Read and write. Died.
October 22. Charles Williams. No. 1. (c) Aged 20. Laborer can read taught shoemaking. Time Out.
November 9: James Allen. No. 45 (c) Aged 44. Laborer. Cannot read or write. was a slave. Time Out.

Howard Moore, an old convict, was let out on November 11. John Curran, a gardener, on the 17th. John Starne, a paper maker, on the 25th. He was the last to be freed that year.

To Gustave de Beaumont and Alexis de Tocqueville, Eastern State and its competing system at Auburn let different kinds of citizens back into the world, perhaps a little at odds with Rush's hope for the conforming soul: "The Philadelphia system being also that which produces the deepest impressions on the soul of the convict, must effect more reformation than that of Auburn. The latter, however, is perhaps more conformable to the habits of men in society, and on this account effects a greater number of reformations, which might be called 'legal,' inasmuch as they produce the external fulfillment of social obligations . . . If it be so, the Philadelphia system produces more honest men, and that of New York more obedient citizens."

But whether released from Eastern State, Auburn, or any number of other silent prisons, the inmates couldn't help but be unanchored upon their discharge. Their bearing would have been different after years of solitude and silence, and even the feel of their old clothes must have been strange. Their gait may have changed, and their size. They would need to recover their voices. The muscles used for speech are also used for breathing and eating, so they wouldn't have atrophied completely, but their voice boxes would have been weak; their ears, sensitive.

For those imprisoned in Yaroslavl, Eugenia Ginzburg notes in her memoir, the sound of voices for the newly released was its own reward. She recalls being transferred from her solitary cell to the car of a freight train, which would spell the start of her journey to the Gulag. She traveled with a crowd of other prisoners who'd also been in solitary: "None of us stopped talking for a single moment. No one listened to anyone else, and there was no common theme: each of us talked about her own affairs from the moment the train left Yaroslavl. Some began to recite verses, sing, and tell stories . . . It was the first time for two years that we had been surrounded by fellow human beings, and every one of us was rejoicing in the sound of her own voice . . . Those in solitary confinement had virtually not spoken for seven hundred and thirty days. For all that time they had heard some six or seven words a day: Get up, hot water, walk, washroom, dinner, lights out." The entire trainload lost their voices within half an hour but spoke on in hoarse whispers.

Ginzburg emerged from her cell in the company of her companion solitaries. They were all being moved together to the Gulag, though the true horror of what that would mean was still mercifully unknown to them. The prisoners at Eastern State, let out singly like birds lifting off a winter branch, would be left to themselves to find their voices in a world becoming more and more talkative. Sounds—increasing, and increasing in volume—included the pounding and clanging of factory production. The lights of the cities were growing brighter. Even those who stood up well under their sentence would carry scars. Psychologist Stuart Grassian has argued that many people who have been subjected to solitary confinement—"including some who did not become overtly psychiatrically ill during their confinement in solitary—will likely suffer permanent harm as a result of such confinement." They'll have difficulty in social situations, difficulty fitting back into world.

Political activist and anarchist Alexander Berkman, confined at Western State Penitentiary, in Pittsburgh, at the end of the nineteenth century, gave an extensive account of how it felt to be released into the world after time in solitary. He was discharged in 1906. Both the rush of the world and the sheer fact of the world seemed utterly strange and unsettling to him. He was stunned by the experience, and also outside it. At times it was too much to bear: "The gates of the penitentiary open to leave me out, and I pause involuntarily at the fascinating sight. It is a street: a line of houses stretches before me; a woman, young and wonderfully sweet-faced, is passing on the opposite side. My eyes follow her graceful lines, as she turns the corner. Men stand about. They wear citizen clothes, and scan me with a curious, insistent gaze."

His years in silence had caused him to become inordinately sensitive to the busy modern world: "The din and noise rend my ears; the rushing cars, the clanging bells, bewilder me. I am afraid to cross the street; the flying monsters pursue me on every side. The crowds jostle me on the sidewalk, and I am constantly running into the passers-by. The turmoil, the ceaseless movement, disconcerts me. A horseless carriage whizzes close by me; I turn to look at the first automobile I have ever seen, but the living current sweeps me helplessly along."

Unrestricted for the first time in years, Berkman found the freedom to be a true wilderness, which forced him to again acknowledge his apartness: "A sudden impulse seizes me at the sight of a passing car, and I dash after it . . . 'Fare, please!' the conductor sings out, and I almost laugh out aloud at the fleeting sense of the material reality of freedom. Conscious of the strangeness of my action, I produce a dollar bill, and a sense of exhilarating independence comes over me, as the man counts out the silver coins."

Memories of confinement were also lying in wait: "It seems strange to be in a regular room: there is paper on the walls, and it feels so peculiar to the touch, so different from the whitewashed cell. I pass my hand over it caressingly, with a keen sense of pleasure. The chairs, too, look strange, and those quaint things on the table. The bric-a-brac absorbs my attention—the people in the room look hazy, their voices sound distant and confused." However much he may have longed to talk, once given that freedom, once he was surrounded by those who talked without a second thought, he felt hindered: "It requires an effort to talk. The last year, in the workhouse, I have barely spoken a dozen words; there was always absolute silence. The voices disturb me. The presence of so many people—there are three or four about me—is oppressive. The room reminds me of the cell, and the desire seizes me to rush out into the open, to breathe the air and see the sky."

Even if a prisoner was able to adjust to the crowds, the noise, and the lights upon release from Eastern State, it's very likely that he would have had difficulty finding employment. The prisoners worked in isolation at their benches, which was hardly the equivalent of training as an apprentice in a shop. Their work probably bore the signs of the homemade. After being sentenced for his second offense, one of the inmates at Eastern State claimed to the prison chaplain that it had been "impossible to get work, [he] was turned out of every situation as all knew by his work that he had been in the penitentiary."

It's also true that silence and solitude don't inhabit the future. They separate one from the common flow of time. Upon his release after his two-year sentence, Charles Williams would have been given the clothes with which he had arrived, and any possessions he'd had with him then would also have been returned to him. The mandates of the penitentiary stated: "If the inspectors and warden have been satisfied with the morality, industry, and order of his conduct, they shall furnish the discharged convict with four dollars, whereby the temptation immediately to commit offenses against society, before employment can be obtained, may be obviated."

During his two years of confinement, the city of Philadelphia had grown incrementally closer to the penitentiary walls, but Williams would have had barely any news of his family, and he'd have had no news of all the things commonly recorded in the papers: inventions, cholera outbreaks, wars, prominent deaths. Even events that occurred the day before his release would have been unknown to him. As he emerged from his sentence, Williams would have left his number behind. His name would have been returned to him, and he would have walked out of the gate as a free man in a wilderness. But there remained this question: Did society really want him back, this prisoner who'd spent considerable time in solitary, and then was released into the world with a few dollars in his pocket? Williams had likely read the Gospel according to Luke: "[They] found the man, out of whom the devils were departed, sitting at the feet of Jesus, clothed, and in his right mind: and they were afraid."

I haven't been able to trace Williams's life after his release from Eastern State. There is no notice in the *Philadelphia Inquirer* about his departure. By then the newspaper had decided against naming any prisoners confined to the penitentiary, as it was "thought that a publication of the names of the convicts would have a tendency to defeat the main object of the institution —their REFORMATION." Charles Williams—age twenty, laborer, shoemaker, able to read—seems to have disappeared into the world and is remembered now because he was sentenced to be forgotten.

PART IV

The Silence of Women

What becometh a woman best, and first of all? Silence.
What second? Silence. What third? Silence.
What fourth? Silence. Yea, if a man should aske me
till Domes daie I would still crie silence, silence.

—Thomas Wilson, *The Arte of Rhetorique*

16

silencing silence

FOR WOMEN, SILENCE within the world of judicial punishment has its own complex history. It's less recorded than the silence of men, and fragmented. Details must be teased out of obscurity and can be distorted by what is absent. Often there are more questions than answers for punishment that amounts to silencing on top of silence, since women have long been expected to govern their tongue.

In colonial America this presumption of silence was reinforced by women's subordinate place in society and bolstered by centuries of English common law. No woman had the right to vote, and once she married—in an age when most women married—she became subject to the law of coverture, which meant that she not only became dependent on her husband but, as William Blackstone in his eighteenth-century work *Commentaries on the Laws of England* explains: "By marriage, the husband and wife are one person in law: that is, the very being or legal existence of the woman is suspended during the marriage, or at least is incorporated and consolidated into that of the husband; under whose wing, protection, and *cover,* she performs every thing, and . . . therefore her condition during her marriage is called her *coverture.*"

When it came to punishment in the colonies, however, the law could be as harsh for women as it was for men. Women, married or single, who committed crimes were hanged, pilloried, whipped, or branded. And for some offenses the law dealt more harshly with women than with men. In part because it was often difficult to name the father, women usually suffered the brunt of the consequences for giving birth to a bastard child, for which they could be fined and whipped. If a woman killed her husband, hanging wasn't good enough. She could be gibbeted—a more severe punishment than a man received for killing his wife—for to kill a husband, as a slave his master, was deemed a greater crime. It upset the natural social order.

One set of laws applied almost entirely to women and was aimed specifically at muting their voices. Women could be harshly punished and humiliated simply for talking too much or too publicly, or in a tone of voice that seemed grating or nagging. Such women were labeled scolds or gossips, and unlike for the crimes of theft, assault, or murder, no concrete measure defined their transgression. English law specified a scold as "a troublesome angry woman who, by her brawling and wrangling among her neighbors, doth break the public peace, and beget, cherish and increase public discord." What evidence could be brought before the courts? To whom was she troublesome? What determined a breach of peace? And what constituted gossip? Imagine the streets on market day, where women stood in small clusters, their heads inclined toward one another in the lane, in the shadow of a cart. A hand at the mouth. Who was to say when a friendly whisper crossed over into malicious gossip? These were more than curious questions. Gossip itself could amplify the accusations. Even in the nineteenth century, gossip was defined by evidence not "of particular acts, but of common fame." The vagaries of the law left room to unfairly accuse an enemy—or a woman who was odd, unpopular, or outspoken—which was no small thing. The punishment for the crime—brutal and feared—was meant to draw a crowd and publicly humiliate the accused.

In colonial towns and villages, the "engines of punishment" for gossips and scolds were varied and specific. Women might be gagged and made to stand in the market square with a placard describing their crime. Their tongues might be fastened with a cleft stick. Commonly, they were sentenced to the ducking stool. Although on rare occasions a double stool might be used to punish a married couple for incessant bickering, it was a punishment that was only infrequently used to punish men. In 1634 Thomas Hartley of Hungars Parish, Virginia, described what we would today call a water-based torture that was "given to one Betsey wife of John Tucker who by ye violence of her tongue has made his house and ye neighborhood uncomfortable."

According to Hartley's account, Betsey Tucker "was taken to ye pond . . . They had a machine for ye purpose yt belongs to ye parish, and which I was so told had been so used three times this Summer. It is a platform with 4 small rollers or wheels and two upright posts between which works a Lever by a Rope fastened to its shorter or heavier end. At ye end of ye longer arm is fixed a stool upon which sd Betsey was fastened by cords, her gown tied fast around her feete. The Machine was then moved up to ye edge of ye pond, ye Rope was slackened . . . and ye woman was allowed to go down under ye water for ye space of half a minute."

Tucker was ducked five times before she begged her persecutors to stop and agreed to "sin no more." She then walked home in her wet clothes.

The punishment for being accused of spreading gossip and rumors was even harsher in the English Midlands in the sixteenth century, and the craft of the village blacksmith was essential to this particular silencing. At the time, the sound of the blacksmith at his anvil was one of the loudest sounds made by a human hand. He was at his work daily, fashioning the ordinary tools and utensils for his village: hinges and clasps, knives and hoes, scythes and plows, shoes for the horses and oxen. Hearthside utensils: pokers, grates, pots, cauldrons, peals, spiders, frying pans, Dutch ovens.

Hard iron, softened by fire, was turned into useful things with a flourish and a musical beat. Did his work sound any different as he forged a scold's bridle? Every sixteenth- and seventeenth-century Midlands town seems to have had its version. Always there was a collar and strip of iron that arched back to front and splayed when it crossed the face so as to pass on either side of a woman's nose. The iron might press down on her cheeks or against the sides of her nose, which made it difficult to take in more than a sip of air at a time. If a scold's bridle left little room for breath, it left none for words. Usually another strip of iron attached to the collar and arched ear to ear over her head, and a bar—or two or three—crossed her face below her nose. Attached to one of the bars was a slab anywhere from one and one-half to three inches long—a bit—to be inserted between her lips to hold down her tongue. The bit made it hard for her to swallow her saliva, and some bits were long enough to make a woman gag.

Sometimes the bit curved upward or downward. It could be smooth, but more often it was stippled with small spikes or comprised of barbs. If a woman moved at all, the barbs would burrow into the roof of her mouth or into her tongue, and crying out in pain only made it worse. The women of the village of Stockport, England, must have known it well, for the one in that town—its slab was two inches long—ended in a cylinder set with spikes upward, downward, and backward: a nettle that, however still a woman sat, cut her palate and tongue at the same time.

For gossiping or any kind of public speaking out of turn, a woman might be fitted with the bridle, which was sometimes decorated with red and white cloth. She was then paraded through the streets to stand at the market cross or by the church. Quaker Dorothy Waugh has left one of the rare firsthand accounts of such a punishment. In 1655 she was taken into custody for publicly preaching in the market of Carlisle, England. At the time women were expected to remain silent in public—it would be more than a decade before Margaret Fell published her pamphlet *Womens Speaking Justified, Proved and Allowed of by the Scriptures,* which argued in favor of women preaching publicly. Waugh was bridled for three hours. "That which they called so was like a steele cap . . . which was a stone weight of Iron . . . & three barrs of Iron to come over my face, and a peece of it was put in my mouth, which was so unreasonable a big thing for that place as cannot be well-related, which was locked to my head, and so I stood their time with my hands bound behind me with the stone weight of Iron upon my head, and the bitt in my mouth to keep me from speaking," she recalled. The prison keeper demanded that all who came to see her pay two pence, and the mayor, intent on making an example of her, had her forced out of the city while she was still bridled, and had her whipped as she was driven from town to town, "from Constable to Constable . . . till I came to my owne home," wrote Waugh, "when as they had not anything to lay to my Charge."

The mere threat of being bridled could be enough to mute a soul. There is an account of a woman who refused to walk bridled through her town, so she was wheeled in a barrow. It was said that for the rest of her life "she kept a quiet tongue."

Bridling had its hidden side as well. Though Dorothy Waugh found refuge in her home, not every woman could depend upon home as a haven. Accounts in Cheshire, England, describe an iron hook by the hearth, right where a wife could always see it as she fed the smoky embers of her fire, as she stirred her cooking pots or spun her wool. If ever she spoke too much or acted out of turn or disobeyed, her husband might send for the jailer to bring the scold's bridle, which was then chained to the hook at the hearth and clamped around her head.

In the American colonies, the ducking stool remained the favored punishment for scolds. Accounts of the use of the scold's bridle for gossips are rare; less rare are those of its use as a slave's punishment for insubordination. Sometimes it also was used if a slave ate more food than was allotted. "I was very much affrighted at some things I saw," writes Olaudah Equiano in his slave narrative as he recounts his time in Virginia. "I had seen a black woman slave as I came through the house, who was cooking the dinner, and the poor creature was cruelly loaded with various kinds of iron machines; she had one particularly on her head, which locked her mouth so fast that she could scarcely speak, and could not eat or drink. I [was] much astonished and shocked at this contrivance, which I afterwards learned was called the iron muzzle."

As for being confined in jail while awaiting trial and sentencing, in England women were sometimes held in the same common room as men, where they, too, paid for their food or begged from the grates and were required to pay to be unlocked from their chains. But such punishments were their own experience for women, who were vulnerable to molestation and rape. They were additionally burdened because they often had no choice but to bring their young children along with them into the chaotic world of confinement and to provide for them as well.

Even when women were confined in quarters separate from men, they weren't secure. When famed English prison reformer Elizabeth Fry made her first visit to the women jailed in London's Newgate Prison in 1813, she remarked: "At that time, all the female prisoners in Newgate were confined in that part, now known as the untried side . . . The partition wall was not of a sufficient height to prevent the state-prisoners from overlooking the narrow yard." Fry offered a firsthand account of the harrowing conditions women and their children were made to endure: "Nearly three hundred women with their numerous children, were crowded; tried and untried, misdemeanants and felons, without classification, without employment, and with no other superintendence than that given by a man and his son." And they were forced to live in squalor: "In the same rooms, in rags and dirt, destitute of sufficient clothing (for which there was no provision) sleeping without bedding on the floor, the boards of which were in part raised to supply a sort of pillow, they lived, cooked, and washed."

Fry understood that women without support had limited options in the world, and she believed the path to helping them was best begun through their children. She began reform efforts by persuading a handful of women Quakers to help her establish a school for the children of jailed women. Several years later, in 1817, the group formed the Association for the Improvement of the Female Prisoners at Newgate. Their goal, in addition to teaching the children, was to instruct the women in reading and in crafts such as spinning, weaving, and sewing, which could give them a means of supporting themselves. The society supplied them with clean clothes and bedding. Members concentrated on speech and manners, and perhaps most distinctly developed a system in which the women would be overseen by matrons rather than male keepers.

The situation in Philadelphia's jails was little better when Mary Wistar and two companions undertook visits to the women in Arch Street Prison in 1823. The city's prisons and jails suffered from overcrowding at the time, and Arch Street had been built to contain the overflow from Walnut Street Jail, which then also served as the city's penitentiary. While convicted felons were sent to Walnut Street, Arch Street held vagrants, streetwalkers, debtors, and the untried. The debtors had separate quarters from the others, and living conditions for vagrants and streetwalkers were particularly crowded and filthy.

Wistar was intimate with the hopes for prison reform that were abroad in her city. Her husband, Thomas, was a founding member of the Philadelphia Society for Alleviating the Miseries of Public Prisons and the son of Richard Wistar, the glass manufacturer who had first brought soup to those imprisoned in Philadelphia's jails. She was also familiar with, and had been profoundly influenced by, Elizabeth Fry's work at Newgate and other English prisons. Wistar hoped to undertake a program similar to Fry's, although her effort wasn't without critics. Even some promulgators of the penitentiary were skeptical of women's capacity to be reformed. Immediately after her initial visit to Arch Street, Wistar was cautioned about committing her time and energy to the cause by her son-in-law Roberts Vaux. Vaux, an early and longstanding advocate of Rush's ideas for a penitentiary, believed in reformation and redemption for men who transgressed. In 1823 he gave the keynote speech at the laying of the cornerstone for Eastern State. But he warned Wistar:

> The unhappy females whom you visited yester-day form a circulation medium of poverty and vice . . . They are known to almost every watch-man in the City & their names are to be found on the docket of almost every magistrate. Their habits have become chronic, & I fear in most instances past restoration. If many of them were *"arrayed in purple & fine linnen"* by an unbounded charity, & set at liberty through the agency of a generous sympathy, such is the depravity of their minds that in a few hours their garment would be surrendered as the price of some sensual appetite, the indulgence of which in a few more hours would insure their return to Prison.

Wistar persisted in the wake of criticism, and eventually her companions for visits to Arch Street and other prisons numbered more than a dozen. She established the Female Prison Association of Friends in Philadelphia, whose practical concerns included seeing that imprisoned women's physical conditions improved, that they were properly clothed and fed, and that their spiritual care was attended to. They worked to establish a system in which matrons would oversee female prisoners, and advocated for a halfway house to be established to help women return to society once their sentence was complete.

At times they had to patiently petition again and again for change. In 1824, after an outbreak of "infectious disease," Wistar and her companions requested that a bathhouse be provided for the women. The bathhouse was approved, but their accompanying petition to employ "a conscientious matron" to oversee woman prisoners was rejected. It took more than a decade of further efforts on Wistar's part before matrons appeared in Philadelphia prisons.

Mary Wistar's prison visits occurred at a time when Philadelphia was growing denser and more diverse, and the factory system was beginning to supplant craftwork. Not surprisingly, the perceived role of women in society was also increasing in complexity. The law of coverture still held, and women still couldn't vote, but the need for a politically discerning citizenry in the new Republic fostered an emphasis on the role of education for women beyond the domestic arts.

Women were still pressured to remain at home to tend to their family and hearth in a world separate from the public sphere of politics and discourse, and their education wasn't meant for themselves alone, but also to provide support and create the proper household atmosphere for husbands and sons. Benjamin Rush, writing on the education of women, remarked: "I am sensible that they must concur in all our plans of education for young men, or no laws will ever render them effectual. To qualify our women for this purpose, they should not only be instructed in the usual branches of female education but they should be instructed in the principles of liberty and government, and the obligations of patriotism should be inculcated upon them." More specifically he suggested: "The opinions and conduct of men are often regulated by the women . . . Besides, the *first* impressions upon the minds of children are generally derived from the women. Of how much consequence, therefore, is it in a republic that they should think justly upon the great subject of liberty and government."

Still, women weren't absent from public life, and prominent women often found their voices as writers and as advocates for social causes. Among the more prominent were Margaret Fuller, Lucretia Coffin Mott, Elizabeth Cady Stanton, and Lucy Stone. But their public place was by no means met with wide approval. The experience of journalist Anne Newport Royall provides a clear example of the price outspoken women could pay. In 1829 Royall was charged in Maryland with being a common scold. She was nearly sixty by then, a widow and prominent public figure who, for decades, had supported herself as a travel writer and newspaper publisher—professions she was forced into by circumstance.

Royall was raised on the frontier of western Pennsylvania on a subsistence farm and had little formal education in her youth. She recalled that "no such thing as salt had we for three months at one time, and as for sugar we could make enough of that from the trees, but for tea we drank the johnsworth, and pinned our clothes (when we had any) with thorns." Her fortunes changed when she married William Royall, a wealthy older man, who provided her with a far more comfortable life than she had previously known and oversaw her education. After his death in 1812, Anne Royall, who was well provided for in his will, became nearly destitute when her deceased husband's family successfully contested her inheritance.

It was then she turned to writing travel books to earn a living, at a time when even a day's journey was slow, difficult, and often unpredictable. Royall traveled many thousands of miles in what was then the frontier—as far south as Louisiana, west to Illinois, and north to Maine. She was jolted along on roads "causewayed with huge logs" and more than once had to travel rough ground on foot. She later recalled one such experience while crossing Cumberland Mountain in Tennessee: "This was an unlucky day throughout, we were so heavily laden, the mountain to ascend, and the rain had rendered the road deep and difficult. Such being the case we had to walk on foot a great part of the way up the mountain." She often visited the places she wrote about more than once, returning to promote her books and sell them by subscription.

Her books, as was typical of the time, describe the roads, her traveling companions, the countryside and farms, and the cities with their museums and institutions. But she had a reputation for being quite frank concerning the people she encountered on her sojourns. She detailed their manner and appearance, at times in an unflattering light: "The Tennessean was a middle-aged man, of the inferior order, he was ugly, ignorant, and in short, he was a complete boor." She also penned denigrating descriptions of prominent figures—a tendency that her biographer, Elizabeth Clapp, suggests was an outgrowth of her brusque and confrontational manner. Royall had a reputation for being prickly, so much so, Clapp notes, that her essential womanhood was challenged in public. "She is no woman at all," declared New England writer John Neal, "but a stout, saucy, swaggering, two fisted chap, with a skull of his own, who having a mind to live an easy life and be impudent with safety, has turned author, and equipped himself in petticoats for protection."

At the time Royall faced charges for being a scold, she was between travels and living in Washington, DC. Her second-story rooms happened to be near a congregation of Presbyterians, and their dealings with Royall in the neighborhood were contentious. Royall reserved a particular ire for Presbyterians, who were fierce promulgators of the evangelical movement, which sought to reassert women's traditional place in the home. In their grievance against her, they accused her of harassing the congregation from her window as they headed for church. She had, church leaders claimed, particularly unnerved the women of the congregation. Clapp notes: "They charged that Royall had used 'opprobrious and indecent language to respectable females and Gentlemen when on the publick street, whilst going to publick worship.' Moreover, she had uttered 'other malicious and false sayings and writing such as Thief, Villain, Hypocrite, etc. etc. to the Great annoyance of Females.'"

Royall was convicted of being a scold and sentenced to the ducking stool decades after the stocks and whipping post had disappeared from the market squares of American cities. Her lawyer argued that the punishment was inappropriate, and the judge agreed. He fined her $10 and charged that she behave well for a year, demanding another $250 in surety for that year. A woman's silence, after all, was intimately linked with obedience.

Though Royall was spared a ducking, the newspapers at the time delighted in imagining it. One editor suggested that she deserved far more than public humiliation. He seemed to recommend the ultimate silencing for Royall—a sentence of death—when he proposed that "perhaps from two to four hours will be thought long enough for her to remain underwater" for her crime of speaking her mind. That at a time when public shaming and punishment had been done away with for highway robbers and horse thieves, and in the same year the penitentiary was being prepared to sequester such offenders in their individual stone cells, away from all observation and humiliation.

17

"or perhaps the women . . ."

WAS THERE A place for women in the penitentiary? Punishment was one thing; redemption, another. And as Roberts Vaux's remarks to Mary Wistar attest, even the most ardent promulgators of the penitentiary weren't certain that drunken women and prostitutes could find redemption, or that they were capable of bearing up under a sentence of solitude and silence. Benjamin Rush himself equivocated. In his address regarding the penitentiary delivered at Benjamin Franklin's house on that March evening in 1787, it's not clear whether he imagined women in his vision. When he condemned the blood punishments, however, he did say that "the men, or perhaps the women whose persons we detest, possess souls and bodies composed of the same materials as those of our friends and relations." Or perhaps . . .

In post-Revolutionary America, people commonly believed that women fell farther and more quickly than men. Even the tough-minded, independent, convicted scold Anne Royall made a distinction between fallen men and fallen women. In her travels to cities, Royall often visited medical schools, museums, prisons, asylums, and bridewells, which wasn't uncommon for a travel writer of the time. In her collection of "sketches," she gives a striking account of the women held in the bridewell and jail in New York City:

> But the tender sex, I am sorry for them. Here was a lamentable proof of depravity, of which I thought human nature incapable! There were about forty females in bridewell, for crimes, no doubt . . . They were the most abandoned, vicious, impudent; they were audacity itself, without one particle of aught besides. Alas! once more for human nature—alas! for frail woman. Lost to the blush of shame . . . They laughed, they romped, they gigled, and saluted me with the familiarity of an old acquaintance! . . . And is this woman? I asked, mentally . . . But what a poor piece of creation is woman! man when he comes finally to take leave of virtue, he pauses, he hesitates, he proceeds by degrees; but woman makes one plunge, and is gone forever.

And when women fell, it was claimed, they took men down with them. Francis Lieber, a nineteenth-century German jurist living in Philadelphia and the English translator of Gustave de Beaumont and Alexis de Tocqueville's *On the Penitentiary System in the United States and Its Application in France,* writes in his preface to their work that if a woman "is unprincipled, the whole house is lost . . . The injury done to society by a criminal woman, is in most cases much greater than that suffered from a male criminal." He specifies that "there is, almost without an exception, some unprincipled or abandoned woman, who plays a prominent part in the life of every convict, be it a worthless mother . . . or a slothful and intemperate wife, who disgusts her husband with his home, a prostitute whose wants must be satisfied by theft . . . I maintain that I found that most criminals have been led on to crime, in a considerable degree, by the unhappy influence of some corrupted female." Lieber believed that women committed fewer crimes not because they were more virtuous by nature, but because they had fewer opportunities: Their constricted place in society prevented them from becoming forgers or abusing power. He suggested that they didn't have the same courage or strength as men, but he thought their reform so essential that he advocated for separate penitentiaries for women, overseen by matrons.

In his initial notes for the design of the penitentiary, John Haviland envisions the central rotunda as having "twenty-six cells . . . this number of cells being under the same roof as the wash-house and laundry would be a very appropriate situation for the confinement of the Female Prisoners." He didn't include those cells in his final design, though, so there wasn't a separate and specific place provided for women when the penitentiary opened in 1829. Ultimately, he may not have perceived a need to accommodate women. Traditionally, the number of women charged with crimes was small, and often their common crimes—such as vagrancy, prostitution, and public drunkenness—weren't violent, so they were likely to be fined or to serve a short time in a local jail like the Arch Street Prison. He may also have excluded them for practical reasons. Promulgators of the penitentiary didn't regard women as capable of earning money for the penitentiary through work at traditional crafts. Additionally, women were perceived to present a danger to the order of the penitentiary: they would tempt men, both prisoners and guards.

The first women prisoners arrived at Eastern State in April 1831. Two women walked through the oaken doors, and two more joined them in December of that year. All four women were black and charged with manslaughter. Amy Rogers, Henrietta Johnson, Ann Hinson, and Eliza Anderson were each sentenced to two years for their crimes. There were eighty-three men in the prison at the time. The wardens and keepers were all men. The sole woman on the ten-acre property until the first female prisoners arrived was the wife of one of the keepers, Mrs. Blundin, who undertook some housekeeping, cooking, and laundry for the penitentiary. She was charged with overseeing the women, for which she received no further compensation. Mary Wistar's desire to establish women matrons wouldn't be realized at Eastern State for another five years.

Little is known about these four women prisoners other than what can be gleaned from the intake and outtake logs and the wardens' journals. The dearth of information is typical. As historian Lucia Zedner has noted: "The lives of female prisoners and their relationships to one another in nineteenth century prisons are all but hidden from us today. For the most part their experiences remained unrecorded. Building up any picture of what their lives were like relies on those occasions when their misbehavior was so blatant as to attract the attention of the prison authorities."

And so it was with the first women incarcerated at Eastern State. There is no record of what work they did in their cells, or if they worked in their cells at all, but just as men moved about the prison—shoveled coal, helped build the prison, worked in the yard—women assisted with the kitchen work, laundry, and cooking. They also helped serve meals at the warden's dinner parties. Such work wasn't officially permitted, but it is recorded in testimony from the investigation into the finances and management of Eastern State undertaken in 1834, which included charges of illicit sexual relations, the spread of venereal disease, indecent conversation, embezzlement, misappropriation of provisions, unsanctioned use of convict labor, and cruel and unusual punishment. The testimony of the guards and keepers offers the briefest glimpse into the lives of these women: "There were some dinner or entertainments given by Mr. Wood . . . One colored woman, a prisoner, I saw there—I don't recollect her name—she was helping at that dinner, doing one thing or another in the kitchen." And this: "No. 74 was a woman—she did the cooking for the sick down in front—it was for a considerable time after I went there—a coloured woman—she remained until she committed some depredations and gave some sauciness, and then she was put back to her cell."

Interestingly enough, although men had charge of almost everything at Eastern State—they controlled supplies, decided on employment, and subjected prisoners to extraordinary punishments—the majority report of the 1834 investigation largely exonerates the wardens and keepers, and centers much of the blame for wrongdoing on the overseer of the women prisoners, Mrs. Blundin: "We consider it unfortunate, that Mrs. Blundin, of whom we have already spoken, was ever permitted to reside within the walls of the penitentiary, and perhaps to this circumstance most of the mischiefs complained of may be traced." She stood accused of illicit assignations and with holding dancing parties on the premises. Witnesses claimed to have seen her drunk about the penitentiary and pilfering bread and the cream off the milk. One witness proclaimed: "She was a very improper woman."

Some years later, Charles Dickens offered another glimpse of women prisoners at Eastern State. During his 1842 tour of the penitentiary, he visited three women who occupied adjoining cells. He suggested that the strictures of the punishment—the solitude and silence—resulted in a markedly different outcome for women than for men. While he described men as being hampered and deformed by their sentence, he wrote of the women:

> In the silence and solitude of their lives they had grown to be quite beautiful. Their looks were very sad, and might have moved the sternest visitor to tears, but not to that kind of sorrow which the contemplation of the men, awakens. One was a young girl . . . She was very penitent and quiet; had come to be resigned, she said (and I believe her); and had a mind at peace. 'In a word, you are happy here?' said one of my companions. She struggled—she did struggle very hard—to answer, Yes; but raising her eyes, and meeting that glimpse of freedom overhead, she burst into tears, and said: 'She tried to be'; she uttered no complaint; but it was natural that she should sometimes long to go out of that one cell; 'she could not help *that*,' she sobbed, poor thing!

William Peter, the official who had countered Dickens's claims regarding male prisoners, also provided a far less sanguine assessment of the women Dickens observed. He asserted that they "have nothing 'very sad' in their looks, or in any way calculated to move 'the sternest visitor to tears.' They have been a kind of decoy-ducks for keepers of low brothels, and were convicted of a conspiracy to rob their prosecutor." Peter noted that they were illiterate when they entered prison but could, when he encountered them, read and write well, and the one that Dickens particularly engaged claimed she'd been nothing more than a drunk "from morning to night" and that prison "had been 'a very good thing' for them all, and that she did not know what would have become of them, had they not been sent there."

At Eastern State, the treatment of women at least approximated the treatment of men. The same could not be said of Auburn State Prison, in New York. While the men gathered silently in workrooms by day and were locked in their individual cells at night, there was no official place for women in the prison. They were viewed as a danger to the male prisoners and the prison itself, and so were removed from view. All the incarcerated women lived and slept together in an unventilated third-floor room above the prison kitchen. The windows were sealed to prevent the possibility of association with any of the men. A steward delivered their food, and another prison worker came to take their waste away. One observer who toured the prison in 1826 called the room "a specimen of the most disgusting and appalling features of the old system of Prison management at the worst period of its history. Crowded, as these females are, about thirty in number, into a single room, of small dimensions and very imperfect ventilation, in the fourth story of the south wing, remote from the post of any officer, and accessible only through four bolted doors, where they are obliged to remain night and day, in an atmosphere absolutely nauseating to a visitor." Harriet Martineau described what she saw during her visit in the 1830s, when it seems little had changed: "The arrangements for the women were extremely bad at that time . . . The women were all in one large room, sewing. The attempt to enforce silence was soon given up as hopeless; and the gabble of tongues among the few who were there was enough to paralyze any matron." She also saw evidence that the sanguinary laws had not been left behind: "There was an engine in sight which made me doubt the evidence of my own eyes.—stocks of a terrible construction; a chair, with a fastening for the head and for all the limbs. Any lunatic asylum ought to be ashamed of such an instrument. The governor [of the prison] liked it no better than we; but he pleaded that it was his only means of keeping his refractory female prisoners quiet, while he was allowed only one room to put them all into." Martineau concluded: "I hope these stocks have been used for fire-wood before this."

What Martineau described approximates all of history's punishments heaped together in that one room: the crowded, filthy jails; Fry's efforts at reformation suggested in their sewing; the colonial engines of physical punishment. Time and any notion of progress had not separated these treatments regarding women, only piled one on top of the other, and concentrated their cruelties and miseries.

In ensuing decades, the course of incarceration of women would continue to be distinct from that of men. Mary Wistar's prison visit programs in Philadelphia helped initiate the work of women reformers throughout the nineteenth century, who concentrated on rehabilitating women and providing them with skills to return to society. Women convicts, in general, were eventually housed in separate institutions from men, which were often organized as group cottages, and were far less imposing than Eastern State Penitentiary.

But women's voices still remain suspect in the world of incarceration. Historian Cristina Rathbone, writing in 2005 about Massachusetts Correctional Institution Framingham, a prison for women, noted that while "violence is the main concern in a male prison, at Framingham it is the creation of intimacy that most worries authorities. For this reason, the population is kept fluid. Women are not allowed, officially, to hold the same job for more than six months and roommates are routinely moved around." It seems that authorities in the twenty-first century are as concerned about what might be shared in whispers as were the sheriffs in sixteenth-century England who forced the bridle upon women as punishment for gossiping. Keeping the population at Framingham fluid serves as its own kind of silencing.

18

monastic women: more shadow than light

THE STORY OF early women monastics, like that of early women prisoners, is little recorded and often fragmented. It must be teased out of obscurity, pieced together, and filtered through our time, now, in the twenty-first century, when women's lives both carry the burdens of the past and have broken free from expectations. Although changes in monastic life have been incremental compared with those in the secular world, in some respects the lives of contemporary women religious have grown markedly distinct from those of the women who joined orders centuries ago. While they continue to take vows of poverty, stability, obedience, and chastity; observe the liturgical hours; and support themselves with their labors, in modern times the decision to join an order is usually a profound personal choice, or a calling.

Although a commitment to the religious life has always been a choice for some women—as far back as the fourth century women, too, joined desert communities in search of a more profound spiritual experience—up until modern times, the decision to enter a monastery was often made *for* women rather than *by* them, and the arrangement was usually a practical one. Most commonly, wealthy fathers sent daughters without marriage prospects to the convent. At times, even daughters in a position to marry might end up in a convent, since it was cheaper to dower a daughter to a monastery than to a husband. In a world where single women in particular had few choices, monastic life also offered an alternative for women who wanted to leave a marriage or avoid one. Older women often joined after having raised their children. Widows.

They entered a world in which they had little say. While almost all women brought bequests, legacies, or donations to a monastery, they had no control over the revenue. And convents, even those headed by powerful and prominent abbesses, were subject to rule by men. Women weren't represented in the Church hierarchy and didn't serve on the councils that determined the monastic regulations that profoundly affected their lives.

Perhaps no regulations were more consequential than those regarding enclosure, which has been prescribed for all monastics since the time of the Desert Fathers, who believed that separation from the world helped create an ideal spiritual space for devotion to God. But enclosure for men wasn't absolute. Monks routinely traveled to tend to their holdings and carry on other financial obligations of the monastery. By contrast, enclosure for women was deemed essential and was imposed in a far more rigid way than for men.

While keeping women securely behind walls might safeguard them against the possibility of being carried off, attacked, or raped, how women were viewed also played a considerable role in the insistence on strict enclosure. Women were considered unable to organize and govern themselves, and prone to moral weakness and sin. They were, it was believed, easily tempted by men, so the Church councils regarded protecting their purity as paramount. Historian Jane Tibbetts Schulenburg wrote: "As brides of Christ they were to be concealed from the world." But women were also regarded as descendants of Eve, a temptation for men. Not for nothing was the Cistercian sign for the apple "by far the worst and most evil sign."

As far back as the rules of Pachomius, men were forbidden to enter convents except under strict conditions: "The female monks among them live on the other side of the river [Nile], and the men among them, opposite them on this side. And when a nun dies, her sisters, the nuns, wrap her in linen; and having wrapped her in, they bring her to the bank of the river, and the brethren cross over on a raft with palm branches and olive boughs, and bring her across with psalm-singing to themselves, and bury her in their burial-place. With the exception of priest and deacon alone, nobody crosses over into the women cloister, and this takes place on each Sabbath of the Christians."

Under the strictest conditions, women religious couldn't leave the monastery for any reason without permission from the bishop or their superior. It was a rule for which there were few exceptions: abbesses had to travel; members of the order became sick and needed outside attention. One early council regulation warns: "If a girl leaving her parents desires to renounce the world and enter the holy fold . . . she must never, up to the time of her death, go out of the monastery, nor into the basilica where there is a door." In some monasteries, outside doors opened only to allow a newcomer in or for the burial of a deceased nun, and the penalties for breaking enclosure could be severe. One bishop warned that if a woman, "at the Devil's urging, like Eve expelled from Paradise, shall venture forth from the cloisters of her convent, as if from the Kingdom of Heaven itself, to visit this place and that, to be bustled and trodden under foot in the vile mud of our public streets, she shall be cut off from our communion and shall be stricken with the awful wound of anathema."

Although already isolated from the world, many women monastics were, as a further safeguard, rarely permitted to be alone within their own monastery, especially in church, and novices were almost always required to be in the presence of older nuns. Even their visual world was narrowed and obscured. They saw the world beyond their walls only through the small openings and grilles meant to keep them separate, and the windows that did open could be shielded with a dark covering. Their male counterparts lived in a world of shadow and light; they, in a world of more shadow than light.

While women could not leave their enclosure, priests—of necessity—entered convents, since not even the most powerful abbess could celebrate Mass or hear confession. Yet, just as their view of the exterior world was narrowed and obscured, so was the ritual of the Mass, which they most often witnessed from behind a distant grille. In some convents the sisters could only view the Mass from a high window and saw little more than the priest's hands. So the ritual was primarily heard. As historian Caroline Bruzelius has remarked: "Christianity has always contained a tradition that especially blessed are those who can believe *without* seeing, touching, or tasting . . . For women in religious life, that which was most holy often came only through the ear." Her observation recalls Bernard de Clairvaux's question: "Why do you strain to see?" Strict enclosure was also meant to accentuate silence and increase the opportunity to listen for the Word of God.

While Church councils throughout the early Middle Ages imposed various degrees of enclosure for women, exacting rules were broadly asserted in 1298. In that year Pope Boniface VIII, concerned about heresies that might foment within the informal monastic world, and equally worried about outside influences on the monasteries, ordered strict enclosure for all women religious who took solemn vows. His papal decree *Periculoso,* so named because of its first word, meaning "dangerous," was sweeping in its scope: "Nuns collectively and individually, both at present and in future . . . in whatever part of the world they may be, ought henceforth to remain perpetually cloistered in their monasteries, so that none of them . . . shall or may for whatever reason or cause . . . have permission hereafter to leave their monasteries; and no persons, in any way disreputable, or even respectable, shall be allowed to enter or leave the same . . . so that [the nuns will] be able to serve God more freely, wholly separated from the public and worldly gaze and, occasions of lasciviousness having been removed, may most diligently safeguard their hearts and bodies in complete chastity."

In the Middle Ages there were far fewer monasteries for women than for men, and their monasteries, in general, were smaller and more obscure, though not always. Any one monastery's fortunes could shift with the times, and the living conditions for both monks and nuns were rarely stable. In a world of slow and difficult travel, with considerable distances between monasteries, and between the center of the Church and its outposts, the rules set down by councils weren't always uniformly followed, and not all orders embraced the restrictions or submitted to them willingly.

Especially as monasticism matured, urban convents could have a thriving and intricate relationship with the surrounding community, and women in the mendicant orders, who led lives of service, of necessity were more involved in local life than cloistered orders. Their silence would not have been as extreme as that of the Cistercians or Benedictines; their observance of the liturgical hours, less elaborate. Historian Silvia Evangelisti has noted: "Since the Middle Ages convents had played a fundamental public role within the cities. By praying and devoting their lives to divine perfection, the 'brides of Christ' fulfilled a crucial intercessory function, and acted as mediators between Heaven and worldly society . . . The nuns' intercessory role strengthened their social presence and connections with the city. For instance, the nuns took an active part in public processions and in the organization of public festivities, and they held public religious ceremonies in their convents' churches." Some tended the sick and poor within the community and worshipped with the townspeople at services. Nuns copied manuscripts or wove tapestries and made embroideries, which they sold to support themselves. They might also take in boarders: older single women who would be paying guests; young women seeking education and instruction.

The permeability between their convent life and the city around them became especially threatened after the Council of Trent, which convened in 1563, reasserted the rules for enclosure set down by Boniface and went even further, subjecting to strict enclosure not only cloistered nuns who'd taken solemn vows, but all women religious in convents, including the mendicant orders. The effect on their lives was profound. For example, the nuns of the convent of Pütrich, in Munich, were accustomed to attending religious services in the city proper, and their place in the church itself was reserved for them with their own chairs. They sold their tapestries and embroidery beyond the walls of the convent, and they tended the sick and the poor of the city. When one of their sisters died, they customarily accompanied her body to the burial ground outside the convent.

Then the reformers arrived. "Anno 1620 on the third of May, the day of the Holy Cross, there came hither an Italian Franciscan and ten others with him from Milan, so-called Reformati in wooden shoes," wrote the convent's gatekeeper of the approaching officials who would enforce their enclosure. The officials took the chairs out of the church in the city and brought them within the convent walls. They forbade the sisters to accompany their dead beyond the walls and ordered them to pray more frequently throughout the day, which took time away from their other activities.

Some of the sisters protested as they were able. Historian Ulrike Strasser has noted that nearly a third of the women in the convent "refused altogether to learn and pray the breviary. These women, mainly of the older generation, and some of them in poor health, stubbornly clung to their customary way of doing things . . . It was a powerful way of claiming agency in a situation of meagre options." But ultimately, the lives of the women within the walls of Pütrich changed radically.

Likewise, the sisters in convents throughout Florence found their customary world upended by forced enclosure. They, too, were accustomed to going out into the city to visit the poor and tend the sick. Church officials not only called for their movement about the city to cease, but they also instructed that the grilles, windows, and gates of their convent facing the street were to be walled. Daylight could come only through windows with fixed, dark glass. The entrance gates were to be locked from the outside. The writing and receiving of letters was severely limited, as were visits from anyone other than relatives.

Strict enclosure seemed untenable, not only for the sisters, but for the city as well, for the convents had become part of the social and economic fabric of Florence. When the pope directed the sisters to adhere to the tenets of enclosure, city authorities objected, citing it would compromise both the convent and the city. They urged that the sisters be allowed to continue to visit the sick and poor and to practice medicine, and they expressed fears that the number of professed religious would decline. The pope denied their petitions, asserting that the Church had to guard against the particular nature of women, "for there is no doubt that women must be governed and cannot govern themselves, and this is so evident that it requires no further persuasion."

At the convent of St. Catherine of Siena in Florence, the sisters protested the enforcement of strict enclosure, but in the end they were made to conform to the decree. "They resisted for nearly three months," notes Silvia Evangelisti, "but . . . events turned definitively against them: 'The 29 [August] we were ordered by the Reverend father . . . to wall the door of our church within five days; otherwise he was going to give us excommunication; and so this door was walled that day . . . and we were the first with our great sorrow.'"

• • •

What burdened an active order might be welcomed by a cloistered order. One finds sustenance and even freedom where another finds confinement and restriction. Some women monastics embraced strict enclosure, seeing it as providing its own opportunities and expansiveness in the way that it secured the interior community and offered an intensification of the experience of the cell and concentration on the spiritual. This embrace of enclosure was most famously expressed by Saint Teresa of Avila, the sixteenth-century Spanish mystic: "Only those who have experienced it will believe what pleasure we get from these foundations when we find ourselves at last in a cloister which can be entered by no one from the world . . . Nuns who find themselves desirous of going out among worldly people . . . may well fear that they have not found the living water of which the Lord spoke to the woman of Samaria, and that the Spouse has hidden himself from them; and they are right to fear this, since they are not content to remain with him."

The women who chose such lives during the Middle Ages often remain a mystery to us now. Their remoteness, isolation, and poverty mean there is only sparse evidence of their material lives, and almost no documentation of their voices, which is the case with the Cistercian convent of Coyroux, in southwestern France. It was the sister house to Obazine (or Aubazine) Abbey —a grand structure, sturdily built on a broad hill overlooking the Coyroux River. During the Middle Ages, the abbey's property was extensive. Obazine was surrounded by farmland that not only supported the monks but also supplied provisions and fuel to pilgrims on their way to Rocamadour.

The women's convent of Coyroux stood less than half a mile from Obazine. The nuns were completely cloistered and had no resources of their own. They depended on the monks at Obazine —who collected their dowers—to provide everything for them. Bernadette Barrière, a French scholar of medieval history, has observed that, as part of a double monastery, the monks likely saw the women monastics as a burden and wanted the convent "close . . . so as to facilitate the performance of ecclesiastical duties." While part of the reason for locating the women's house nearby might have been practical, Barrière suggests that the site was probably also chosen "so that any contact with the outside world, even were it only visual, would be rendered difficult."

The convent stood precariously on the banks of the Coyroux River, in a wild and forbidding environment. As Barrière described it in the 1990s, "Rapids exit from a deep, narrow gorge . . . still turbulent because of the strong current, and enhanced by seasonal floods . . . The valley, completely cut off from all human activity and distant from all roads, is a kind of cul-de-sac, very narrow (less than 100 meters wide), with steep and rocky wooded slopes that shut out the horizon." So the site was also very dark.

Although the walls of the convent's buildings were constructed of local stone, the roofs were timber, and the dormitory, refectory, and storage rooms were mortared with earth. Only the church was built with lime mortar. "No function was neglected, no element was missing, all the necessary technical services were there, yet nothing was conceived to last," Barrière observed. The temporal nature of these buildings stood in stark contrast not only to those of Obazine, but also to the ideal of Cistercian architecture and to all that was prized in the building of the great monasteries: the proportion, the quality of the work, the sense of permanence of these structures painstakingly erected for the glory of God.

The buildings of Coyroux, which surrounded a modest cloister, covered about half an acre. Within that confined space, at one time a hundred nuns lived—more religious than resided at Obazine. They had no reliable source of water, depending on an aqueduct over the river that was periodically damaged during storms and floods. Nor did they have any way of securing their own food; rather, they relied on an elaborate system of delivery meant to keep the women from encountering the monks they depended upon for their survival. A document from the Middle Ages describing life at Obazine notes that "the way out of the enclosure [at Coyroux] is through two doors facing each other, at either end of a small corridor. The prioress keeps the key to the inner door while that of the outer door is in the keeping of an elderly, experienced friar [who] . . . gathers the various supplies between the two doors: bread, wine, herbs, wood, vegetables, all that is useful to the healthy and to the sick, then locks the outer door which he then strikes with a stick. The porter nun, thus notified, opens her own door and removes what has been placed in the corridor."

Although the nuns had almost no privacy, silence would have been as strictly enforced at Coyroux as at any other Cistercian monastery, and compared with the severe restrictions women faced in the greater world, the silence of even that crowded and strict enclosure might have bestowed on them a certain freedom. Did the remoteness and isolation of Coyroux intensify their silence, their belief, their community bonds? Might they have come to embrace the narrowness of their earth-mortared, flood-threatened world? Without any record of their voices, historians today must rely on imagination and conjecture to answer those questions. In the early seventeenth century, Barrière notes, when the nuns were "offered the opportunity to move to a newly built convent in town . . . most of them refuse[d] to leave." Their decision seems staggering when viewed from the material comforts of our secular lives. Barrière asks: "Are we to consider that such a way of life was deliberately chosen by the original nucleus of the female community, and that nuns deliberately accepted it for several centuries with no desire to alter it?"

No answers come to us from the gorge. Obazine Abbey, always more prominent than the convent of Coyroux, retains its place today: it serves as the parish church of the community of Aubazine. All that remains of Coyroux are some partial walls of the church, the sole building constructed with lime mortar. Only the foundations of most of the other buildings survive. There is little more than Barrière's research to bring Coyroux forward into our own time, as the dedicated patiently block and sweep the ruins, and sift and conjecture and question the evidence of the past.

PART V

The Ends of Silence

But these still remain: the quietness of dawn, and the furtive fall of night . . . Never was the silence of these things more perfect than now; never was it more beautiful. The silence of these things is lonely.

—Max Picard, *The World of Silence*

19

thomas merton: questioning silence

NO SILENCE IS stable, perhaps especially an enduring commitment to it. Thomas Merton spent half his life at the Abbey of Gethsemani, and during that time he never stopped inquiring into the solitude and silence he'd chosen. "Inner silence depends on a continual seeking," he remarked. "If we cling to a silence we think we have found forever, we stop seeking God and the silence goes dead within us." By the early 1950s, however, his writings had brought him increasing renown, and more and more of his time was taken up with visitors and responding to letters and inquiries from his readers. He received so much correspondence that he resorted to replying to most of it with a form letter. Between his obligations to his community—he was master of the scholastics, in charge of their spiritual education—and his renown as a writer, it had become more and more difficult for him to find the smallest measure of silence.

So, after more than a decade at the monastery, he petitioned for, and was granted by his superior, time in a small toolshed in the wooded hills of the monastery grounds, which he could use as a hermitage. Merton christened this makeshift, spartan shed St. Anne's. Its surrounding landscape reminded him of walks during his youth throughout Sussex, England, and the silence, simplicity, and solitude it offered was exactly what he felt he needed. "I am now almost completely convinced that I am only really a monk when I am alone in the old toolshed Reverend Father gave me (It is back in the woods beyond the horse pasture where Bro. Aelred hauled it with the traxcavator the day before Trinity Sunday.)," he wrote in his diary in September 1952. "True, I have the will of a monk in the community. But I have the *prayer* of a monk in the silence of the woods and the toolshed. To begin with: the place is simple, and really poor with the bare poverty I need . . . And silent. And inactive—materially. Therefore the Spirit is busy here."

He'd always grappled with the tensions and complexities, the mass and mess, of the social self. St. Anne's offered him a respite from all that, and a rediscovery of the simple soul. He wrote: "I need solitude for the true fulfillment which I seek—that of being *ordinary* . . . In solitude, at last, I shall be just a person, no longer corrupted by being known." The idea of being no longer corrupted was also inextricably tied to the natural world surrounding him at Gethsemani. His intense love of the beauty of the days threads through his first journal writings at St. Anne's. He could not take his eyes off the world, and he could forget himself in it. It was—as it always had been—a dependable solace, a vision of the spiritual. On September 15, 1952, he noted in his journal: "High up in the late Summer sky I watch the silent flight of a vulture, and the day goes by in prayer. This solitude confirms my call to solitude. The more I am in it, the more I love it. One day it will possess me entirely and no man will ever see me again."

Although he remained an integral part of the monastic community at Gethsemani—he continued to teach and take meals in the refectory, and prayed and worked with his fellow monks—Merton, at least at times, found that under the protection of St. Anne's, away from the community and settled in silence, he was more able to bear the incidental and necessary modern noises of the monastery: "The tractors in the bottoms would have exasperated me two years ago. I hardly notice them now." Nevertheless, during this time and in spite of his best efforts to embrace the particular spiritual life within the community, he questioned his place in it, thinking again of making a request to join a more hermetic order, something he'd desired throughout his monastic life.

At the same time, he increasingly came to believe that in any hermitage, no matter how remote, the twentieth century could not be ignored. He was aware of Cold War tensions and the buildup of nuclear arms in the post–World War II era, which was evident even in the choice of monastic readings during meals. On most days, when the monks ate together in silence, one of the members likely read to them many of the same spiritual writings and commentaries that their order had listened to for centuries. In November 1957, however, as the Trappist community leaned over their meal as prescribed since their founding—milk, vegetables, beans, bread, fish, or cheese; nothing with four legs—Merton noted that the reading consisted of something that would have been unfathomable even a few years prior: "Yesterday and today in the refectory first a news article about the two sputniks and the dog in the second one. Then Eisenhower's speech about science and defense—a fantastic future which, I suppose, we have to take for granted from now on."

If the reader that day happened to be drawing on the article from the *New York Times,* he might have ended with the reporter's observation that "what the late British astronomer, Sir Arthur S. Eddington, said a generation ago was no longer true—that man in his search for knowledge of the universe was like a potato bug in a potato in the hold of a ship trying to fathom from the ship's motions the nature of the vast sea." That realignment of human knowledge in relation to the universe was one kind of challenge to traditional thinking; the response of Eisenhower, another. In the president's televised speech following the launch of the satellite, he outlined the defenses of the country in an attempt to allay fears about what Sputnik would mean for Russian nuclear missile capabilities. "In numbers, our stock of nuclear weapons is so large and so rapidly growing that we are able safely to disperse it to positions assuring its instant availability against attack, and still keep strong reserves," he proclaimed.

How strange the news must have seemed when heard from the monastery, steeped in its observances, its dark nights of chants and prayers reverberating in the oratory amid the language of light and shadow. As the reader relayed news of the first man-made moon circling Earth every ninety-six minutes, perhaps a monk turned to another and placed the palm of one hand over the outside of the other to ask for more bread. Their sign language had developed in a world of fewer than 400 million humans. Since then, their communities had been repeatedly scattered by political decree, their monasteries had been raided and ravaged by war. Communities reestablished themselves in the wake of each tragedy. The very name of the order to which Merton belonged—the Trappists—had emerged out of the dissolutions of the Cistercian monasteries during the nineteenth century, when fugitive monks resettled the Abbey of La Trappe in northern France.

Trappist monks, by the time of Sputnik's launch, numbered far fewer than their Cistercian predecessors who had settled the valleys of France in the eleventh and twelfth centuries, and they were dispersed across a globe that supported more than three billion people.

Merton knew that the twentieth-century monastery could not be the twelfth, and the contemplative life could not be an escape from the political turmoil in his own country. In the days following news of the satellite launches and Eisenhower's speech, he wrote: "It is futile to try and live in an expanding universe with atomic fission an ever present possibility and try to think and act exclusively as if the cosmos were fixed in an immutable order centered upon man's earth. Modern physics has repercussions in the monastery and to be a monk one must take them into account, though that does nothing whatever to make one's spirituality either simple or neat."

To read his journals of the 1950s and '60s is to see a man coming to a more profound sense of his place in the larger world. "The freedom of the Christian contemplative is not freedom *from* time, but freedom *in* time," he insisted. Merton saw the monk's flight from society, in imitation of the Desert Fathers, not as a withdrawal or denial of the world, but a rejection, a refusal to participate in its aggression and selfishness, its limited and shortsighted goals. Merton called it "withdrawal from secular time." He was fully aware of the long, complex history of his monastic order—its braveries, its purities, its collusions, its corruptions—but in his time alone at St. Anne's, the decision he felt he faced was intensely personal: He was a contemplative monk who was by no means obscure, whose words carried weight. The questions he asked himself were those of a monk and of a citizen: When is silence power? When is it an accomplice to fear? A means of control? What did it mean to remain silent when faced with the intolerable?

As the Cold War deepened, he could not help but see removal from the world as potentially destructive to the monastic calling: "The contemplative life is not, and cannot be, a mere withdrawal, a pure negation, a turning of one's back on the world with its sufferings, its crises, its confusions and its errors . . . The monastic community is deeply implicated, for better or for worse, in the economic, political, and social structures of the contemporary world. To forget or to ignore this does not absolve the monk from responsibility for participation in events in which his very silence and 'not knowing' may constitute a form of complicity. The mere fact of 'ignoring' what goes on can become a political decision."

Further, he wrote that the very fact of his long silence, of being accustomed to deliberateness in speech, could add weight to words: "Genuine communication is becoming more and more difficult, and when speech is in danger of perishing or being perverted in the amplified noise of beasts, perhaps it becomes obligatory for a monk to try to speak." He must have felt a double pressure: a responsibility as a monk and also as a writer. He was an admirer of Bertolt Brecht, especially his poems. You can imagine him encountering Brecht's "In Dark Times":

> . . . they won't say: the times were dark
> Rather: why were their poets silent?

In questioning silence, Merton was also testing his vow of obedience, one of the solemn vows, which had emerged in a feudal society. What place did it have in a twentieth-century democracy? In 1961 he wrote: "Yesterday afternoon at the hermitage, surely a decisive clarity came. That I must definitely commit myself to opposition to, and non-cooperation with, nuclear war." In the medium available to him: print. Still, he did not fail to understand his voice in the world as being inextricably tied to his place in the Church. For Merton, this went to the very heart of his vocation: "My position loses its meaning unless I continue to speak from the Center of the Church. Yet that is exactly the point: where is the true center? From the bosom of complacent approbation by Monsignors?"

He wanted more for the Church than the Church seemed to want for itself. Vatican II, initiated by Pope John XXIII, had let in some fresh air: dialogue with other religions, parish priests turning to face their congregations, the celebration of the Mass in the vernacular, relaxed rules concerning silence in the monastery and restrictions on travel for monks. These changes would make possible Merton's eventual dialogue with Eastern monasticism, but there remained dark, airless corners of the institution, and he was still obligated to obey his superiors.

Although Merton was free to write as he wished, his final manuscripts were screened by two officially appointed censors of the Cistercian Order. They had to declare that the work contained no doctrinal or moral errors, after which Merton's abbot had to grant his approval for publication. But approval by the order wasn't the end. A Church censor, usually from the archdiocese, had to authorize the work before Merton could be granted final permission to publish. Only then could his book be stamped with the imprimatur. This was rarely a straightforward process. Of his first book Merton wrote:

> *The Seven Storey Mountain* has been rejected by one of the Censors of the Order: not on theological grounds but as unripe for publication. Our censors are also editors. They determine whether or not the Order will benefit by the publication of the books submitted to them. This time the decision is no. I am held to be incapable of writing an autobiography "with his present literary equipment" and I am advised to take a correspondence course in English grammar. Urged by Father Abbot, I sent back the manuscript with three pages of single-spaced self-defense, pointing out that Harcourt, Brace did not agree that the book was unripe for publication. Another objection was that I had been too frank about my past . . . Secretly I am delighted to have a cross that I can understand. It falls into a nice flattering literary context: I am a misunderstood author.

In the early 1950s he also had trouble with the censors over his second autobiographical work, *The Sign of Jonas,* an edited journal of his first years of monastic life. By the 1960s, the Church went beyond questioning individual books. It specifically forbade him to write on matters of war and civil rights. "I am being silenced on the subject of war and peace," Merton wrote to James Forest, a peace activist and editor at Dorothy Day's newspaper, the *Catholic Worker.* The reasons given were that it was inappropriate for a monk to write on such subjects, that it was a distraction from his calling, and that it falsified the message of monasticism.

Although he was forbidden to publish, Merton found ways of getting around the censors. He wrote articles for the *Catho-*

lic Worker under the pen names Benedict Monk and Benedict Moore. He was a great admirer of Day and her Catholic Worker movement, with its commitment to nonviolence and the alleviation of poverty. Merton once wrote to her: "If there were no Catholic Worker and such forms of witness, I would never have joined the Catholic Church." And, in another letter: "As for writing: I don't feel that I can in conscience, at a time like this, go on writing just about things like meditation, though that has its point . . . I think I have to face the big issues."

Merton's shorter works and those of limited circulation weren't subject to the formal censors; they required only the consent of his abbot. So he broke down his long works into shorter pieces and disseminated them in the form of mimeographed sheets. He sent out essays and declarations to his wide network of influential people—other writers, university professors, political activists—and his friends mimeographed them and distributed them further. They discussed these works in their classrooms. Regarding one collection of his writings, *Peace in the Post-Christian Era,* which he was repeatedly denied permission to publish (it was eventually published in 2004), he wrote to his friend John Harris: "I have just been instructed to shut my trap and behave, which I do since these are orders that must be obeyed and I have said what I had to say. I will send you a mimeographed copy of the book if I can. Meanwhile with the letters of course you can use them discreetly, and I see no objection to their being quoted in class in a private school." To Forest at the *Catholic Worker* he suggested: "You could write a short article reporting on the appearance of my article and quoting bits from it . . . I think this is a feasible way of handling material that would otherwise just get jammed up in the censorship machine forever." And later: "I have been considering the possibility of writing a kind of statement—'Where I stand,' as a declaration of my position as a Christian, a writer and a Priest in the present war crisis. There seems to be little that I can do other than this. There is *no other activity* available to me."

As much as Merton pushed the boundaries, he was also cognizant of them. In April 1962, he wrote to Forest reasserting his place within the Church and stepping back from his most resolute stance: "I am where I am. I have freely chosen this state, and have freely chosen to stay in it . . . This means accepting such limitation as may be placed on me by authority . . . but out of love for God who is using these things to attain an end which I myself cannot at the moment see or comprehend . . . Once again, please don't print anything of mine in a letter or anything else about peace . . . and above all don't print any of this one."

Merton would one day admit that obedience was the most difficult of his solemn vows to keep. He tested the boundaries of his freedom and also retreated from them again and again. In 1964, several years after his caution to Forest, he wrote even more boldly: "To have a vow of obedience seems to me to be absurd if it does not imply a deep concern for the most fundamental of all expressions of God's will: the love of His truth and of our neighbor."

For Bertolt Brecht, one of the greatest freedoms for a poet was to be able to write as you wish rather than as you must. Part of the insidiousness of Nazism was the way it undercut his freedom to celebrate the joy and beauty of the world. During the time in which he lived, writing as he wished could feel like its own silence. The celebration of beauty, a kind of silence. In his poem "To Those Born Later," Brecht asks:

> What kind of times are they, when
> A talk about trees is almost a crime
> Because it implies silence about so many horrors?

Perhaps existence in uncomplicated times is a dream as elusive as the dream of peace in solitude. All during the buildup of the Cold War, Merton's solitude was becoming more expansive. He was granted more and more time in the toolshed. Then, in the 1960s, his abbot approved the building of a larger hermitage for him that would also serve as a conference center. His renown had always brought renown to Gethsemani, and the conference center was a means of both granting Merton his solitude and gathering the energy and interest in the order that his writings had attracted.

In his new hermitage—a modest cement block cabin set back in the woods—he said Vespers, cooked his oatmeal, listened to the rain. He toasted bread in the fireplace; sat on the porch, cordwood stacked behind him. At the desk, which faced a large set of windows, he wrote poems and journal entries and created ink drawings. Such solitude, he understood, was never for himself alone. He maintained that the solitary, stripped of the help and hindrances of social life and material comfort, "far from enclosing himself in himself, becomes every man. He dwells in the solitude, the poverty, the indigence of every man."

If silence grew more precious and joyful to him, it was no less complex. Even in his more solid hermitage, the world intruded.

Deep in a storm-soaked night he could celebrate the intensity of the rain: "There is no clock that can measure the speech of this rain that falls all night on the drowned and lonely forest." But the beauty of that rain, even in the countryside and within his monastery's grounds, could no longer be separated from the larger powers of human aggression. Fort Knox wasn't far away: "Of course at three-thirty A.M. the SAC plane goes over, red light winking low under the clouds, skimming the wooded summits on the south side of the valley, loaded with strong medicine. Very strong. Strong enough to burn up all these woods."

Still, he had limits to the kinds of protest he would support. He was suspicious of mass gatherings. Though he would always be a friend of Jesuit priest and antiwar activist Daniel Berrigan, he broke with him over street demonstrations and the burning of draft cards, believing such actions led to violence and could also overwhelm an individual soul. And he warned his friend James Forest: "It seems everything is happening at once in your life . . . Don't let it become an avalanche. You want to keep your footing and be able to look about you and see what you are doing. The trouble with movements is that they sweep you off your feet and carry you away with the tide of activism and then you become another kind of mass man."

Even speaking out had its limits for a man who believed at heart the world could change through the transformation of individual souls. By 1965 Merton suggested he was growing disenchanted with activism. In a letter to Polish poet Czeslaw Milosz, with whom he'd corresponded for nearly a decade, the two of them often troubling out the tensions between contemplation and engagement, he wrote: "I think the monastic life is a life of liberation from movements. This is of course in many ways reprehensible and open to criticism, and it has immense disadvantages. But there you are . . . I have come around a corner, as you have, and I simply feel that there is so much of significance simply in my own living and doing or not doing such work as I do or don't do, that there is no further reason to imagine having an identity that is made up of relationships with new movements." And yet he couldn't entirely separate himself from political involvement. Near the end of the letter he admits: "Still, it is true I do write for pacifist publications."

From all outward appearances Merton, by entering the monastery, had chosen the most clear-cut of lives, with its orderly days of observances, its hierarchies and regulations, but he never saw his place within it in a simple or exclusive way. His allegiance to opposing forces, forged by his own conscience and the consciences of his friends and supporters, was always with him: the contemplative life, which requires silence and solitude; the life of engagement, with its demands of articulation and its outward pull. He could write to Milosz of his exhaustion with movements, and with equal conviction to Brazilian writer and activist Alceu Amoroso Lima suggesting that monastic cover was no less problematic than political engagement:

> This is a crucial and perhaps calamitous moment in history, a moment in which reason and understanding threaten to be swallowed up . . . It is all very well for me to meditate on these things in the shelter of the monastery: but there are times when this shelter itself is deceptive . . . And grains of error planted innocently in a well-kept greenhouse can become giant poisonous trees . . . Everything healthy, everything certain, everything holy, if we

> can find such things, they all need to be emphasized and articulated. For this it is necessary that there be a genuine and deep communication between the hearts and minds of men, communication and not the noise of slogans or the repetition of clichés.

Still, in the end, his allegiance to contemplation could not be denied. Merton's conviction that silence and solitude had much to offer a troubled world—perhaps enough to save it—and that the renewal of a society had to come from the transformation of individual souls was not only at the heart of his Catholic monastic practice; it was also reinforced by his longtime interest in Eastern contemplative practices, which he'd brought with him to the monastery. He continued to read Eastern religious thinkers and study Eastern art during his years at Gethsemani, and in 1968, in the spirit of aggiornamento fostered by Vatican II, he was granted the opportunity to travel to Asia to attend several conferences and visit established Cistercian monasteries in the East.

Whatever his official duties, he also saw the journey as a deeply personal one, an opportunity to expand his own thinking about the contemplative life and how it might be beneficial to a modern, secular society. "Serious communication . . . among contemplatives of different traditions, disciplines, and religions . . . can contribute much to the development of man at this crucial point of his history," he wrote. ". . . We find ourselves in a crisis, a moment of crucial choice. We are in grave danger of losing a spiritual heritage that has been painfully accumulated by thousands of generations of saints and contemplatives. It is the peculiar office of the monk in the modern world to keep alive the contemplative experience and to keep the way open for modern technological man to recover the integrity of his own inner depths."

Asia offered him a simplification of his life as well. As the trip approached, he expressed relief at being able, for a few months at least, to leave behind not only his correspondence but his public role. Before his departure he wrote a circular letter to friends in which he explained that he would not be receiving most of his mail and that any correspondence would be minimal. He further advised: "It will be impossible for me to think of keeping in touch with political issues, still less to comment on them or to sign various petitions, protests, etc. Even though the need for them may be even greater: but will they now have lost any usefulness? Has the signing of protests become a pointless exercise? In any case, anything I do on this trip will be absolutely nonpolitical."

It was his own chance for renewal and deepening, and it was not insignificant that he ended his letter to friends by reasserting the value of the contemplative life, no matter the crises of the world and its violence. "Our real journey in life is interior," he wrote. "It is a matter of growth, deepening, and of an ever greater surrender to the creative action of love and grace in our hearts. Never was it more necessary for us to respond to that action."

He left Gethsemani in October of 1968, stopping first on the West Coast to visit some fellow monastics and search, perhaps, for a place for a hermitage away from his increasingly complex and demanding life back home. Merton had traveled infrequently since joining the Trappists. He carried far too many books with him and keenly recorded all that he saw: his fellow travelers, the temperature of the air, the vegetation, the sounds of the world.

As the time for departure for Asia grew near, his anticipation and energy rose. He was, he believed, approaching the culmination of his lifelong search. "Joy," he wrote. "We left the ground —I with Christian mantras and a great sense of destiny, of being at last on my true way after years of waiting and wondering and fooling around."

Soon after landing in Bangkok he departed for Calcutta, then New Delhi, Darjeeling, the Himalayas. In northern India he visited with the Dalai Lama in exile. Merton had long wanted such a meeting, and as they spoke over the course of three consecutive days, he felt he'd found a deeply spiritual brother, as did the Dalai Lama, who recalled the visits decades later, his memory still fresh: "Merton was a well-built man of medium height, with even less hair than me, though that was not because his head was shaved as mine is. He had big boots and wore a thick leather belt round the middle of his heavy, white cassock. But more striking than his outward appearance, which was memorable in itself, was the inner life that he manifested. I could see he was a truly humble and deeply spiritual man."

Then Merton traveled on to Madras and Ceylon (now Sri Lanka) before returning to Bangkok. After several months of lectures, conversations, talks, panels, and immersion in foreign landscapes, he was deeply energized by his travels, particularly his encounters with cultures where religion remained at the heart of daily life, and by his conversations with rimpoches about spiritual matters. Yet he also felt a little homesick, perhaps especially because it was Advent, the same time of year he'd entered the order more than twenty years before. The distance from his home had given him a new angle of vision on the rush of his life there and prompted him to contemplate ever more seriously time away from it. But his sojourn in Asia had also deepened his affection for Gethsemani. "It is my monastery," he wrote, "and being away has helped me see it in perspective and love it more." Although rumor had it that Merton might leave Kentucky, he made it clear that even if he were to find a hermitage on the West Coast or in Alaska, he had no intention of cutting ties with Gethsemani. "Keep telling everyone I am a monk of Gethsemani," he wrote to his friend Brother Patrick Hart, "and intend to remain one all my days."

On December 10, at a Red Cross center near Bangkok, Merton gave a lecture in which he affirmed the place of the monastic as an outsider. "The monk is essentially someone who takes up a critical attitude toward the world and its structures," he remarked. "In other words, the monk is somebody who says in one way or another, that the claims of the world are fraudulent." Afterward, he went back to his cottage to rest and to shower before a scheduled evening panel discussion. He emerged from his shower, walking with wet feet on a wet floor. It's surmised that he reached for a fan, which later was shown to have faulty wiring, and suffered a fatal electric shock.

Merton's body was flown back to the United States on an Air Force transport to Oakland, then sent on a commercial carrier to Louisville. He was laid to rest on December 17 as snow fell in the waning light of day, at the monastery in the Knobs of Kentucky where he had spent half of his fifty-three years. His burial place is marked, as are all the other graves of the monks of Gethsemani, with a simple white cross.

20

the monastic world: what remains

THERE WERE MORE than seven hundred Cistercian monasteries in the valleys and on the plains of Europe on the eve of the Reformation. Many now stand in ruins. A limestone foundation in a grass field. The remnant of an exposed water system. Two walls of a nave against the hills at Aulps, ivy growing over the stumps of columns at Notre Dame de Ré, the lone squat bell tower and windows open to the sky at Châalis, a domed vault at Boschaud. In Yorkshire, England, in winter, snow spits through the arches at Rievaulx, landing on horses grazing in what had been the transept and falling softly on the remaining wall with its lancet windows, on the last standing stones from an age of faith. Henry Moore, who grew up within Rievaulx's reach, would say: "When it is no longer usable, architecture inevitably becomes aesthetically like sculpture."

Of those monasteries that remain, some have been converted to secular uses that would have been unimaginable to the medieval monks who devoted their lives to raising walls and building arches for the glory of God; who planted orchards, pastured sheep, and ate their pottage out of wooden bowls. Coombe Abbey near Coventry, England, has become a fine hotel with sunken baths, gilded mirrors, and down pillows on the beds. Its restaurant offers lamb and beef, along with spring chicken; recordings of Gregorian chant are piped into the lobby.

The fate of the monastery at Clairvaux, in northeastern France, is strange in an entirely different way. Founded by Bernard, it is also his burial place and was once at the center of the Cistercian world. Many of the original buildings have long fallen into ruin, though some were rebuilt in the seventeenth century. After the French Revolution, the monastery became the property of the state and was converted to a high-security prison. Victor Hugo noted that the monastic cells had been turned "into dungeons, and the altar itself into a pillory," which would not have been unimaginable to the boys John Howard encountered in the Hospice of San Michele in Rome, who worked at tables flanked on one end by an altar, on the other by a whipping post.

The pillory may be gone, but Clairvaux remains a high-security prison. The ruins of medieval Clairvaux also remain, and the site is overseen by both the Ministry of Justice and the Ministry of Culture. Visitors who tour the monastery must adhere to some of the rules for prison visits. They are required to present a photo ID, for instance, and are forbidden to take photographs.

The Cistercian order has shrunk drastically over the centuries. There are now about four thousand souls housed in fewer than two hundred monasteries throughout the world. The ruined far outnumber the inhabited ones, and while many of the lost have been abandoned to time and weather, violence has also played its role, even in modern times. Saint Benedict's Monte Cassino, where he wrote his Rule in the sixth century, was raided by Lombards and later toppled by an earthquake. It was sacked by Napoleon's troops. But it took the age of aerial bombing to destroy it completely. Perched atop a hill northeast of Naples, the monastery had always been considered a strategic location. At more than 1,700 feet above the road to Rome, it afforded an expansive view of travelers, or enemies, crossing the Liri Valley below.

During the fall and early winter of 1943, German soldiers, bunkered in the hillside below the monastery, assaulted the Allied forces in the valley, most of whom had been working their way up from the south on their way to Rome. Troops from fifteen different countries, including the United States, France, Poland, South Africa, New Zealand, Great Britain, India, and Tunisia, toiled through a wet, harsh Italian winter. The destruction and the dying had followed them north, and the advance from Naples had been especially slow, with their jeeps and tanks often mired in the mud. At times they had to rely on mules to carry supplies. They had to ford the swift currents of the Rapido River. They were never warm and never dry. The bare winter landscape provided little natural cover for them, and they suffered heavy casualties.

Fighting in the vicinity of the monastery went on for months, and the Allies suspected the Germans were launching their attacks from within the monastery, even though it had been designated as a historic sanctuary. During that time the monastery itself took on outsized meaning. The Allied troops, perhaps, couldn't escape the feeling of being watched, and the feeling only increased and folded into the complex sentiments of war-weary soldiers. "Day and night they had lived under its baleful eye," wrote one observer. "It was a constant intruding presence, it looked into everything, it nagged at their nerves and became a phobia and an obsession." Was their anger aimed at belief, at God? Or at the centuries of men steeped in silence and contemplation, seemingly above it all and away from the world?

By the time the worst ground fighting had begun, most of the monks had gone to Rome, but a handful remained at Monte Cassino and attempted to continue life as they'd known it, even as the monastery filled with starving, wounded, shell-shocked refugees fleeing the fighting below. One monk kept a diary throughout the ground assault:

> December 19, 1943: In the afternoon about 3:15, while we were saying the rosary . . . the explosions were very powerful and close, shaking the whole building; we went on praying. After vespers we realized that Monte Cassino was saved by a miracle, because the closest of the bombs fell hardly six meters from the Novitiate . . .
>
> . . .
>
> December 22: This morning we settled more or less on what we would do for the liturgical celebration of Christmas. We shall do the best we can.
>
> . . .
>
> January 5[, 1944]: The saddest of days . . . All civilians without any exception must be evacuated; German trucks would come for that purpose . . . If we remained we would do so at our own risk . . . It is useless to try to say what this day meant to our little community.
>
> . . .
>
> January 7: The situation of those who remain is that we have no contact with the outside world and no one is allowed

in . . . We do not know, from one moment to the next, what will happen to us monks.

. . .

January 10: The Germans now surround us. They have even made lodgings in the cave under the main wing of the monastery . . .

. . .

January 18: One day perhaps we will find out the reason for things that seem somewhat mysterious.

On January 21 Allied bombs smashed the confessionals in the church and destroyed some of the marble statues, the stained-glass window, and a cherished painting by the late baroque artist Luca Giordano. The diarist wrote: "From now on entering the church is forbidden." The monks continued to observe the Liturgy of the Hours and hold Mass in a makeshift chapel even after white leaflets, printed in Italian and English, floated down from the sky warning the remaining monks and refugees to leave immediately: "The time has come when we must train our guns on the monastery itself." The next day, February 15, 1944, aerial bombing began while the monks were praying in their makeshift chapel.

In the valley below, at the sight of the planes dropping their first payload on the monastery, and of the plumes of black smoke rising from the mountaintop, Allied soldiers cheered. American reporters cheered. "I watched it sitting on a stone wall and saw the monastery turning into a muddle of dust and heard the big bangs and was absolutely delighted and cheered like all the other fools," remarked American war correspondent Martha Gellhorn. The monks had no choice but to flee down an ancient mule path that had first been used in the sixth century, when

Benedict established Monte Cassino. In less than four hours, five hundred bombers dropped more than one thousand tons of explosives on the monastery.

In the wake of the bombing, when almost all that was left of Monte Cassino was a partial wall and endless rubble, it was deemed likely that no Germans had occupied it, though they moved in quickly after the bombing ceased. The ruins provided a great bulwark, and for another three months they fought amid the bodies of more than a hundred refugees who'd once sought shelter in the monastery.

In May 1944 the Allies finally broke through the German line and proceeded toward Rome. By then the Battle of Monte Cassino was considered a strategic failure. The death toll for Allied soldiers alone reached over fifty thousand.

Film footage shows the monks of Monte Cassino in the aftermath of the war, carting away stones in wheelbarrows, picking out manuscript pages and torn books from the dust and rubble. The ruin around them is massive. "Up until 1948, we did only that," remembered one of the monks. In the footage they are moving quickly—shaking the books, stacking them up, showing some of the pages to the camera. The dust settles on the hems of their cassocks, which distinguish them from the other men working to clear the rubble and move the fallen stones. Their legendary library had contained more than forty thousand books, manuscripts, and documents. Some of the most valuable had been transported to Rome prior to the fighting, but countless others were destroyed or damaged in the bombing.

The monastery was eventually rebuilt, using the old plans, as the image of its prewar self. Of the reconstruction, one of the monks who'd remained at the abbey throughout the ground assault remarked: "What you see today is exactly what I saw when I first came here in 1922." Still, nothing could bring back the painting by Luca Giordano, the broken statuary, or the ruined books and manuscripts, which went the way of all the other monastic documents destroyed by fires, floods, or mold; subject to foxing, stains, or tears; raided for their precious paper; or lost when their libraries were sacked or dispersed in the wake of dissolutions.

Perhaps all that loss is part of what makes even the most modest pages of surviving medieval books and manuscripts more highly valued than belief itself—or so it seems by the way they are so carefully preserved in rooms in Boston or Paris or London, where gauges continuously monitor humidity and temperature. On occasion they are taken out and displayed in low light. I've been among the visitors slowly moving through hushed rooms, bent to the display cases—one of those useless readers separated from the parchment and ink by glass, and unaccustomed to the beautiful, careful script of centuries past. Some of us might try for a little while to silently mouth what we see, but the strangeness of the script slows us down. "Legibility, in practice," remarked type designer Eric Gill, "amounts simply to what one is accustomed to."

21

the prison cell in our time

THE PENITENTIARY HAS mostly slipped its name. We now have prisons, or houses of incarceration, or houses of correction. Just as Eastern State was when the first prisoners arrived, they are almost always sited beyond the edges of cities. Every now and again a voice rises to object to our distance from them. "If there are prisons, they ought to be in the neighborhood, near a subway," remarked writer and activist Grace Paley, "not way out in distant suburbs, where families have to take buses, ferries, trains, and the population that considers itself innocent forgets, denies, chooses to never know."

The sheer size of contemporary prisons precludes their being built in urban areas. Eastern State occupied 10 acres and was first envisioned as housing fewer than three hundred souls at any one time. Pelican Bay State Prison, eight miles outside the center of Crescent City, California, is a 275-acre compound that can hold over three thousand prisoners. It's just one correctional facility in California's state system, in a country with nearly two thousand state and federal prisons and over three thousand county jails. In the nearly two hundred years since Charles Williams was sentenced, the prison population of the United States has grown to over one and a half million men and women in state and federal correctional institutions. Minorities still comprise a disproportionate percentage of the prison population.

No one is officially punished by being sentenced to solitary confinement by the courts. Offenders in the general prison population live in a crowd—eating meals together, working together, exercising together, gathering for classes and instruction. Usually more than one prisoner occupies a cell, and sometimes one cell is separated from the next only by bars. Nothing could be further from the steeped solitude and silence of the first prisoners at Eastern State. "You must be careful to move around people rather than against or through them," one late-twentieth-century inmate remarked, noting that he and his cellmate "take care neither by what we say nor in any other way to let the other know about . . . ways in which, living so close to one another as we do, we annoy one another. It is better that way. We have not yet had an argument that leads to a fight, even a shouting match, but we live so close that someday that will happen, and we will both probably end up in the hole, hating one another."

The idea of order and control instituted at Eastern State remains evident: in the number of prison guards; the surveillance equipment; the strict, straight utilitarian lines of the architecture; the lock systems for entrance and exit. But the incessant noise is reminiscent of the chaos of old jails. One modern inmate's record of a typical day begins like this: "5:30 a.m. I was awakened by the wake-up call for the kitchen detail. I am not on that detail, but the banging on the bars of the cell near me, to awaken a prisoner who is on the kitchen detail, wakes me every morning . . . 6:00 a.m. The keys were rattled across the bars of our cells." The overall noise is most likely worse than that experienced in, say, London's eighteenth-century Newgate, because it's now amplified by the electronic age. The inmate's record of the day continues: "As F House came to life, the noise began—radios, TVs, shouting from cell to cell—and so it would go on till night, with an occasional scream of rage or fear through the night." The noise is so profound that trying to minimize it can be a decisive factor in choosing how to negotiate the day: "The food is often worse in the evening than at lunch, but it is better to go than to stay in what is by now the thundering noise of F House, with TVs and radios blaring and, it seems to me, every prisoner shouting to another prisoner and nobody listening." Time and ideas seem to have made little difference since one visitor described Newgate as "a tower of Babel where all are speakers and no hearers."

Within the chaos of noise, which defeats communication in its own way, groups of inmates develop their own slang, often arcane languages or codes, so they can talk freely among themselves even when surrounded by guards and the general population. It's a concentrated Babel: the Aryan Brotherhood might base their communication on old Anglo-Saxon; blacks, on Swahili; Hispanics, on Aztec or the old Chinese alphabet. Such diverse communication not only separates rival from rival, but enforcers from inmates. In a century when people travel back and forth around the globe and prisoners are shunted across borders, ignorance of a language or languages at times separates one prisoner from all others, and such linguistic isolation can be lonelier than imposed silence.

By the second half of the twentieth century, there were new ways of muting prisoners, as political activist Angela Davis noted while she awaited extradition to California in the Women's House of Detention in Greenwich Village, New York, in 1970. She'd been charged with conspiracy for her part in buying firearms that were used in the armed takeover of a Marin County courthouse. Her cell, in a section of the jail reserved for the mentally unstable, was less than five feet wide and contained little more than a cot bolted to the floor and a toilet. Since she had no table, her breakfast—cornflakes and watery milk, two slices of white bread, and coffee—was set on the unswept floor. All prisoners, no matter their age, were called "girls." She had no reading materials; no pen or paper; no soap, toothbrush, or toilet paper. But the lack of these things was hardly the greatest source of her suffering: "The week I spent in 4b was far worse than my worst fantasies of solitary confinement. It was torture to be surrounded by these women who urgently needed professional help. It was all the more torturous because each time I tried to help one of them out of her misery, I would discover a wall—far more impervious than the walls of our cells—stood between us. I could not keep from becoming depressed myself when their 'doctor' came to examine them—he simply prescribed larger doses of Thorazine, chloral hydrate, or other tranquilizers."

Isolation, too, has taken on a life of its own as a form of punishment within punishment, akin to the dark cells at Eastern State in the early nineteenth century. Its use increased markedly in the second half of the twentieth century, when incarceration rates also increased in the wake of the War on Drugs and the closing of institutions for the mentally ill. This modern exile within exile has various names: supermax, SHU (special housing unit), isolation, segregation, seg. Little remains to link solitary confinement to Benjamin Rush's ideas. Even the small shaft of light, the oculus, the "Eye of God," has disappeared. There may be some natural daylight in a cell, but inmates now live on the other side of Edison's dream. Fluorescent lights stare back at them, even at night, and some prisoners are watched by a more sinister eye. They may be continually monitored by video feed, which only increases the feeling expressed two hundred years ago by the Marquis de Lafayette upon seeing Eastern State for the first time: "None have exceeded—none have equalled that single oppression of being . . . exposed to the view of two eyes, watching my every motion, taking from my very thoughts every idea of privacy."

This sentence within a sentence, not prescribed in manner or length by a court, is indeterminate in length and sometimes can be extraordinarily long. At Pelican Bay's SHUs, which can hold over a thousand prisoners in isolation, seventy-eight prisoners have been in isolation—with few visits and rarely a human touch—for more than twenty years. Almost five hundred have lived in SHUs for at least ten years, and many hundreds have been confined there for between three months and five years. They might have access to some books, less often to television or radio.

Nationwide, this solitary population is more fluid than the general prison population, so estimates of its numbers are not as certain as those for general prisoners. Solitary Watch, an organization that investigates prison conditions and publicizes the use of solitary confinement, estimates that there may be over eighty thousand prisoners in solitary confinement at any one time in the United States. Other estimates hover closer to twenty-five thousand.

Even in solitude, the noise is unceasing. Random cries and howls. Screams. Rattling. Banging. Shouting. Prisoners in solitary continue to find ways to communicate by speaking through conduits, passing notes, or simply calling to one another. There is no work, but those who know something about survival would certainly understand a man getting up to hammer his leather before daybreak. As prison advocate and writer Keramet Reiter has observed, the ones who do best "develop rigid, repetitive routines to get through the long days." Exercise, preparing legal work, reading, learning a language.

The dimensions of the solitary cell haven't changed much over time. For the modern imagination, its size has been compared to that of a parking space, and it shares the same basic features of Charles Williams's cell: a bed bolted to the wall, a toilet and sink. Instead of Williams's workbench, perhaps a small desk. "Even in these sparse conditions, ingenuity abounds," Reiter notes. "Prisoners describe mixing colored candies such as M&Ms or jellybeans with droplets of water to make paint." There may be modern versions of homey touches in the cell—akin to the dyed walls and homemade clocks of the early Eastern State cells—such as photographs on the desk or wall, though what is allowed into the cells is severely restricted.

Time doesn't separate us from these prisoners' solitude. No matter how remote the facility, they live along with us in this moment, absent the slant of old light, without the surround of rust and crumbling stone. Now the size and sparseness of a solitary cell stands in greater contrast to the world beyond the prison walls, where American kitchens and dining rooms and bedrooms have grown considerably since the early nineteenth century. Houses where six people once lived now shelter two. Most Americans have far more possessions than their economic counterparts of the early nineteenth century, and even the country's working poor are surrounded by material goods that would be unimaginable to Charles Williams and his contemporaries. As well, Americans today are accustomed to a mobility any early-nineteenth-century citizen could not have imagined, moving farther and more quickly than in the past. It seems as if the dimensions of everything in society have increased except those of a solitary cell.

The comments of any modern prisoner in solitary would likely sound familiar to Charles Williams, Eugenia Ginzburg, and Vera Figner. "The first three years of my sentence I spent in solitary confinement on death row," recalled Sharon Wiggins, who was incarcerated in a modern Pennsylvania prison. "It's like what I perceive blindness to be: you kind of lose your balance; there's nothing that steadies you. When you lose contact with other people it leaves you in a kind of darkness, a limbo. It's like being in a dark room with a blindfold on. There's no visual light, but, after a time, your imagination creates light for you."

It's difficult for those confined in solitary even to return to the general prison population. One prisoner serving time in the Maine State Prison remarked: "And then they let me out into population. And to be honest with you, I was weirded out because you're in a cell 23 hours a day, you're not used to people walking behind you, talking to you out loud. And getting out felt really weird, kind of like the first day at a school, except, like, 100 times worse, you know what I mean? It's weird being around groups of people after being so segregated for so long."

The challenges are even more daunting when those incarcerated in solitary are released into the world. A former prisoner's sense of isolation from the human community also is likely more profound now than it was in 1829, since the distance between prison's solitude and silence and daily life is more pronounced than ever; the pace of life, faster. "You lose all feeling," remarked one young prisoner upon release from solitary in the Maine State Prison. "You become immune to everything. You're not the same after spending so much time by yourself in those conditions. I don't care who you are, you don't come out the same person. I did 11 months in a seg unit and went from there straight home . . . I got home, there was five people there, and I felt like there was 5,000 people there. And ultimately, for my first couple of months, I locked myself in my camper."

And what of Benjamin Rush's vision of transformation in a prison population that includes agnostics, atheists, Christians, Muslims, Jews, Hindus, Buddhists, Sikhs, Native Americans . . . The formal spiritual programs are more various now than Eastern State's Bible study and Christian Sunday worship, listened to through the food drawer. Often an assortment of communal contemplative practices, such as centering prayer, Transcendental Meditation, and Buddhist rituals, are offered within the same prison. Participation is voluntary, and the aims are not only spiritual. They're practical, too: helping the incarcerated to deal with their restlessness and tendency toward violence, and with the crushing circumstances of daily life; helping them to find a way of acceptance—to bear the moment and the years, the crowds and the noise.

There may not be silence in a contemporary prison, but there is time, and in that time some prisoners find more than practical help. Joe Labriola, incarcerated at the Massachusetts Correctional Institution Shirley, had been sentenced as a young man to life in prison for first-degree murder. "I immersed myself in the library with the purpose of reading every book in it to escape facing what I had done," he wrote. Later, when he was placed in solitary—where the reading choices were limited to the Bible and the Koran—he began reading the Bible "out of mind-numbing boredom." Labriola was what he himself called "a dedicated recalcitrant," and he found himself in solitary more than a few times. Eventually reading as an escape became reading as reckoning: "Soon I found myself not just reading but understanding and, most importantly of all, believing."

On one trip to solitary, Labriola found a book under the mattress, left there by the man who'd occupied the cell before him. It was Thomas Merton's *Seeds of Contemplation.* "The book was illegal . . . I could only read it when I was sure the guard was not making a round," Labriola recalled. "I read it, I ate it. I wrote down lines page by page with the nub of a pencil. I shouted out passages to men in other cells through the barred window." Eventually a priest smuggled more of Merton's work in to him. "I read his poetry aloud to hear the words echo off the steel and cement enclosure."

For Merton, the formality and structure of the monastic observances weren't unimportant—he taught them to the novices for two decades; explained their meaning; was invested in the Church and abided its authority, even when he chafed against it —but he understood that the spiritual journey was beyond ritual, custom, architecture, or authority: "What is essential in the monastic life is not embedded in buildings, is not embedded in clothing, is not necessarily embedded even in a rule. It is somewhere along the lines of something deeper than a rule. It is concerned with this business of total inner transformation. All other things serve that end."

At Shirley razor wire and locks and guards and surveillance equipment stand between the prisoners and anything of the outside world—its cities and countryside and citizens. But Merton's words made their way in, and more than forty years after Labriola first picked up the Bible, then *Seeds of Contemplation,* and with the help of a Merton scholar who visited the prison, he and a handful of other prisoners formed the forty-first chapter of the International Thomas Merton Society. Labriola wasn't the only one of its members serving life for murder.

The men have access to a donated library, perhaps one of the largest collections of Merton's work outside of Bellarmine University in Kentucky, where his papers are kept. They read Merton's writings and meet regularly, gathering benches in a circle, to discuss them. In a noisy place where almost everything has been taken away—their loved ones and their privacy, the liberty to walk through a door or eat what they'd like, their control of time—the books offer both communication and a chance to find what silence can offer—the freedom to think, to form one's own ideas, and, perhaps, to be changed.

22

intervals of silence

EVEN AS CONTEMPORARY life pushes silence to the corners, a longing for it persists, as does faith that it offers something the noise of the world cannot provide. And just as Benjamin Rush did in the eighteenth century, we moderns often accord silence a moral weight and invest it with hope of discovery. Some of us deliberately seek intervals of it—weeks, days, hours, even just a few minutes every morning. Some of us find what we can. American writer Doris Grumbach recalled a conversation she had with a physician who told her he didn't mind undergoing an MRI, a medical test that required him to lie inside a cylinder for an extended period while the machine produced images of his internal organs: "He said it was the only quiet time he had had in a long time, and he was able to think very well in the stillness and silence the examination provided."

Grumbach recorded her own conscious inquiry into silence. For fifty days one winter during the 1990s, while her partner was away on an extended trip, she deliberately kept to herself within the world they ordinarily inhabited together. In their house on a cove along the coast of Maine, her silence was by no means total. She often listened to music, and at times to the news. She drove into town on necessary errands, to the library, to Sunday services. But she tamped down her social interactions and outside intrusions in order to spend her days largely in silence and solitude. To begin with, her expectations were akin to the austerity most of us imagine of monastic life. "Did I think talking to my acquaintances would affect the purity of my fifty days?" asked Grumbach. "I suppose I did, being an intolerant absolutist and believing, I think, that any break in the tapestry of silence would cause the whole plan, the unconditional experiment, to come undone." And later she remarked that the sound of crows, or of logs collapsing into the ash in the woodstove, "roughed up the smooth nothingness I hoped for."

But as she began to inhabit the silence, she discovered its nuances, its demands and complexities. At times it felt like an exposure, both expansive and unsettling. With nothing to cut off thought or distract her, she found herself deeply investigating the world, her memory, her work, the habits of her own mind, all the while dwelling in a silence that seemed to expand over time and amplify not only the smallest sounds, but thought and memory as well. She was prompted to question her social self, the world in which "our points of reference are always our neighbors, the people in the village or in the city, our acquaintance at school." Life without those reassurances could be sobering, and sometimes frightening: "In the silence I eagerly sought, I *could* hear myself think, and what I heard was, sadly, not often worth listening to."

But the moods and meanings of her silence shifted every bit as much as the sea smoke rising from the cold Atlantic in the distance. There was also a great richness in it, and it presented the opportunity to forge something deeper, or perhaps new: "The absence of other voices compelled me to listen more intently to the inner one. I became aware that the interior voice, so often before stifled or stilled entirely by what I thought others wanted to hear, or what I considered to be socially acceptable, grew gratifyingly louder, more insistent . . . and I became aware that, with nothing to interrupt it, it now commanded my entire attention . . . In this way, living alone in quiet . . . I was apt to hear news of an inner terrain, an endolithic self, resembling the condition of lichens embedded in rock."

Just as Merton was so often to insist, Grumbach found this interior journey wasn't selfish. She wasn't rejecting her friends or the wider world. Rather, her silence and solitude provided an opportunity for deepening social connections. In it she realized that friendship was not merely companionship, but an ongoing conversation that inhabited even solitude: "What others regard as retreat from them or rejection of them is not those things at all but instead a breeding ground for greater friendship, a culture for deeper involvement, eventually, with them."

And if it could expose, it could also magnify the meaning of so much that mattered to her. Words, for one: "Care in the use of language came with seldom hearing it or using it aloud. I discovered that when I began to write in those dark, early mornings I approached the whole act of word choice warily . . . Every word I put down on paper seemed to take on a kind of holiness, a special, single precision." Additionally, the aural world provided a deepening no less complex. The winter possessed its own acoustics—sounds reverberating off the cold clear air, off frost and ice—in a season that amplified her interiority, with its low temperatures, storms, and early dark: "I felt the human force of the sun rising and setting, the temperature, atmosphere, weather. Nothing came between them and me."

Her home, which sheltered her in her silence for those fifty days, was also inextricably tied up with her exploration: "The house expanded. It now seemed to have more rooms than before, even with three upstairs rooms closed off. I found that the silence I maintained also increased until it filled every space, pushed out the walls, invaded closets, drawers, and cupboards. Eventually it seeped out through the house's seams and surrounded the whole property with a blessed, protective wall of quiet." Surely she would have recognized William of St. Thierry's words to the novices at Mont Dieu: "Love your inner cell then, love your outward cell too, and give to each of them the care which belongs to it. Let the outward cell shelter you, not hide you away."

Her days—difficult, meaningful, questioning—illustrate the complexity of what we often take for austerity. Her sojourn into silence did have an end point, marked by departure. One March day she left the house to join her partner in Washington, DC. Even a few months prior, she could not have imagined where the days of snow and cold would take her. And the same undertaking in another place or at another time could have gone much differently, of course. But Grumbach's experience fell on the side of richness, and as she closed the door to return to the world, a deep affection for her outer shell rose up. She felt as if she was abandoning an old friend.

While Grumbach's engagement with silence was anticipated and intentional, and undertaken in familiar surroundings, British writer Patrick Leigh Fermor had a more happenstance encounter with silence, though it was no less profound. Exhausted by the demands of his mid-twentieth-century urban life, he traveled from Paris to the Benedictine abbey of St. Wandrille, in northern France, on the advice of a friend. He knew almost nothing about the place or the monks and arrived unannounced, "without even the excuse that I wished to go on retreat," he remembered. He was looking for little more than "somewhere quiet and cheap" to work on a book.

Having arrived unprepared for what he would find, Fermor, predictably enough, wasn't immediately at ease among the monks. He had a difficult time settling into the silence. The abbey felt like a tomb to him. Overcome as he was by depression and loneliness, his first impulse was to sleep, and sleep deeply. But after a few days he fell into the rhythms of the monastic world and its rituals. As his nerved-up life dropped away, the silence began to feel expansive rather than oppressive. He was able to sleep in a way he'd never had before. His concentration deepened, and the monastery itself became "a silent university, a country house, a castle hanging in mid-air beyond the reach of ordinary troubles and vexations."

Fermor, who unlike Grumbach had cut himself off from his daily life and contemporary events, realized that the journey had brought him to another world entirely. The monks, hidden deep in their cowls, had at first seemed indistinguishable from one another, but after a while they began to take on complex dimensions. Some of their mystery fell away: "I found no trace of the Dark Ages here . . . There was no doubt of the respect in which they held the cause to which their lives were devoted; but their company was like that of any civilised well educated Frenchman . . . the only difference being a gentleness, a lack of haste, and a calmness which is common to the whole community."

Still, the monks, in their silence, poverty, obedience, and abstinence, presented a "staggering difference from the ordinary life that we lead." Their world had changed little over the centuries, while every aspect of society beyond their walls had evolved and speeded up. He perceived that the things most of us take as life itself, and value as essential, meant almost nothing to them. "The two ways of life do not share a single attribute," he observed, "and the thoughts, ambitions, sounds, light, time and mood that surround the inhabitants of a cloister are not only unlike anything to which one is accustomed, but in some curious way, seem its exact reverse."

While the world he'd left behind seemed marked by the pressure of time, within the monastery time seemed, to Fermor, to pass "with disconcerting speed . . . There are no landmarks to divide it up except the cycle of the seasons." But he also discovered silence's amplitude. In their quest for the spiritual, the monks created something helpful even to the nonbeliever, or half believer, looking to silence for entirely secular ends. "I, not the monks, was the escapist," remarked Fermor. "For my hosts, the Abbey was a springboard into eternity; for me a retiring place to write a book and spring more effectively back into the maelstrom. Strange that the same habitat should prove favourable to ambitions so glaringly opposed."

As a visitor to their world, Fermor may well have had fewer obligations in his day—and perhaps more quiet—than the monks themselves, although while they looked intently toward the infinite, Fermor, for whatever respite St. Wandrille provided, remained oriented toward his world. "World" in its old meaning: "the age of man." Yet his few weeks' stay marked him profoundly.

His departure, if anything, was more wrenching than his arrival had been. Once he stepped outside the monastery walls, he felt he was entering an "inferno of noise and vulgarity." The billboards along the roadways appeared impossibly garish. However harsh the world was, he reaccustomed himself to the glare and noise—it was his world, after all—but he would return to St. Wandrille, and he would visit numerous other monasteries—Solesmes, La Trappe, the rock monasteries of Cappadocia, and the ruins of Monte Cassino among them—to record a vanishing way of life.

Like Fermor, my most profound encounter with silence—almost forty years ago now—was unwitting. I was just out of college, living on Nantucket Island and trying to figure out a direction for my life. One winter I agreed to house-sit a small cape down a dirt road on the remote eastern edge of the island, in a place called Squam. I hadn't really thought out how the house would feel in winter, when so much of Nantucket was tamped down and almost all the other homes on the road were closed up for the season. No sounds but what the wind and the cold Atlantic made. I had a staticky radio for distraction, and there was a telephone. But other than that, I was pretty much on my own with the wide sky, the marsh hawks, the bare scrub oaks, the winter surf.

My silence and solitude were by no means complete. I'd drive the eight or so miles into town to work in a small bakery and restaurant. I'd spend time with friends in town, and friends would come out to visit me. Even so, the huge silence of winter was the defining note of those months. It could be difficult, especially during the nights when the house took the brunt of the wind, the sound of which could only be allayed by the crackling of a wood fire. During the fiercest storms I'd gather some blankets and sleep next to the hearth.

But that winter was also my first serious attempt at a writing life, and I think those days allowed me to glean an understanding of what was possible in silence. I believe now that the time in Squam gave me the freedom to begin, and once I'd begun, to work intently. It also gave me room to inquire into the life that I hoped for and allowed me to make large decisions. I think I was more daring with my choices than I otherwise might have been.

The silence may have been unsought to begin with, but it became a complex part of my life after a while. I grew to love the days when I could so intently focus on my work. Grew to love the long walks in that austere landscape, and the continuity of thought that silence allowed. I also feared it at times. It could seem like a test, and I wondered the same things the world always wonders about silence: Was it an avoidance, an escape?

Squam, and Nantucket itself, wasn't a place for me to spend my whole life. I knew that. I eventually left the house and the island, and joined the fray. I reaccustomed myself to a world dense with the human sounds of crowds and chaos, of cars persisting through swirling snow that lost its whiteness once fallen —a world that will hardly suffer stillness, or even delay. I'd associated silence so much with wildness that equally hard to hear were the sounds of tameness, of church bells and ice cream trucks.

I've had to learn to maneuver my way around more than noise. During the nearly forty years since I left Squam, the same tools that have so thoroughly changed my writing life have also assaulted silence. The quiet key clicks that replaced the scratch of a pen and the clacking of a typewriter eventually opened my house to the world in a profound way. I became intimately connected with almost everyone and everything. Then the machines became portable, and after a while they shrank to the size of a pocket. Like nearly everyone else, I live in a world where there is never any need to be alone, never any need to listen to the surrounding silence. And once you stop listening to it, you become impatient with it. Perhaps such connection with the world has proved to be a greater threat than noise to silence—for distraction is also its opposite.

Just as forty years ago I questioned what I was closing myself off from, now at times I wonder what I left behind in that silence, what I have lost in my accommodation to the world. Even so, that winter on the island stays with me. Sometimes during a harried day or a time of overwhelming obligations—when silence feels more difficult to reach than the other side of the globe—I remind myself of the house in Squam. I can still conjure the feeling of space around me, especially around my ears, and I have felt something similar—the enclosed expansiveness allowed by austerity—in the chapter house and warming room at Sénanque.

I know one thing for certain: silence will not present itself unbidden amid the noise of the world. If I want it, I have to make space for it, and there is always a choice to make that space. It may be Thomas Merton's lifelong commitment, or Doris Grumbach's deliberate inquiry, or Patrick Leigh Fermor's last resort. The decision to seek silence is the beginning of the encounter, with all its attendant hopes and destabilizations. And in our time now, every decision in favor of silence is profound, even if it involves no more than deliberately turning away other things for hours or days in a week.

Silence can seem like a luxury. Or the fraught world has labeled it that way. But from what I know of it, I would argue that silence is as necessary as the constitutionally guaranteed freedom of speech that we so carefully guard and endlessly ponder, for it affirms the meaning of speech even as it provides a path to inner life, to beauty and observation and appreciation. It presents the opportunity for a true reckoning with the self, with external obligation, and with power.

As much as we need silence, it needs us. It needs more than a few hundred monasteries where a few thousand souls guard most of what's left of it. Like all else threatened by our onslaught, it must be attended to and valued, given space and time in which to gain strength again. And the stronger the silence, the more it will be able to withstand the noise and distractions of our world.

Coda

For every form retains life, and a fossil is not merely a being that once lived, but one that is still alive, asleep in its form.

—Gaston Bachelard, *The Poetics of Space*

in ruins

IT'S KNOWN AS the Ghost House—the tubular steel outline of Benjamin Franklin's Philadelphia home on Market Street where Benjamin Rush articulated his idea for the penitentiary on that March night in 1787, just a few blocks from the wharves along the Delaware, among pubs and printers, wheelwrights, apothecaries, and carpenters. Franklin's house was razed early in the nineteenth century, and now the only remaining in-place artifacts—vestiges of the privy pits, wells, and foundation—are visible through glass portals in the ground. Those charged with restoring his home in the late twentieth century knew the house was three stories high and included ten rooms. They could trace its perimeter. But beyond that, they uncovered only scant details concerning household goods and furnishings. So, rather than imagine the lost from fragments, they reconstructed the house's frame alone. Now, certain lines—without flourish, open to wind and rain—rise for the imagination. Nothing to speak of time passing. Nothing further from the feel of an eighteenth-century home, with its tea steeping, voices in close quarters, cinders falling from a stirred fire.

I stood in the midst of the steel frame enjoying the light spring wind, but I couldn't seem to conjure the library or dining room where Franklin's friends congregated to hear Rush deliver his vision of the future of justice. So I turned in the direction of the city center and began the scant three-mile walk to Eastern State. The architecture of later centuries crowded in around me. I threaded through high-rises that narrowed my view of the sky above, past cafés, restaurants, investment firms, and clothing stores built upon what had been open country back in 1829. Traffic and construction noises closed off distant sounds.

Eventually I turned right onto one of the numbered streets —21st or 22nd—and began a gentle uphill walk that skirted the museums. The sky opened up again and the world grew quieter as I approached the old row houses of the Fairmount neighborhood. Then, a few streets away, blocking my view of the city beyond, I saw the thirty-foot wall of Schuylkill stone that seemed to interrupt the neighborhood that had long since inched up from the city center and then flowed around the penitentiary wall. Eastern State and the neighborhood lived side by side for many decades—the world within keeping its own time, separate from ordinary days, though the sounds of the world beyond and the bustle of its freedoms surely leaked in to haunt its prisoners in the quieter hours.

Strangely, the penitentiary stands more stable in its afterlife than it did as a working prison. It began to change almost as soon as it opened on that October day in 1829 when Charles Williams arrived, for it soon became apparent that there would not be adequate space to accommodate all the prisoners to come. So John Haviland altered his dream of symmetry to include upper floors on the yet unbuilt ranges, each with an extra room to compensate for the lack of an outdoor exercise yard. His original plan would house fewer than 300. Once it was finally completed in 1844, it could house 586. Even so, in the aftermath of the Civil War, the demand for cells outgrew even the added space, and the warden had no choice but to double up prisoners in the cells. There is a photograph from the later decades of the nineteenth century showing two men in one cell, each at work at his cobbler's bench. They are facing each other, though their heads are bent to their tasks. In the twelve-by-eight-foot room, among the shoes and shoe lasts, the leather and cords: a rocking chair, a small pile of books, a model schooner, pictures on the walls, hanging lace adorning a shelf.

Yet the official practice of silent and separate incarceration didn't end until 1913, when Eastern State converted to a congregate system of incarceration and strict silence was no longer formally enforced. Prison authorities then squeezed in more cell blocks constructed of reinforced concrete, and built communal areas, mostly where Haviland's exercise yards had stood: a long, narrow dining hall, workrooms, a chapel, a synagogue. They fashioned a large outdoor exercise space. But the world built for isolation was never really suited for a communal prison and could not be satisfactorily reconfigured. The cells were small. No renovation could create adequate common areas. Prisoners and officials continued to struggle with overcrowding.

In its jerry-rigged state, the old penitentiary functioned as a congregate prison for more than a half century, during which time it published its own magazine. The inmates played chess with each other and formed singing clubs. They watched movies together and, eventually, television. Brief, silent films show prisoners playing football, or standing in groups in the open, or sitting together atop the walls of the same exercise yards that once kept Charles Williams and his contemporaries from seeing one another. Their legs dangle from the top of the walls as they cheer on a boxing match on the prison grounds.

Even before Eastern State closed in 1970 and the remaining inmates were transferred to another state prison, there had been discussions regarding what to do with the ten acres that by then stood in the middle of Philadelphia. The land had extraordinary value, but the penitentiary had been designed as a fortress. Its wall and structures would be prohibitively expensive to demolish. So, once it closed, the prison stood abandoned for decades while ideas for preservation or redevelopment were proposed and defeated time and again. A shopping center? An industrial park? Residences? Create a monument to Eastern State by demolishing all but one wing? Tear down everything and create a park?

By 1987, less than two decades after the last prisoners at Eastern State left on the last bus, what was left to preserve had become its own question. A good part of John Haviland's early nineteenth-century design had long been obscured by the subsequent renovations, and once all care was abandoned, the fate of the penitentiary seemed, in some respects, not much different from that of a neglected cherry orchard. Trees between the ranges overtopped the roofs. A colony of feral cats thrived. Weed seeds blew into the old exercise yards and took hold. They flourished, and then their seed heads dried and scattered.

The remnants of Haviland's design and all the renovations that succeeded it were subject to the same winds and rain, though they were not all equal in their disintegration. One engineer who visited the decaying penitentiary suggested that "the forces of nature represented the construction history played in reverse. Those buildings and building systems added most recently were proving to be the least durable and were in the most advanced state of deterioration; followed by those of the early twentieth century and then of the late nineteenth, with the likelihood being that the process would leave, in the end, only the Haviland work remaining."

As the neighborhoods around Eastern State prospered and grew, the world within the walls further decayed. Flooding destroyed the electrical and plumbing systems. Ceilings collapsed. Rust spread. The City of Philadelphia, which by then owned the property, decided, finally, to honor Eastern State by preserving it as a stabilized ruin. When it opened to the public in 1994, the danger of collapse remained appreciable, so the first visitors had to wear hard hats and sign liability waivers.

Those requirements were lifted by the time I visited in the twenty-first century. During my last trip I walked freely for hours through peeling corridors and the weedy prison grounds. From one corner of the compound, I could see skyscrapers beyond. Then I entered one of the few remaining original walled-in exercise yards, and I looked up to the measured portion of bright sky that was equal in its dimension to what Williams would have beheld in 1829. I circled back to the first range to peer into the mock-up of the original cell as Charles Williams would have known it. The eight-inch circular window, even on that sunny day, let in so little light that the cell seemed shrouded in perpetual dusk. Things that could have been his were sitting in their shadows with all the futures of the penitentiary decaying around them: the bed, the workbench, the shoemaker's tools. The metal toilet rusted in a corner.

What is emphasized here in the exhibits is not the silence in particular. The extraordinary, the small but spectacular washes of history, get attention: escapes and attempted escapes; a dog held as a prisoner; Al Capone's cell with its Oriental rugs and wingback chair and velvet bedspread. Time also has had a say in what has come forward. The prison records become clearer, more complete, more fully illustrated, as they grow closer to the present day. The largest share of information about the prisoners has been gleaned from the records of the twentieth century, which contain photographs and voices on tape. Some of the photos are displayed on the walls of one of the ranges—prisoners and guards, a few who were both. The 1950s and '60s are largely represented.

The strangest photograph may be from the 1950s. Two men crouch in the open yard, each holding the end of a miniature clothesline with doll-size dresses and pants hanging on it. A table fan brought into the open blows on the clothes. There is no explanation for what is going on. It reminded me of the room of diminutive replicas in the tomb of the Egyptian king Meketre. The room, closed off for thousands of years, might be hidden still had not a worker on an archaeological dig noticed the way stone chips kept falling into a crack. When archaeologist H. E. Winlock shone a light into the crack, a miniature world revealed itself. "A tall slender girl gazed across at me perfectly composed," he wrote. "A gang of little men with sticks in their upraised hands drove spotted oxen; rowers tugged at their oars on a fleet of boats . . . in uncanny silence, as though the distance back over the forty centuries I looked across was too great for even an echo to reach my ears." The diggers uncovered a bakery with men kneading dough, a brewhouse, fishing and sailing vessels, weaving rooms, a dozen houses all carefully carved for the tomb so that in the afterlife the animals and people and homes familiar to Meketre could accompany him on the passage to the next world, where he could possess the life he'd always known.

Among the stabilization efforts of the prison there are modest restorations. What has been restored is what has been funded through special revenue-raising campaigns: most commonly those large spaces for congregation built during the later years of the prison, and in particular the synagogue, which was a rarity for a prison—usually one meeting place served for the services of all denominations. Restoration involved clearing away six inches of collapsed plaster and crumbling masonry, which turned up, buried underneath the debris, Hanukkah song sheets, remnants of the Torah ark, fragments of paint.

After hours of sober puzzlement among the ruins, I walked down a swept path. On either side of me I saw piles of crumbled plaster, wire mesh, rotting lumber. Then I opened a pale blue door, clear and clean in the midst of old dust, and stepped into the pristine blue and white synagogue, lovingly restored. Star on the ceiling, the Torah ark, the reader's table centered in its own world of consolation. I sat on one of the benches that had been made by prisoners, which may be considered imperfect in the world beyond the wall, where its homemade inaccuracies might not stand up to expectations. But it is beautifully serviceable here. Out of the wind in a silence beyond the ruins of silence, amid all the thoughts darkening the already dark places: a moment of peace.

By the time I roused myself to leave, the light felt late, the day was leaning toward its close. The wall, once built to keep hundreds of the convicted in, now keeps everyone out past five o'clock, when, I imagine, other than the hums and clicks of modern surveillance equipment, nothing interferes with the old silence. But it is absent anyone to hear the scurryings, absent human will or desire. No one imposing silence. No one enduring it. No one to fear the small things. The preserved and the ruined are equally lit, and equally dark.

acknowledgments

I'm grateful once again to the MacDowell Colony, a place that has been a help to me during my entire writing life, for providing me with the quietest of places to work. Visits to Mount St. Mary's Abbey in Wrentham, Massachusetts, and Emery House in West Newbury, Massachusetts, steeped me in silence. Thanks to the Lesley University Professional Development Fund and the Maine Arts Commission for providing funding for research.

The Curtis Memorial Library in Brunswick Maine, the Bowdoin College Library, and the Maine Interlibrary Loan Service were indispensable to me during my years of research. Gratitude also to the Historical Society of Pennsylvania and the Kislak Center for Special Collections at the University of Pennsylvania. Thanks to all the individuals and organizations who chose to preserve Eastern State Penitentiary. And, *in memoriam,* thanks to Mimi Beman, who once lent me use of her house in Squam.

I've had the support of many friends during the writing of this book. Thanks, in particular, to Elizabeth Brown, who accompanied me on my initial visit to Sénanque, where the first thoughts for *Silence* began; and to Sandrine Robin Brox for the second visit. I'm grateful to Alex Johnson and Kyoko Mori for their candid insights; to Pam Petro for her affirming friendship; to Andrea Sulzer for talks over tea; to John Bisbee for his ear.

I am grateful to Barbara Jatkola for her careful work copyediting the manuscript.

Silence took many years to write, and the process was often bewildering. I don't know how I would have proceeded had I not had the enduring and enthusiastic support of my agent, Cynthia Cannell, and my editor, Deanne Urmy.

bibliographic note

Silence owes much to the works of Thomas Merton, in particular: *The Seven Storey Mountain: An Autobiography of Faith* (New York: Harcourt, 1998); *The Sign of Jonas* (New York: Harcourt, 1981); *A Search for Solitude: The Journals of Thomas Merton,* vol. 3, *1952–1960* (New York: HarperSanFrancisco, 1997); *Turning Toward the World: The Journals of Thomas Merton,* vol. 4, *1960–1963* (New York: HarperSanFrancisco, 1997); and *The Asian Journal of Thomas Merton* (New York: New Directions, 1975). I'm grateful to all the collections of Merton's correspondence, in particular *Striving Toward Being: The Letters of Thomas Merton and Czeslaw Milosz* (New York: Farrar, Straus and Giroux, 1997).

Merton's writings led me to Max Picard's unstinting and beautiful *The World of Silence* (Wichita, KS: Eighth Day Press, 2002), which is one of the books I returned to again and again during my years of work in an attempt to understand the meaning of silence. I'm indebted, too, to the accounts of chosen sojourns:

Doris Grumbach, *Fifty Days of Solitude* (Boston: Beacon Press, 1994); Patrick Leigh Fermor, *A Time to Keep Silence* (New York: New York Review Books, 2007); and Sara Maitland, *A Book of Silence* (Berkeley, CA: Counterpoint Press, 2008).

David Heald's photographs and Terryl N. Kinder's essay in *Architecture of Silence: Cistercian Abbeys of France* (New York: Harry N. Abrams, 2000), as well as Terryl N. Kinder's *Cistercian Europe: Architecture of Contemplation* (Kalamazoo, MI: Cistercian Publications, 2002), helped me to understand the practice and the architecture of the Cistercian world. So, too, did Benedict of Nursia, *The Rule of Saint Benedict* (New York: Doubleday, 1975); Michael Casey, *Strangers to the City: Reflections on the Beliefs and Values of the Rule of Saint Benedict* (Brewster, MA: Paraclete Press, 2010); and William of St. Thierry, *The Golden Epistle: A Letter to the Brethren at Mont Dieu* (Kalamazoo, MI: Cistercian Publications, 1980).

The experiences of women monastics were brought to life by a series of works: Silvia Evangelisti, "'We Do Not Have It, and We Do Not Want It': Women, Power, and Convent Reform in Florence," *Sixteenth Century Journal* 34, no. 3 (Fall 2003); Ulrike Strasser, "Cloistering Women's Past: Conflicting Accounts of Enclosure in a Seventeenth-Century Munich Nunnery," in *Gender in Early Modern German History* (Cambridge: Cambridge University Press, 2002); and Bernadette Barrière, "The Cistercian Convent of Coyroux in the Twelfth and Thirteenth Centuries," in "Monastic Architecture for Women," special issue, *Gesta* 31, no. 2 (1992).

Several authors helped me understand the bridge between the world of chosen and imposed silence: Andrew Skotnicki's works *Criminal Justice and the Catholic Church* (Lanham, MD: Rowman & Littlefield, 2007) and "God's Prisoners: Penal Confinement and the Creation of Purgatory," *Modern Theology* 22, no. 1 (January 2006); Thorsten Sellin's essays "The House of Correction for Boys in the Hospice of Saint Michael in Rome," *Journal of the American Institute of Criminal Law and Criminology* 20, no. 4 (February 1930), and "Dom Jean Mabillon, A Prison Reformer of the Seventeenth Century," *Journal of the American Institute of Criminal Law and Criminology* 17, no. 4 (February 1927).

For information concerning Eastern State Penitentiary, I am indebted to Negley K. Teeters and John D. Shearer, *The Prison at Philadelphia, Cherry Hill: The Separate System of Penal Discipline, 1829–1913* (New York: Columbia University Press for Temple University Publications, 1957); and Thomas B. McElwee, *A Concise History of the Eastern Penitentiary of Pennsylvania: Together with a Detailed Statement of the Proceedings of the Committee . . .* (Philadelphia: Neall & Massey, 1835). For an understanding of the nineteenth-century penitentiary and prison systems in general: Jodi Schorb, *Reading Prisoners: Literature, Literacy, and the Transformation of American Punishment, 1700–1845* (New Brunswick, NJ: Rutgers University Press, 2014); Adam J. Hirsch, *The Rise of the Penitentiary: Prisons and Punishment in Early America* (New Haven, CT: Yale University Press, 1992); W. David Lewis, *From Newgate to Dannemora: The Rise of the Penitentiary in New York, 1796–1848* (Ithaca, NY: Cornell University

Press, 2009); Orlando Faulkland Lewis, *The Development of American Prisons and Prison Customs, 1776–1845* (Montclair, NJ: Patterson Smith, 1967); *The Oxford History of the Prison: The Practice of Punishment in Western Society,* ed. Norval Morris and David J. Rothman (New York: Oxford University Press, 1998); and Michael Meranze, *Laboratories of Virtue: Punishment, Revolution, and Authority in Philadelphia, 1760–1835* (Chapel Hill: University of North Carolina Press, 1996).

Two profound meditations on Piranesi's *Carceri* helped deepen my understanding of the wages of imposed silence: Marguerite Yourcenar's "The Dark Brain of Piranesi," in *The Dark Brain of Piranesi and Other Essays* (New York: Farrar, Straus and Giroux, 1984); and Aldous Huxley's introduction to the *Carceri,* "Aldous Huxley on Piranesi's Prisons," *{feuilleton},* August 25, 2006, http://www.johncoulthart.com/feuilleton/2006/08/25/aldous-huxley-on-piranesis-prisons/. In addition, I owe a debt of gratitude to three memoirs of solitary incarceration: Austin Reed, *The Life and Adventures of a Haunted Convict* (New York: Random House, 2016); Eugenia Semyonovna Ginzburg, *Journey into the Whirlwind* (New York: Harcourt, 1995); and Vera Figner, *Memoirs of a Revolutionist* (DeKalb: Northern Illinois University Press, 1991).

notes

1. MAN OF SORROWS

PAGE

4 *"such an entire seclusion": Journal of the Senate of the Commonwealth of Pennsylvania . . .*, vol. 31 (Harrisburg, PA: William F. Buyers, 1820), 339.

6 *"convey to the mind":* Quoted in Negley K. Teeters and John D. Shearer, *The Prison at Philadelphia, Cherry Hill: The Separate System of Penal Discipline, 1829–1913* (New York: Columbia University Press for Temple University Publications, 1957), 59.

"Let its doors": Benjamin Rush, *An Enquiry into the Effects of Public Punishments upon Criminals, and upon Society,* quoted in Michael Meranze, *Laboratories of Virtue: Punishment, Revolution, and Authority in Philadelphia, 1760–1835* (Chapel Hill: University of North Carolina Press, 1996), 133.

7 *"Suffering is one":* Oscar Wilde, "De Profundis," in *De Profundis and Other Writings* (Harmondsworth, England: Penguin English Library, 1973), 140–41.

8 *The first prisoner:* Information on the structure of the penitentiary, the contents of the cells, and the meals provided is from Teeters and Shearer, *The Prison at Philadelphia,* 56–57, 62–64, 77–78.

10 *"deadeye":* Teeters and Shearer, *The Prison at Philadelphia,* 69.

"I never met with": Harriet Martineau, *Retrospect of Western Travel,* vol. 1, *Prisons* (London: Saunders and Otley, 1838), 208–9.

"I already hear": Benjamin Rush, *An Enquiry into the Effects of Public Punishments upon Criminals, and upon Society . . . ,* in *Essays: Literary, Moral and Philosophical,* ed. Michael Meranze (Schenectady, NY: Union College Press, 1988), 91.

11 *narrower than:* For the comparison of the cell size to a cherry tree, I am indebted to John Berger's essay "An Apple Orchard (An Open Letter to Raymond Barre, Mayor of Lyon)," in *The Shape of a Pocket* (New York: Pantheon Books, 2001). Berger suggests that the mayor plant an orchard on the site of an old prison and compares the spacing of the trees to the size of the cells.

2. BENJAMIN RUSH'S VISION

13 *"the nearest resemblance":* Quoted in Henry Wilder Foote, *Annals of the King's Chapel from the Puritan Age of New England to the Present Day,* vol. 1 (Boston: Little, Brown, 1882), 86.

14 *"a bottomless pit":* Captain Alexander Smith, quoted in Peter Linebaugh, *The London Hanged: Crime and Civil Society in the Eighteenth Century* (London: Verso, 2003), 28.

"Behind the façade": "Aldous Huxley on Piranesi's Prisons," *{feuilleton},* August 25, 2006, http://www.johncoulthart.com/feuilleton/2006/08/25/aldous-huxley-on-piranesis-prisons/.

16 *called a gibbet iron:* The information on the gibbet iron is from Thorsten Sellin, "The Philadelphia Gibbet Iron," *Journal of Criminal Law, Criminology, and Police Science* 46, no. 1 (May–June 1955): 11–25.

17 *"passed Charlestown neck":* Paul Revere, letter to Rev. Dr. Jeremy Belknap, quoted in Elbridge Henry Goss, *The Life of Colonel Paul Revere,* vol. 1 (Boston: Joseph George Cupples, 1891), 193.

"a man of strife*":* Benjamin Rush, quoted in David Freeman Hawke, *Benjamin Rush: Revolutionary Gadfly* (New York: Bobbs-Merrill, 1971), 5.

"'There was no formality'": Quoted in Hawke, *Benjamin Rush,* 364.

18 *"I cannot help entertaining":* Benjamin Rush, *An Enquiry into the Effects of Public Punishments upon Criminals, and upon Society . . . ,* in *Essays: Literary, Moral and Philosophical,* ed. Michael Meranze (Schenectady, NY: Union College Press, 1988), 94.

"make bad men worse": Ibid., 80.

"destroys . . . the sense": Ibid.
"A man who has lost": Ibid.
"The men, or perhaps": Ibid., 84.

20 *"There are three kinds":* Miguel de Molinos, *The Spiritual Guide*, quoted in Richard Phillips, *Concise Remarks on Watchfulness and Silence* (London: W. Phillips, 1815), 8.
"The one corner-stone": Caroline Stephen, "Selections from *Quaker Strongholds*," in *Quaker Spirituality: Selected Writings*, ed. Douglas V. Steere (New York: Paulist Press, 1984), 246, 250.

21 *"amongst the moss-troopers":* George Fox, *An Autobiography*, ed. Rufus M. Jones (Philadelphia: Ferris and Leach, 1919), 190–91.

22 *"Who takes away":* George Fox, *An Instruction to Judges and Lawyers That They May Act . . .* (London, 1657; Early English Books Online, print edition), 7.

25 *"They were encumbered":* Roberts Vaux, *Notices of the Original, and Successive Efforts, to Improve the Discipline of the Prison at Philadelphia* (Philadelphia: Kimber and Sharpless, 1826), 22.

26 *"It took an accidental":* Hawke, *Benjamin Rush*, 364.
"All public *punishments":* Rush, *An Enquiry into the Effects of Public Punishments*, 80.
"But may not the benefit": Ibid., 85.
"An attachment to kindred": Ibid., 87.
"It is the prerogative": Ibid., 84.

3. "GOOD BY DISCIPLINE"

29 *"Let the laws be clear":* Cesare Beccaria, *An Essay on Crimes and Punishments*, trans. Edward D. Ingraham (Philadelphia: Philip H. Nicklin, 1819), 149, https://books.google.com/books/about/An_Essay_on_Crimes_and_Punishments.html?id=FRDtZqosmnEC&printsec=frontcover&source=kp_read_button#v=onepage&q="Let%20the%20laws%20be%20clear%20and%20simple%2C"%20&f=false.
"What right . . . *have men":* Ibid., 97.
"moderate the ferocity": Ibid., 104.
"What must men think": Ibid., 105–6.
"the end of punishment": Ibid., 47.

30 *"there is no allowance":* John Howard, *The State of the Prisons in England and Wales with Preliminary Observations, and an Account of Some Foreign Prisons* (Warrington, England: William Eyres, 1777), 15.

"There the petty offender": Ibid., 16.

31 *"My cloaths were":* Ibid., 13.

32 *"I was present":* Ibid., 142.

"The idea of being excluded": Jonas Hanway, *Solitude in Imprisonment: With Proper Profitable Labour and a Spare Diet, the Most Human and Effectual Means of Bringing Malefactors . . .* (London: J. Bew, 1776), 109.

"keep the greater awe": Ibid., 114.

"Solitude and silence": Howard, *The State of the Prisons in England,* 43.

33 *"It is of little advantage":* Thorsten Sellin, "The House of Correction for Boys in the Hospice of Saint Michael in Rome," *Journal of the American Institute of Criminal Law and Criminology* 20, no. 4 (February 1930): 534.

34 *"Here were sixty boys":* John Howard, quoted ibid.

"the softest conversation": Carlo Fontana, quoted in Luigi Cajani, "Surveillance and Redemption: The Casa di Correzione of San Michele a Ripa in Rome," in *Institution of Confinement: Hospitals, Asylums, and Prisons in Western Europe and North America, 1500–1950,* ed. Norbert Finzsch and Robert Jütte (Cambridge: Cambridge University Press for German Historical Institute, 1996), 306.

35 *"provided for the solitary confinement":* Benjamin Rush, *An Enquiry into the Effects of Public Punishments upon Criminals, and upon Society,* quoted in Michael Meranze, *Laboratories of Virtue: Punishment, Revolution, and Authority in Philadelphia, 1760–1835* (Chapel Hill: University of North Carolina Press, 1996), 87.

36 *"There have been many opinions":* Caleb Lownes, *An Account of the Alteration and Present State of the Penal Laws of Pennsylvania, Containing Also an Account of the Gaol and Penitentiary House of Philadelphia . . .* (Boston: Young & Minns, 1799), 12.

"adopted a plan": Ibid.

"second conviction would consign": Ibid., 22.

"at the outset branded": Orlando Faulkland Lewis, *The Development of American Prisons and Prison Customs, 1776–1845* (Montclair, NJ: Patterson Smith, 1967), 26.

37 *"put ill-behaved prisoners":* Thomas Jefferson, quoted in David McNair, "Jefferson's Jail: Lovingston's New Discovery," *The Hook,* January 26, 2006, http://www.readthehook.com/98325/architecture-jeffersons-jail-lovingstons-new-discovery.

"It was probably not": Lewis, *The Development of American Prisons,* 27.

"To acquaintances he did appear": David Freeman Hawke, *Benjamin Rush: Revolutionary Gadfly* (New York: Bobbs-Merrill, 1971), 310.
"I have no more doubt": Rush, *An Enquiry into the Effects of Public Punishments,* 90.

38 "Venerate the Lancet": Benjamin Rush, quoted in Paul E. Kopperman, "'Venerate the Lancet': Benjamin Rush's Yellow Fever Therapy in Context," *Bulletin of the History of Medicine* 78, no. 3 (Fall 2004): 573.
"To many practitioners": Kopperman, "'Venerate the Lancet'," 558.

4. JOHN HAVILAND'S STAR OF SOLITUDES

40 *"The windows are inserted":* John Haviland, daybook, vol. 1, 21, Manuscript Collection 176, Rare Books and Manuscripts, Kislak Center for Special Collections, University of Pennsylvania.
"of iron strongly secured": Ibid., 21, 23–24.
"dark and comfortless abodes": Negley K. Teeters, "Early Days of the Maine State Prison at Thomaston," *Journal of Criminal Law and Criminology* 38, no. 2 (1947): 108.
"were literally jugs*":* Ibid., 107.

41 *Haviland's heating plan:* Mention of the Derbyshire Infirmary can be found in Haviland, daybook, vol. 1, 22.

42 *"best calculated for* watching*":* Ibid., 19.
"any sort of establishment": Jeremy Bentham, *The Panopticon Writings,* ed. Miran Bozovic (London: Verso, 1995), title page.

43 *"To the keeper":* Ibid., 50.
"Ideal perfection": Ibid., 34.
"Noise," he wrote: Ibid., 49.
"To save the troublesome": Ibid., 36.

44 *"Only in one field":* "Aldous Huxley on Piranesi's Prisons," *{feuilleton},* August 25, 2006, http://www.johncoulthart.com/feuilleton/2006/08/25/aldous-huxley-on-piranesis-prisons/.

46 *"I have been subjected":* Marquis de Lafayette, quoted in Negley K. Teeters and John D. Shearer, *The Prison at Philadelphia, Cherry Hill: The Separate System of Penal Discipline, 1829–1913* (New York: Columbia University Press for Temple University Publications, 1957), 28.

47 *"This man works":* Gustave de Beaumont and Alexis de Tocqueville, *On the Penitentiary System in the United States and Its Application in France,* quoted ibid., 84.
"I am the good shepherd": John 10:14, 16 (King James Version).

"each living solitude": "Aldous Huxley on Piranesi's Prisons."

48 *"But if there is a chaplain":* Louis Dwight, quoted in Teeters and Shearer, *The Prison at Philadelphia,* 151.

49 *"Hither, thither, downward":* Dante Alighieri, *The Divine Comedy: Inferno,* trans. Charles S. Singleton (Princeton, NJ: Princeton University Press, Bollingen Series LXXX, 1970), canto 5, verses 41–43, p. 49.

"Go, then, and see": Dante Alighieri, *The Divine Comedy: Purgatorio,* trans. Charles S. Singleton (Princeton, NJ: Princeton University Press, Bollingen Series LXXX, 1973), canto 1, verses 94–96, p. 9.

"When, lo, the venerable": Ibid., canto 2, verses 119–23, p. 21.

"The criminal is what": Andrew Skotnicki, *Criminal Justice and the Catholic Church* (Lanham, MD: Rowman & Littlefield, 2007), 73.

5. IN PROPORTION

53 *"You have one cell":* William of St. Thierry, *The Golden Epistle: A Letter to the Brethren at Mont Dieu,* trans. Theodore Berkeley (Kalamazoo, MI: Cistercian Publications, 1980), 47.

54 *"Love your inner cell":* Ibid.

"if anyone among you": Ibid., 19.

"Solitude, like poverty": Saint Thomas Aquinas, *Summa Theologiae,* vol. 47, *The Pastoral and Religious Lives,* ed. Jordan Aumann (Cambridge: Cambridge University Press, 2006), 221.

55 *"Like doves are those monks":* Saint Pachomius, "The Rules of Pachomius: Part III," trans. G. H. Schodde, http://www.ecatholic2000.com/pachomius/untitled-05.shtml.

"are not neophytes": Benedict of Nursia, *The Rule of Saint Benedict,* trans. Anthony C. Meisel and M. L. del Mastro (New York: Doubleday, 1975), 47.

56 *"Monks should try":* Ibid., 82.

"In liturgical prayer": Pius Parsch, quoted in Rita Ferrone, "Praying with the Psalms, Part 1," *Commonweal,* February 20, 2014, https://www.commonwealmagazine.org/praying-psalms-part-i.

57 *"The silence with people":* Thomas Merton, *The Seven Storey Mountain: An Autobiography of Faith* (New York: Harcourt, 1998), 354.

"How did I live": Ibid.

"This exclusion means": Benedict of Nursia, *The Rule of Saint Benedict,* 71.

58 *"more retreat than":* Quoted in Thorsten Sellin, "Dom Jean Mabillon, a Prison Reformer of the Seventeenth Century," *Journal of the American Institute of Criminal Law and Criminology* 17, no. 4 (February 1927): 584–85.

"The harshness of some priors": Ibid., 584.

59 *"a frightful kind of prison":* Ibid., 585.

"The measure of unhappiness": Ibid., 585, 587.

"to entertain them": Ibid., 588.

60 *"One knows but too well":* Ibid., 587.

61 *"There must be no decoration":* Bernard de Clairvaux, quoted in Thomas Barrie, *The Sacred In-Between: The Mediating Roles of Architecture* (New York: Routledge, 2010), 39.

"In the cloister": Bernard de Clairvaux, letter to William of St. Thierry, quoted in George Zarnecki, *Art of the Medieval World: Architecture, Sculpture, Painting, the Sacred Arts* (Englewood Cliffs, NJ: Prentice-Hall, 1975), 222.

"The Churches of our Fathers": Thomas Merton, *The Sign of Jonas* (New York: Harcourt, 1981), 24.

"They knew a good building": Ibid.

62 *"The monastery should be planned":* Benedict of Nursia, *The Rule of Saint Benedict*, 102.

63 "All *guests to the monastery":* Ibid., 89.

"A wise old monk": Ibid., 102.

64 *"Medieval comfort":* Siegfried Giedion, *Mechanization Takes Command: A Contribution to Anonymous History* (New York: Oxford University Press, 1948), 301–2.

"Confession shall be": Quoted in Jeffrey F. Hamburger, "Art, Enclosure and the Cura Monialium: Prolegomena in the Guise of a Postscript Author(s)," in "Monastic Architecture for Women," special issue, *Gesta* 31, no. 2 (1992): 111.

"The whole and its details": Le Corbusier, introduction to *Architecture of Truth: The Cistercian Abbey of Le Thoronet*, by Lucien Hervé (London: Phaidon, 2001), 7.

65 *"any medieval person":* Marshall McLuhan, *The Gutenberg Galaxy: The Making of Typographic Man* (Toronto: University of Toronto Press, 1965), 106.

"it is as though": Roger Hinks, quoted ibid., 106.

"Why do you strain": Bernard de Clairvaux, quoted in Robert Lawlor, "Geometry at the Service of Prayer: Reflections on Cistercian Mystic Architecture," *Parabola* 3, no. 1 (1978): 16.

"So then faith cometh*":* Romans 10:17 (King James Version).

66 *"The eye does not see":* Lawlor, "Geometry at the Service of Prayer," 12–13, 17.

"No outside sound": Ibid., 17.

68 *"was considered to be":* Emma Hornby, "Preliminary Thoughts About Silence in Early Western Chant," in *Silence, Music, Silent Music,* ed. Nicky Losseff and Jenny Doctor (Aldershot, England: Ashgate, 2007), 143.

"Both the Hebrew": Ibid., 142–43.

6. SPEECH AND SILENCE

69 *"Let us do":* Benedict of Nursia, *The Rule of Saint Benedict,* trans. Anthony C. Meisel and M. L. del Mastro (New York: Doubleday, 1975), 56.

70 *"The master should speak":* Ibid.

"Speech and silence": Max Picard, *The World of Silence,* trans. Stanley Godwin (Wichita, KS: Eighth Day Press, 2002), 36.

"Listening requires": Jean-Louis Chrétien, *The Ark of Speech,* trans. Andrew Brown (London: Routledge, 2013), 53.

71 *"Silence itself":* Thomas Merton, "Lecture 4: Benefits of Religious Silence," in *Thomas Merton on Contemplation: 6 Talks on 4 CDs,* Now You Know Media, 2014.

"With all the mixture": Quoted in Thomas Merton, *The Seven Storey Mountain: An Autobiography of Faith* (New York: Harcourt, 1998), 288.

72 *"The imperfections":* Merton, *The Seven Storey Mountain,* 419.

"The brothers should wait": Benedict of Nursia, *The Rule of Saint Benedict,* 77.

73 *"may uplift the listeners":* Ibid., 80.

"The colour they're painted": Vincent van Gogh to his brother Theo, letter 499, http://vangoghletters.org/vg/letters/let499/letter.html.

74 *Some sign lists:* For this segment on Cistercian sign language, I am indebted to Robert A. Barakat, *The Cistercian Sign Language: A Study in Non-verbal Communication* (Kalamazoo, MI: Cistercian Publications, 1975).

"For the sign of bread": Kirk Ambrose, "A Medieval Food List from the Monastery of Cluny," *Gastronomica* 6, no. 1 (Winter 2006): 16.

"For the sign of cheese": Ibid., 17.
"for the sign of apples": Ibid., 18.
"kidded one another": Merton, *The Seven Storey Mountain,* 420.
75 *"The usefulness of silence":* Quoted in Barakat, *The Cistercian Sign Language,* 14.
"The two words exclude": Michele Federico Sciacca, "Meaningful Silence," *Philosophy Today* 1, no. 4 (Winter 1957): 250.
76 *"An appreciation and respect":* Sister Joann Ottenstroer, "A Position Paper on a Functional Approach to Silence," *Review for Religious* 27, no. 2 (March 1968): 216.
"Possibly the effort": Ibid., 220.
"Do they not talk": Henry David Thoreau, *Walden,* in *Walden and Civil Disobedience* (New York: Penguin, 1986), 163.
"What a disaster": A Search for Solitude: The Journals of Thomas Merton, vol. 3, *1952–1960,* ed. Lawrence S. Cunningham (New York: HarperSanFrancisco, 1997), 71.
77 *"Those who have enjoyed":* Michael Sweetman, S.J., "Silence," *Review for Religious,* 22, no. 4 (July 1963): 430.
78 *"The positive reason":* Ibid., 431.
"A silence which is nothing": Ibid.
"Since, then, we adopt": Ibid., 430.
"Babel": Thomas Merton, *The Sign of Jonas* (New York: Harcourt, 1981), 311.
"But if silence itself: Merton, *A Search for Solitude,* 253.

7. THOMAS MERTON: SILENCE AND THE WORLD

79 *"advises his monks":* Michael Casey, *Strangers to the City: Reflections on the Beliefs and Values of the Rule of Saint Benedict* (Brewster, MA: Paraclete Press, 2010), xii.
"seem to lie": Max Picard, *The World of Silence,* trans. Stanley Godwin (Wichita, KS: Eighth Day Press, 2002), 131.
80 *"would crawl around":* Thomas Merton, *The Seven Storey Mountain: An Autobiography of Faith* (New York: Harcourt, 1998), 173.
"It was nothing unusual": Ibid., 276.
81 *"What I needed":* Ibid., 285.
"excessive rejection of": Ibid., 289.
"I was relieved": Ibid., 288.
82 *"The atmosphere of the city":* Ibid., 233–34.

"That was where": Ibid., 339.

83 *"Then suddenly we saw":* Ibid., 357.

"I had entered into": Ibid., 352.

"and serve in the medical corps": Ibid., 342.

"for the first time": Ibid., 343–44.

84 *"And it was appropriate":* Ibid., 410.

"If I expected": Ibid., 410–11.

"Does the silence": Ibid., 413.

"the abbot is to furnish": Benedict of Nursia, *The Rule of Saint Benedict,* trans. Anthony C. Meisel and M. L. del Mastro (New York: Doubleday, 1975), 92.

"could only use": Scott G. Bruce, *Silence and Sign Language in Medieval Monasticism: The Cluniac Tradition, c. 900–1200* (Cambridge: Cambridge University Press, 2007), 71.

85 *"that was to represent":* Merton, *The Seven Storey Mountain,* 423.

86 *"my double, my shadow":* Ibid., 451.

"One sign of": Robert Giroux, "Thomas Merton's Durable Mountain," *New York Times,* October 11, 1998, http://www.nytimes.com/books/98/10/11/bookend/bookend.html.

"I am a different person": Thomas Merton, *The Sign of Jonas* (New York: Harcourt, 1981), 95, 97, 96.

87 *"It wasn't by reason":* Father Matthew Torpey, Monastery of the Holy Spirit, Conyers, GA, January 31, 2015, "Men Choosing the Monastic Life, After World War II and Today," video, Emory University, https://www.youtube.com/watch?v=4VdMqgnsCAA.

"Let us suppose": Merton, *The Sign of Jonas,* 4.

88 *"The problem of where":* Ibid., 24–25.

"And now it is": Ibid., 25.

"the only justification": Thomas Merton, *New Seeds of Contemplation* (New York: New Directions, 2007), 52.

8. MEASURES OF TIME

90 *In that world:* For the information on bells and their meaning, I am indebted to Alain Corbin, *Village Bells: Sound and Meaning in the 19th-Century French Countryside,* trans. Martin Thom (New York: Columbia University Press, 1998).

91 *"They are to us":* Thomas Merton, *Monastic Observances: Initiation into*

the Monastic Tradition 5, ed. Patrick F. O'Connell (Collegeville, MN: Liturgical Press, 2010), 30.

"The bells call us": Ibid., 32.

92 *"If the mechanical clock":* Lewis Mumford, *Technics and Civilization* (Chicago: University of Chicago Press, 2010), 13.

"helped to give": Ibid., 13–14.

"What was clearly new": Jacques Le Goff, *Time, Work, and Culture in the Middle Ages,* trans. Arthur Goldhammer (Chicago: University of Chicago Press, 1980), 48.

"Rather than the uncertain*":* Ibid.

"marks a perfection": Mumford, *Technics and Civilization,* 15.

93 *"The Franciscans replaced":* Emma Hornby, "Preliminary Thoughts About Silence in Early Western Chant," in *Silence, Music, Silent Music,* ed. Nicky Losseff and Jenny Doctor (Aldershot, England: Ashgate, 2007), 143.

94 *"'What is this'":* Dante Alighieri, *The Divine Comedy: Purgatorio,* trans. Charles S. Singleton (Princeton, NJ: Princeton University Press, Bollingen Series LXXX, 1973), canto 2, verses 120–23, p. 21.

"Punctuality is the sense": Andrew Skotnicki, "God's Prisoners: Penal Confinement and the Creation of Purgatory," *Modern Theology* 22, no. 1 (January 2006): 100–101.

"the apprehension and expectancy": Ibid., 101.

95 *"For a poem to coalesce":* Adrienne Rich, "When We Dead Awaken," in *Arts of the Possible: Essays and Conversations* (New York: Norton, 2002), 20–21.

"a time and space": Michael Casey, *Strangers to the City: Reflections on the Beliefs and Values of the Rule of Saint Benedict* (Brewster, MA: Paraclete Press, 2010), 26.

"above all being attentive": Ibid., 27.

96 *"The contemplative life": The Asian Journal of Thomas Merton,* ed. Naomi Burton, Brother Patrick Hart, and James Laughlin (New York: New Directions, 1975), 117.

"So the monks prayed": Robert Taft, *The Liturgy of the Hours in East and West: The Origins of the Divine Office and Its Meaning for Today* (Collegeville, MN: Liturgical Press, 1986), 363.

97 *"Supposing it's my afternoon":* Thomas Merton, "Lecture 4: Benefits of Religious Silence," in *Thomas Merton on Contemplation: 6 Talks on 4 CDs,* Now You Know Media, 2014.

98 *"Silence . . . stands outside":* Max Picard, *The World of Silence,* trans. Stanley Godwin (Wichita, KS: Eighth Day Press, 2002), 18–19.
"It is not so much": Ibid., 113.
"does not develop": Ibid., 18.

9. THE VOICES OF THE PAGES

100 *"usually, not as today":* Jean Leclercq, *The Love of Learning and the Desire for God: A Study of Monastic Culture,* trans. Catharine Misrahi (New York: Fordham University Press, 1961), 19.
"It's a real": Ibid.
"Should anyone desire": Benedict of Nursia, *The Rule of Saint Benedict,* trans. Anthony C. Meisel and M. L. del Mastro (New York: Doubleday, 1975), 86.
"At fixed hours": William of St. Thierry, *The Golden Epistle: A Letter to the Brethren at Mont Dieu,* trans. Theodore Berkeley (Kalamazoo, MI: Cistercian Publications, 1980), 51.
102 *"The work of writing":* "Silos Apocalypse," Online Gallery: Sacred Texts, British Library, http://www.bl.uk/onlinegallery/sacredtexts/silos.html.
103 *"Some part of":* William of St. Thierry, *The Golden Epistle,* 52.
"You will never": Ibid., 51–52.
"to speak, to think": Leclercq, *The Love of Learning,* 21, 90.
104 *"must always grow":* Jun'icherō Tanizaki, *In Praise of Shadows,* trans. Thomas J. Harper and Edward G. Seidensticker (Stony Creek, CT: Leete's Island Books, 1977), 18.

10. THE GREAT SILENCE

105 *"A servant would":* Cyril of Jerusalem, quoted in Philip Schaff and Henry Wace, eds., *A Select Library of Nicene and Post-Nicene Fathers of the Christian Church,* 2nd ser., vol. 7 (New York: Christian Literature, 1894), 52.
106 *"The faces of":* Patrick Leigh Fermor, *A Time to Keep Silence* (New York: New York Review Books, 2007), 40–41.
"I am tempted": Pius Parsch, quoted in Thomas Merton, *Monastic Observances: Initiation into the Monastic Tradition 5,* ed. Patrick F. O'Connell (Collegeville, MN: Liturgical Press, 2010), 93.
107 *"Monks should try":* Benedict of Nursia, *The Rule of Saint Benedict,* trans. Anthony C. Meisel and M. L. del Mastro (New York: Doubleday, 1975), 82.

"And when is our mind": Cyril of Jerusalem, quoted in Schaff and Wace, *A Select Library,* 52.

"Only man makes": Thomas Merton, *The Sign of Jonas* (New York: Harcourt, 1981), 356.

108 *"does not illuminate":* Gaston Bachelard, *The Flame of a Candle,* trans. Joni Caldwell (Dallas: Dallas Institute, 1984), 37.

"The thing that depressed": Thomas Merton, *The Seven Storey Mountain: An Autobiography of Faith* (New York: Harcourt, 1998), 174.

109 *"I thought of":* Merton, *The Sign of Jonas,* 297.

110 *"You hit strange caverns":* Ibid., 354.

"The walls of the building": Ibid., 352.

"I have prayed": Ibid., 352–53.

"Between the silence": Ibid., 354.

111 *"I know what":* Ibid., 333–34.

"'Vigilers' or 'watchers'": Robert Taft, *The Liturgy of the Hours in East and West: The Origins of the Divine Office and Its Meaning for Today* (Collegeville, MN: Liturgical Press, 1986), 15–16.

"I had learned": Merton, *The Seven Storey Mountain,* 222.

112 *"After two or three":* Ibid., 428.

"Or that was the way": Ibid., 429.

"to deliver oneself up": Thomas Merton, *Thoughts in Solitude* (New York: Farrar, Straus and Giroux, 1958), 101.

11. NIGHT IN STONE

116 *"At a pinch":* Eugenia Semyonovna Ginzburg, *Journey into the Whirlwind,* trans. Paul Stevenson and Max Hayward (New York: Harcourt, 1995), 193.

"what remained of": Ibid., 194.

117 *"From the authorities'":* Ibid., 211–12.

"The time after supper": Ibid., 198.

118 *"A new life began":* Vera Figner, *Memoirs of a Revolutionist,* trans. Camilla Chapin Daniels and G. A. Davidson (DeKalb: Northern Illinois University Press, 1991), 181.

"felt that the silence": Sara Maitland, *A Book of Silence* (Berkeley, CA: Counterpoint Press, 2008), 81.

"My negative experiences": Ibid., 86.

119 *"Accursed sounds":* Figner, *Memoirs of a Revolutionist,* 182.

"And the dreams": Ibid.

120 *"The worst thing of all":* Ginzburg, *Journey into the Whirlwind*, 198–99.
121 *"The night grows wider":* Ibid., 199.

12. "I GET UP AND HAMMER MY LEATHER"

122 *"In the Philadelphia":* Harriet Martineau, *Retrospect of Western Travel*, vol. 1, *Prisons* (London: Saunders and Otley, 1838), 208.
123 *"As solitude is in":* Gustave de Beaumont and Alexis de Tocqueville, *On the Penitentiary System in the United States and Its Application in France*, trans. Francis Lieber (Philadelphia: Carey, Lea & Blanchard, 1833), 23.
"employment diminishes": William Roscoe, *Additional Observations on Penal Jurisprudence and the Reformation of Criminals* (London: T. Cadell and John and Arthur Arch, 1823), 21.
"be abandoned altogether": Ibid., 43.
124 *"Let them walk":* Quoted in Orlando Faulkland Lewis, *The Development of American Prisons and Prison Customs, 1776–1845* (Montclair, NJ: Patterson Smith, 1967), 81.
"The demands of nature": Quoted in W. David Lewis, *From Newgate to Dannemora: The Rise of the Penitentiary in New York, 1796–1848* (Ithaca, NY: Cornell University Press, 2009), 69.
125 *Building the penitentiary:* For information on the building costs of Eastern State, see Lewis, *The Development of American Prisons*, 237–38.
126 *"Every workshop":* David N. Johnson, *Sketches of Lynn, or The Changes of Fifty Years* (Westport, CT: Greenwood Press, 1970), 4–5.
127 *"1830":* Quoted in Lewis, *The Development of American Prisons*, 238.
"Prisons and the social portrait": Andrew Skotnicki, "God's Prisoners: Penal Confinement and the Creation of Purgatory," *Modern Theology* 22, no. 1 (January 2006): 86.
"The penitentiary arose": Adam J. Hirsch, *The Rise of the Penitentiary: Prisons and Punishment in Early America* (New Haven, CT: Yale University Press, 1992), 71.
128 *"Even as they were":* Caleb Smith, introduction to *The Life and Adventures of a Haunted Convict*, by Austin Reed, ed. Caleb Smith (New York: Random House, 2016), xix.
"are now getting work": Quoted in John R. Commons, "American Shoemakers, 1648–1895: A Sketch of Industrial Evolution," *Quarterly Journal of Economics* 24, no. 1 (November 1909): 62.
"in one hour": Ibid., 73–74.
129 *"He arose at 5:15":* Lewis, *From Newgate to Dannemora*, 118.

"The duty of the convicts": Gershon Powers, *Report of Gershon Powers, Agent and Keeper of the State Prison, at Auburn, Made to the Legislature, January 7, 1828* (Albany, NY: Croswell and Van Benthusen, 1828), 24.

130 *"When marching":* Austin Reed, *The Life and Adventures of a Haunted Convict,* ed. Caleb Smith (New York: Random House, 2016), 144.

"must not look up": Ibid., 145.

"In all the shops": Powers, *Report of Gershon Powers,* 26.

131 *"generally admit":* Ibid., 51–52.

"The convicts converse": Martineau, *Retrospect of Western Travel,* 200.

"When sitting at the table": Reed, *The Life and Adventures of a Haunted Convict,* 144.

132 *"5′ plus 5½ inches":* Quoted in Smith, introduction, xix.

"Many was the nights": Reed, *The Life and Adventures of a Haunted Convict,* 174.

"When the day": Beaumont and Tocqueville, *On the Penitentiary System,* 32.

13. PUNISHMENT WITHIN PUNISHMENT

135 *"worked about the yard":* Quoted in Thomas B. McElwee, *A Concise History of the Eastern Penitentiary of Pennsylvania: Together with a Detailed Statement of the Proceedings of the Committee . . .* (Philadelphia: Neall & Massey, 1835), 168.

"frequently employed in cooking": Ibid., 48.

"constantly while at work": Ibid.

"wore a paper hat": Charles Dickens, "Philadelphia, and Its Solitary Prison," in *American Notes and Pictures from Italy* (Oxford: Oxford University Press, 1989), 101.

136 *"a strange stare":* Ibid., 102.

"took one of the visitors": Ibid.

"at his hands": Ibid., 104.

"I am . . . convinced": Ibid., 99.

"I hold this slow": Ibid.

"whose note as a writer": Job R. Tyson, Esq., letter to William Peter, quoted in "Miscellaneous Notices," *Journal of Prison Discipline and Philanthropy* 1 (April 1845): 85.

"superior *to any thing":* William Peter, letter to Job R. Tyson, Esq., quoted ibid., 86.

137 *"I do not think":* Ibid., 88.

"A more dejected": Dickens, "Philadelphia, and Its Solitary Prison," 102.
"he was in": Peter, letter to Tyson, 86.
Negley Teeters and John Shearer: For the official account of Charles Langheimer's incarceration, see Negley K. Teeters and John D. Shearer, *The Prison at Philadelphia, Cherry Hill: The Separate System of Penal Discipline, 1829–1913* (New York: Columbia University Press for Temple University Publications, 1957), 117–22.
138 *"The guard responded":* Teeters and Sheerer, 122.
"No. 50": McElwee, *A Concise History,* 19.
139 *"is almost universally liked":* Ibid., 63.
"The vast majority": Jennifer Lawrence Janofsky, "Hopelessly Hardened," in *Buried Lives: Incarcerated in Early America,* ed. Michele Lise Tarter and Richard Bell (Athens: University of Georgia Press, 2012), 111.
"immediately removed his tools": McElwee, *A Concise History,* 19.
141 *The Cyrillic alphabet:* For an explanation of the prisoners' alphabet, see Anne Applebaum, *Gulag: A History* (New York: Doubleday, 2003), 156–57.
"but hardly had he": Vera Figner, *Memoirs of a Revolutionist,* trans. Camilla Chapin Daniels and G. A. Davidson (DeKalb: Northern Illinois University Press, 1991), 209.
"From then on": Eugenia Semyonovna Ginzburg, *Journey into the Whirlwind,* trans. Paul Stevenson and Max Hayward (New York: Harcourt, 1995), 73.
142 *"opened a new world":* Ibid.
"The most important thing": Ibid., 197.
"They are denied": Harriet Martineau, *Retrospect of Western Travel,* vol. 1, *Prisons* (London: Saunders and Otley, 1838), 200.
143 *"were brief intervals":* Ginzburg, *Journey into the Whirlwind,* 196.
"I waited for them": Ibid.
"To my dying day": Ibid., 196–97.
144 *"if in pride":* Benedict of Nursia, *The Rule of Saint Benedict,* trans. Anthony C. Meisel and M. L. del Mastro (New York: Doubleday, 1975), 73.
"No. 132": McElwee, *A Concise History,* 153.
145 *"What I must do":* Ginzburg, *Journey into the Whirlwind,* 219–20.
"fell, after even a short": Stuart Grassian, "The Psychiatric Effects of Solitary Confinement," *Washington University Journal of Law and Policy* 22 (2006): 329.

146 *"However all . . . individuals":* Ibid., 332.
"ordinary stimuli become": Ibid., 331–32.
"The brain": Oliver Sacks, "The Prisoner's Cinema: Sensory Deprivation," in *Hallucinations* (New York: Knopf, 2012), 34.
"No. 118": McElwee, *A Concise History,* 153.

147 *"tied up against a wall":* Ibid., 41.
"having on several occasions": Pennsylvania State Archives, Harrisburg, PA, Eastern State Penitentiary Wardens' Daily Journals, 1829–1961, RG 15.
"Last evening I ordered": Ibid.
"rough iron instrument": McElwee, *A Concise History,* 18.

148 *"About 9 OCK":* Wardens' Daily Journals, 1833.
"perpetuated in defiance": McElwee, *A Concise History,* 19.

14. SO THAT IT "MAY UPLIFT"

150 *"I was able to observe":* Eugenia Semyonovna Ginzburg, *Journey into the Whirlwind,* trans. Paul Stevenson and Max Hayward (New York: Harcourt, 1995), 71.
"This was the end": Ibid., 204.
"I have never loved": Ibid., 228.

151 *"in my stone sepulcher":* Ibid., 205.
"After I came out": Ibid.
"When a human being": Ibid.
"Sitting in a cell": Ibid., 205–6.

152 *"in obedience to": Philadelphia Inquirer,* October 30, 1829, 1.
"Without written laws": Cesare Beccaria, *An Essay on Crimes and Punishments,* trans. Edward D. Ingraham (Philadelphia: Philip H. Nicklin, 1819), 26–27.

153 *"illuminate, as far as practicable":* Thomas Jefferson, "A Bill for the More General Diffusion of Knowledge," article courtesy of the *Thomas Jefferson Encyclopedia,* Monticello.org, https://www.monticello.org/site/jefferson/bill-more-general-diffusion-knowledge.
"When the clouds": Cesare Beccaria, quoted in Benjamin Rush, "A Plan for the Establishment of Public Schools . . . ," in *Essays on Education in the Early Republic,* ed. Frederick Randolph (Cambridge, MA: Belknap Press, 1965), 3.

154 *"Our schools of learning":* Benjamin Rush, "Thoughts upon the Mode of Education Proper in a Republic," in *Essays on Education in the Early*

Republic, ed. Frederick Randolph (Cambridge, MA: Belknap Press, 1965), 10.
"Of the many criminals": Ibid., 23.
"fewer pillories": Rush, "A Plan for the Establishment of Public Schools" 6.

155 *"The first object": First and Second Annual Report of the Inspectors of the ESP* (1831), quoted in Jodi Schorb, *Reading Prisoners: Literature, Literacy, and the Transformation of American Punishment, 1700–1845* (New Brunswick, NJ: Rutgers University Press, 2014), 119.
"The character of the convict": Ibid., 119–20.
"calculated to imbue": Thomas B. McElwee, *A Concise History of the Eastern Penitentiary of Pennsylvania: Together with a Detailed Statement of the Proceedings of the Committee . . .* (Philadelphia: Neall & Massey, 1835), 14.
"was quite ignorant": William Peter, letter to Job R. Tyson, Esq., quoted in "Miscellaneous Notices," *Journal of Prison Discipline and Philanthropy* 1 (April 1845): 87.

156 *"only four have been":* William Wood, quoted in Schorb, *Reading Prisoners,* 122.
"read or write indifferently": Ibid.
"From the start": Schorb, *Reading Prisoners,* 95.

157 *"Those was dark days":* Austin Reed, *The Life and Adventures of a Haunted Convict,* ed. Caleb Smith (New York: Random House, 2016), 173.
Prior to being sentenced: Details of Austin Reed's life and the writing of his memoir are from Caleb Smith, introduction to *The Life and Adventures of a Haunted Convict,* by Austin Reed, ed. Caleb Smith (New York: Random House, 2016).
"Every spare minute": Ibid., 25.
"I found myself": Ibid., 25–26.

158 *"I say that I use":* Ibid., 26.
"His book is full": Smith, introduction, lxi.
"drifted westward": Ibid.

15. TIME AGAIN

160 *"faint, sweet":* Henry David Thoreau, *Walden,* in *Walden and Civil Disobedience* (New York: Penguin, 1986), 168.
"worth importing": Ibid., 168–69.

"The startings and arrivals": Ibid., 163.

161 *"You may see her":* "A Week in the Mill," in *The Lowell Offering: Writings by New England Mill Women (1840–1845),* ed. Benita Eisler (New York: Harper & Row, 1977), 75.

"The clang of the early bell": Ibid., 76.

"It is their station": Charles Dickens, "Lowell and Its Factory System," in *American Notes and Pictures from Italy* (Oxford: Oxford University Press, 1989), 68.

162 *"Chairs, chairs":* "Editorial: Home in a Boarding-House," in *The Lowell Offering: Writings by New England Mill Women (1840–1845),* ed. Benita Eisler (New York: Harper & Row, 1977), 73.

Philadelphia, by contrast: For the information on Philadelphia's clocks and bells, I am indebted to Alexis McCrossen, "The Sound and Look of Time: Bells and Clocks in Philadelphia," *Common-Place* 13, no. 1 (October 2012), http://www.common-place-archives.org/vol-13/no-01/mccrossen/.

"the time of the citizens": Quoted in McCrossen, "The Sound and Look of Time."

"which is so deficient": Ibid.

"appropriated $12,000": McCrossen, "The Sound and Look of Time."

163 *"from more than one thousand":* Quoted ibid.

"it is always twilight": Oscar Wilde, "De Profundis," in *De Profundis and Other Writings* (Harmondsworth, England: Penguin English Library, 1973), 141.

"Forth you are": Dante Alighieri, *The Divine Comedy: Purgatorio,* trans. Charles S. Singleton (Princeton, NJ: Princeton University Press, 1973), canto 27, verses 132–35, p. 299.

164 *"Free, upright":* Ibid., verses 140–42, p. 301.

The records still remain: Information on the release of prisoners is from Pennsylvania State Archives, Harrisburg, PA, Eastern State Penitentiary Discharge Books, 1830–1858, RG 15.

165 *"The Philadelphia system":* Gustave de Beaumont and Alexis de Tocqueville, *On the Penitentiary System in the United States and Its Application in France,* trans. Francis Lieber (Carbondale: Southern Illinois University Press, 1964), 91.

166 *"None of us stopped":* Eugenia Semyonovna Ginzburg, *Journey into the Whirlwind,* trans. Paul Stevenson and Max Hayward (New York: Harcourt, 1995), 273–74.

167 *"including some who did not":* Stuart Grassian, "The Psychiatric Effects of Solitary Confinement," *Washington University Journal of Law and Policy* 22 (2006): 332.
"The gates of the penitentiary": Alexander Berkman, *Prison Memoirs of an Anarchist* (New York: New York Review Books, 1999), 481.
"The din and noise": Ibid., 494.
"A sudden impulse": Ibid., 495.
168 *"It seems strange":* Ibid., 495–96.
"It requires an effort": Ibid., 496.
169 *"impossible to get work":* Quoted in Negley K. Teeters and John D. Shearer, *The Prison at Philadelphia, Cherry Hill: The Separate System of Penal Discipline, 1829–1913* (New York: Columbia University Press for Temple University Publications, 1957), 126.
"If the inspectors": Ibid., 135.
"[They] found the man": Luke 8:35 (King James Version).
170 *"thought that a publication":* "Eastern Penitentiary," *Philadelphia Inquirer,* February 11, 1830, 2.

16. SILENCING SILENCE

173 *"By marriage, the husband":* William Blackstone, *Commentaries on the Laws of England,* vol. 1 (1765), 442–45, Kentlaw.edu, http://www.kentlaw.edu/faculty/fbatlan/classes/BatlanGender&LawS2007/CourseDocs/coursedoc07/Blackstone.pdf.
174 *"a troublesome angry woman":* Quoted in Elizabeth J. Clapp, *A Notorious Woman: Anne Royall in Jacksonian America* (Charlottesville: University of Virginia Press, 2016), 136.
175 *"of particular acts":* Commonwealth vs. Samanthia Hutchinson, *American Law Register (1852–1891),* 114, http://www.jstor.org/stable/3301740?seq=2#page_scan_tab_contents.
"given to one Betsey": Alice Morse Earle, *Curious Punishments of Bygone Days* (Rutland, VT: Charles E. Tuttle, 1972), 19.
"was taken to ye pond": Ibid., 19–20.
176 *a scold's bridle:* Information on the scold's bridle comes from William Andrews, *Bygone Punishments* (London: printed by the author, 1899), 276–98, http://www.gutenberg.org/files/29117/29117-h/29117-h.htm.
177 *"That which they called":* Dorothy Waugh, "A Relation Concerning Dorothy Waughs Cruell Usage by the Mayor of Carlile," in *The Lambs Defence Against Lyes and a True Testimony Given Concerning the*

Sufferings and Death of James Parnell, and the Ground Thereof (Little Falls, NY: Geoffrey Gilmore, n.d.), 29–30.

178 *"from Constable to Constable:* Ibid., 30.

"she kept a quiet tongue": Andrews, *Bygone Punishments,* 285.

"I was very much": "The Interesting Narrative of the Life of Olaudah Equiano or Gustavus Vassa, the African," in *The Classic Slave Narratives,* ed. Henry Louis Gates Jr. (New York: Penguin, 1987), 39.

179 *"At that time":* Elizabeth Fry, *Memoir of the Life of Elizabeth Fry with Extracts from her Journal and Letters,* ed. Katharine Fry and Rachel Elizabeth Cresswell (Montclair, NJ: Patterson Smith, 1974), 201.

"Nearly three hundred": Ibid., 202.

"In the same rooms": Ibid.

181 *"The unhappy females":* Roberts Vaux, letter to Mary Wistar, quoted in Margaret Hope Bacon, introduction to *Abby Hopper Gibbons: Prison Reformer and Social Activist* (Albany: State University of New York Press, 2000), xv.

182 *"I am sensible":* Benjamin Rush, "A Plan for the Establishment of Public Schools and the Diffusion of Knowledge in Pennsylvania," in *Essays on Education in the Early Republic,* ed. Frederick Rudolph (Cambridge, MA: Belknap Press, 1965), 21–22.

183 *"The opinions and conduct":* Ibid., 22.

"no such thing": Anne Royall, quoted in Clapp, *A Notorious Woman,* 20.

184 *"causewayed with huge logs":* Anne Royall, *Sketches of History, Life, and Manners, in the United* States (New Haven, CT: printed for the author, 1826), 15.

"This was an unlucky day": Ibid., 19.

"The Tennessean": Ibid., 15.

185 *"She is no woman":* John Neal, quoted in Clapp, *A Notorious Woman,* 1.

At the time Royall faced: Information on the trial of Anne Royall is from Clapp, *A Notorious Woman,* 132–47.

"They charged that Royall": Ibid., 133.

186 *"perhaps from two to four":* Quoted ibid., 144.

17. "OR PERHAPS THE WOMEN . . ."

187 *"the men, or perhaps the women":* Benjamin Rush, *An Enquiry into the Effects of Public Punishments upon Criminals, and upon Society . . . ,* in *Essays: Literary, Moral and Philosophical,* ed. Michael Meranze (Schenectady, NY: Union College Press, 1988), 84.

188 *"But the tender sex":* Anne Royall, *Sketches of History, Life, and Manners, in the United States* (New Haven, CT: printed for the author, 1826), 251–52.
"is unprincipled": Francis Lieber, translator's preface to *On the Penitentiary System in the United States and Its Application in France,* by Gustave de Beaumont and Alexis de Tocqueville, trans. Francis Lieber (Carbondale: Southern Illinois University Press, 1964), 9.
"there is, almost without": Ibid.

189 *"twenty-six cells":* John Haviland, daybook, vol. 1, 24, Manuscript Collection 176, Rare Books and Manuscripts, Kislak Center for Special Collections, University of Pennsylvania.

190 *"The lives of female prisoners":* Lucia Zedner, "Wayward Sisters: The Prison for Women," in *The Oxford History of the Prison: The Practice of Punishment in Western Society,* ed. Norval Morris and David J. Rothman (New York: Oxford University Press, 1998), 311.

191 *"There were some":* Quoted in Thomas B. McElwee, *A Concise History of the Eastern Penitentiary of Pennsylvania: Together with a Detailed Statement of the Proceedings of the Committee . . .* (Philadelphia: Neall & Massey, 1835), 145.
"No. 74": Ibid., 150.
"We consider it unfortunate": McElwee, *A Concise History,* 38.

192 *"She was a very":* Quoted ibid., 171.
"In the silence": Charles Dickens, "Philadelphia, and Its Solitary Prison," in *American Notes and Pictures from Italy* (Oxford: Oxford University Press, 1989), 104–5.

193 *"have nothing 'very sad'":* William Peter, letter to Job R. Tyson, Esq., quoted in "Miscellaneous Notices," *Journal of Prison Discipline and Philanthropy* 1 (April 1845): 87.
"from morning to night": Ibid.
"had been 'a very good thing'": Ibid.
"a specimen of the most": The Annual Report of the Board of Managers of the Prison Discipline Society, Boston, June 1, 1827 (Boston: Perkins & Marvin, 1829), 562.

194 *"The arrangements for the women":* Harriet Martineau, *Retrospect of Western Travel,* vol. 1, *Prisons* (London: Saunders and Otley, 1838), 202.
"There was an engine": Ibid.
"I hope these stocks": Ibid.

195 *"violence is the main concern":* Cristina Rathbone, *A World Apart: Women, Prison, and Life Behind Bars* (New York: Random House, 2005), 6.

18. MONASTIC WOMEN: MORE SHADOW THAN LIGHT

198 *"As brides of Christ":* Jane Tibbetts Schulenburg, "Strict Active Enclosure and Its Effects on the Female Monastic Experience (ca. 500–1100)," in *Distant Echoes: Medieval Religious Women,* vol. 1, ed. John A. Nichols and Lillian Thomas Shank (Kalamazoo, MI: Cistercian Publications, 1984), 54.

"The female monks": "The Rules of Pachomius: Part I," trans. George H. Schodde, *Presbyterian Review* 6 (1885): 683, https://books.google.com/books/about/The_Presbyterian_Review.html?id=AkQ9AAAAYAAJ.

"If a girl": Caesarius of Arles, quoted in Schulenburg, "Strict Active Enclosure," 54.

199 *"at the Devil's urging":* Quoted ibid., 55.

"Christianity has always": Caroline A. Bruzelius, "Hearing Is Believing: Clarissan Architecture, ca. 1213–1340," in "Monastic Architecture for Women," special issue, *Gesta* 31, no. 2 (1992): 88.

200 *"Nuns collectively":* Quoted in Elizabeth Makowski, *Canon Law and Cloistered Women: Periculoso and Its Commentators, 1298–1545* (Washington, DC: Catholic University of America Press, 1997), 135.

201 *"Since the Middle Ages":* Silvia Evangelisti, "'We Do Not Have It, and We Do Not Want It': Women, Power, and Convent Reform in Florence," *Sixteenth Century Journal* 34, no. 3 (Fall 2003): 689.

202 *"Anno 1620":* Ulrike Strasser, "Cloistering Women's Past: Conflicting Accounts of Enclosure in a Seventeenth-Century Munich Nunnery," in *Gender in Early Modern German History,* ed. Ulinka Rublack (Cambridge: Cambridge University Press, 2002), 225.

"refused altogether to learn": Ibid., 230–31.

203 *"for there is no doubt":* Quoted in Evangelisti, "'We Do Not Have It,'" 685.

"They resisted": Evangelisti, "'We Do Not Have It,'" 698–99.

204 *"Only those who have":* Teresa of Avila, quoted in *Walled About with God: The History and Spirituality of Enclosure for Cloistered Nuns,* ed. Dom Jean Prou and the Benedictine Nuns of the Solesmes Congregation, trans. B. David Hayes (Leominster, England: Gracewing, 2005), 84.

205 *"close . . . so as to facilitate":* Bernadette Barrière, "The Cistercian Convent of Coyroux in the Twelfth and Thirteenth Centuries," in "Monastic Architecture for Women," special issue, *Gesta* 31, no. 2 (1992): 76.

"so that any contact": Ibid.
"Rapids exit from": Ibid.
"No function was neglected": Ibid., 81.
206 *"the way out of the enclosure":* Quoted ibid., 80.
207 *"offered the opportunity":* Barrière, "The Cistercian Convent of Coyroux," 82.
"Are we to consider": Ibid.

19. THOMAS MERTON: QUESTIONING SILENCE

211 *"Inner silence depends":* Thomas Merton, *Thoughts in Solitude* (New York: Farrar, Straus and Giroux, 1958), 86.
212 *"I am now": A Search for Solitude: The Journals of Thomas Merton,* vol. 3, *1952–1960,* ed. Lawrence S. Cunningham (New York: HarperSanFrancisco, 1997), 14.
"I need solitude": Ibid., 27.
"High up in": Ibid., 16.
213 *"The tractors in the bottoms":* Ibid., 64.
"Yesterday and today": Ibid., 134.
214 *"what the late":* "Round the World; in 96 Minutes," *New York Times,* October 6, 1957, sec. 4, The News of the Week in Review, 1, https://timesmachine.nytimes.com/timesmachine/1957/10/06/91166843.html?pageNumber=193.
"In numbers": Dwight D. Eisenhower, "Radio and Television Address to the American People on Science in National Security," November 7, 1957, The American Presidency Project, http://www.presidency.ucsb.edu/ws/?pid=10946.
215 *"It is futile":* Merton, *A Search for Solitude,* 132.
"The freedom of": Thomas Merton, *Seeds of Destruction* (New York: Farrar, Straus and Giroux, 1964), xiv.
216 *"The contemplative life":* Ibid., xiii.
"Genuine communication": Ibid., 243.
". . . they won't say": Bertolt Brecht, "In Dark Times," in *Poems: 1913–1956,* ed. John Willett and Ralph Manheim (New York: Methuen, 1976), 274.
217 *"Yesterday afternoon": Turning Toward the World: The Journals of Thomas Merton,* vol. 4, *1960–1963,* ed. Victor A. Cramer (New York: HarperSanFrancisco, 1997), 182.
"My position loses": Quoted in Robert Nugent, *Silence Speaks: Teilhard de*

Chardin, Yves Congar, John Courtney Murray, and Thomas Merton (New York: Paulist Press, 2011), 86.

218 "The Seven Storey Mountain": Thomas Merton, *The Sign of Jonas* (New York: Harcourt, 1981), 40.

"I am being silenced": Thomas Merton, letter to James Forest, in *The Hidden Ground of Love: The Letters of Thomas Merton on Religious Experience and Social Concerns,* ed. William H. Shannon (New York: Farrar, Straus and Giroux, 1985), 266.

219 *"If there were":* Thomas Merton, letter to Dorothy Day, in *Thomas Merton: A Life in Letters,* ed. William H. Shannon and Christine M. Bochen (New York: HarperCollins, 2008), 278.

"As for writing": Ibid., 140.

"I have just been instructed": Thomas Merton, letter to John Harris, in ibid., 398.

"You could write": Thomas Merton, letter to James Forest, in *The Hidden Ground of Love,* 258.

220 *"I have been considering":* Thomas Merton, letter to James Forest, in *Turning Toward the World,* 157.

"I am where I am": Thomas Merton, letter to James Forest, in *The Hidden Ground of Love,* 267–68.

"To have a vow": Merton, *Seeds of Destruction,* xvi.

221 *"What kind of times":* Bertolt Brecht, "To Those Born Later," in *Poems: 1913–1956,* ed. John Willett and Ralph Manheim (New York: Methuen, 1976), 318.

"far from enclosing himself": Thomas Merton, "Rain and the Rhinoceros," in *Raids on the Unspeakable* (New York: New Directions, 1964), 18.

222 *"There is no clock":* Ibid., 14.

"Of course at three-thirty": Ibid., 14.

"It seems everything": Thomas Merton, letter to James Forest, in *The Hidden Ground of Love,* 266.

"I think the monastic life": Thomas Merton, letter to Czeslaw Milosz, in *Striving Toward Being: The Letters of Thomas Merton and Czeslaw Milosz,* ed. Robert Faggen (New York: Farrar, Straus and Giroux, 1997), 168–70.

223 *"Still, it is true":* Ibid., 170.

"This is a crucial": Thomas Merton, letter to Alceu Amoroso Lima, in *Thomas Merton: A Life in Letters,* ed. William H. Shannon and Christine M. Bochen (New York: HarperCollins, 2008), 199.

224 *"Serious communication": The Asian Journal of Thomas Merton,* ed. Naomi Burton, Brother Patrick Hart, and James Laughlin (New York: New Directions, 1975), 317.
225 *"It will be impossible":* Ibid., 296.
"Our real journey": Ibid., 29.
226 *"Joy":* Ibid., 4.
Soon after landing: Details about Thomas Merton's last days in Asia and his burial at Gethsemani are from Brother Patrick Hart's foreword and postscript to *The Asian Journal of Thomas Merton,* ed. Naomi Burton, Brother Patrick Hart, and James Laughlin (New York: New Directions, 1975), xxi–xxix, 257–59.
"Merton was a well-built man": Dalai Lama, *Freedom in Exile: The Autobiography of the Dalai Lama* (New York: Harper Perennial, 1991), 189.
227 *"It is my monastery": The Asian Journal,* 149.
"Keep telling everyone": Quoted in Hart, foreword, xxviii.
"The monk is essentially": The Asian Journal, 329.

20. THE MONASTIC WORLD: WHAT REMAINS

228 *Many now stand:* The descriptions of the ruins are derived from David Heald's photographs in *Architecture of Silence: Cistercian Abbeys of France,* text by Terryl N. Kinder (New York: Harry N. Abrams, 2000).
"When it is": Henry Moore and John Hedgecoe, *Henry Moore: My Ideas, Inspiration, and Life as an Artist* (London: Collins & Brown, 1999), 41.
229 *"into dungeons":* Victor Hugo, "Claude Gueux, King of Thieves," in *The Works of Victor Hugo: One Volume Edition* (Roslyn, NY: Black's Readers Service, 1927), 430.
230 *"Day and night":* N. C. Phillips, quoted in Henry Kamm, "40 Years Later, the Message of Monte Cassino: Pax," *New York Times,* February 27, 1984, http://www.nytimes.com/1984/02/27/world/40-years-later-the-message-of-monte-cassino-pax.html?pagewanted=1.
231 *"December 19, 1943":* Quoted in David Hapgood and David Richardson, *Monte Cassino* (New York: Congdon & Weed, 1984), 81.
"December 22": Ibid., 88.
"January 5": Ibid., 98–99.
"January 7": Ibid., 100.
232 *"January 10":* Ibid., 101.
"January 18": Ibid., 109.

"From now on": Ibid., 117.

"The time has come": Ibid., 191.

"I watched it sitting": Martha Gellhorn, quoted in Don North, "The Bloody Victory at Monte Cassino," Consortiumnews.com, May 19, 2014, https://consortiumnews.com/2014/05/19/the-bloody-victory-at-monte-cassino/.

233 *Film footage shows:* For film footage of the monks working in the ruins of Monte Cassino, see "Monks Rebuilding Monte Cassino," video, British Pathé, https://www.youtube.com/watch?v=TlGenc4lJNw.

"Up until 1948": Quoted in Kamm, "40 Years Later."

234 *"What you see today":* Ibid.

"Legibility, in practice": Eric Gill, *An Essay on Typography* (Boston: David R. Godine, 1988), 44.

21. THE PRISON CELL IN OUR TIME

235 *"If there are prisons":* Grace Paley, "Six Days: Some Rememberings," in *The Best American Essays 1995,* ed. Jamaica Kincaid and Robert Atwan (Boston: Houghton Mifflin, 1995), 192.

236 *"You must be careful":* Quoted in Norval Morris, "The Contemporary Prison, 1965–Present," in *The Oxford History of the Prison: The Practice of Punishment in Western Society,* ed. Norval Morris and David J. Rothman (New York: Oxford University Press, 1998), 203.

"take care neither": Ibid., 210.

"5:30 a.m.": Ibid., 204.

237 *"As F House came to life":* Ibid.

"The food is often worse": Ibid., 209.

"a tower of Babel": Captain Alexander Smith, quoted in Peter Linebaugh, *The London Hanged: Crime and Civil Society in the Eighteenth Century* (London: Verso, 2003), 28.

238 *"The week I spent": Angela Davis: An Autobiography* (New York: Random House, 1974), 36.

239 *"None have exceeded":* Marquis de Lafayette, quoted in Negley K. Teeters and John D. Shearer, *The Prison at Philadelphia, Cherry Hill: The Separate System of Penal Discipline, 1829–1913* (New York: Columbia University Press for Temple University Publications, 1957), 28.

At Pelican Bay's SHUs: Statistics on Pelican Bay are from Keramet Reiter, *23/7: Pelican Bay Prison and the Rise of Long-Term Solitary Confinement* (New Haven, CT: Yale University Press, 2016), 29.

Solitary Watch: Solitary Watch, "Solitary Confinement in the United States: FAQ," n.d., http://solitarywatch.com/wp-content/uploads/2017/09/Solitary-Confinement-FAQ-2015.pdf.

240 *"develop rigid, repetitive":* Reiter, *23/7,* 25.

"Even in these sparse conditions": Ibid.

241 *"The first three years":* Sharon Wiggins, quoted in Howard Zehr, *Doing Life: Reflections of Men and Women Serving Life Sentences* (Intercourse, PA: Good Books, 1996), 112.

"And then they let me": Frontline, season 33, episode 19, "Last Days of Solitary," produced by Dan Edge and Lauren Mucciolo, aired April 18, 2017, on PBS, http://www.pbs.org/wgbh/frontline/film/last-days-of-solitary/transcript/.

242 *"You lose all feeling":* Ibid.

"I immersed myself": Joe Labriola, in John P. Collins, Joe Labriola, Shawn Fisher, and Timothy J. Muise, "Thomas Merton Comes to Prison," Merton.org, http://merton.org/ITMS/Seasonal/39/39-4Collins.pdf.

243 *"out of mind-numbing boredom":* Ibid.

"a dedicated recalcitrant": Ibid.

"Soon I found myself": Ibid.

"The book was illegal": Ibid.

"I read his poetry": Ibid.

"What is essential": The Asian Journal of Thomas Merton, ed. Naomi Burton, Brother Patrick Hart, and James Laughlin (New York: New Directions, 1975), 340.

22. INTERVALS OF SILENCE

245 *"He said it was":* Doris Grumbach, *Fifty Days of Solitude* (Boston: Beacon Press, 1994), 47.

246 *"Did I think":* Ibid., 29.

"roughed up the smooth": Ibid., 48

"our points of reference": Ibid., 17.

"In the silence": Ibid., 50.

247 *"The absence of other":* Ibid., 3.

"What others regard": Ibid., 113.

"Care in the use": Ibid., 33.

"I felt the human force": Ibid., 60.

248 *"The house expanded":* Ibid., 98.

249 *"without even the excuse":* Patrick Leigh Fermor, *A Time to Keep Silence* (New York: New York Review Books, 2007), 7.
"somewhere quiet and cheap": Ibid., 8.
"a silent university": Ibid., 23.
"I found no trace": Ibid., 25.
250 *"staggering difference":* Ibid., 21.
"The two ways of life": Ibid., 22.
"with disconcerting speed": Ibid., 33–34.
"I, not the monks": Ibid., 30.
251 *"inferno of noise":* Ibid., 43.

IN RUINS

261 *"the forces of nature": Eastern State Penitentiary Historic Structures Report,* vol. 1 (Philadelphia: Philadelphia Historical Commission, July 21, 1994), 279, https://www.easternstate.org/sites/easternstate/files/inline-files/history-vol1.pdf.
262 *"A tall slender girl":* H. E. Winlock, *Models of Daily Life in Ancient Egypt: From the Tomb of Meket Rē' at Thebes* (Cambridge, MA: Harvard University Press for the Metropolitan Museum of Art, 1955), 3.

permissions

Excerpts from *Journey into the Whirlwind* by Eugenia Semyonovna Ginzburg, translated by Paul Stevenson and Max Hayward. Copyright © 1967 by Arnoldo Mondadori Editorie–Milano. English translation copyright © 1967 by Houghton Mifflin Harcourt Publishing Company. Reprinted by permission of Houghton Mifflin Harcourt Publishing Company. All rights reserved.

Excerpts from *The Rule of Saint Benedict* by Anthony C. Meisel, translated by M. L. del Mastro. Copyright © 1975 by Anthony C. Meisel & M. L. del Mastro. Used by permission of Doubleday, an imprint of the Knopf Doubleday Publishing Group, a division of Penguin Random House LLC. All rights reserved.

A Search for Solitude: The Journals of Thomas Merton, Volume 3, 1952–1960 by Thomas Merton and edited by Lawrence S. Cunningham. Copyright © 1996 by the Merton Legacy Trust. Reprinted by permission of HarperCollins Publishers.

Excerpts from *The Seven Storey Mountain* by Thomas Merton. Copyright © 1948 by Houghton Mifflin Harcourt Publishing Company and renewed 1976 by the Trustees of The Merton Legacy Trust. Reprinted by permission of Houghton Mifflin Harcourt Publishing Company. All rights reserved.

Excerpts from *The Sign of Jonas* by Thomas Merton. Copyright © 1953 by The Abbey of Our Lady of Gethsemani and renewed 1981 by the Trustees of The Merton Legacy Trust. Reprinted by permission of Houghton Mifflin Harcourt Publishing Company. All rights reserved.

Fifty Days of Solitude by Doris Grumbach. Copyright © 1994 by Doris Grumbach. Reprinted by permission of Beacon Press, Boston.

Introduction by Caleb Smith and excerpts from *The Life and Adventures of a Haunted Convict* by Austin Reed, edited and with an introduction by Caleb Smith. Copyright © 2016 by Caleb Smith. Used by permission of Random House, an imprint and division of Penguin Random House LLC. All rights reserved.

"To Those Born Later," originally published in German in 1939 as "An Die Nachgeborenen." Copyright © 1976, 1961 by Bertolt-Brecht-Erben / Suhrkamp Verlag, from *Bertolt Brecht Poems 1913-1956* by Bertolt Brecht, edited by John Willet and Ralph Manheim. Used by permission of Liveright Publishing Corporation.

index